Guide to Military Operations Other Than War

Tactics, Techniques, and Procedures
for Stability and Support Operations

Domestic and International

LTC Keith E. Bonn, USA (Ret.)
and
MSG Anthony E. Baker, USAR (Ret.)

STACKPOLE
BOOKS

Published by
STACKPOLE BOOKS
5067 Ritter Road
Mechanicsburg, PA 17055
www.stackpolebooks.com

Printed in the United States of America

10 9 8 7 6 5 4 3 2 1

First edition

Cover design by Wendy A. Reynolds

Library of Congress Cataloging-in-Publication Data

Bonn, Keith E. (Keith Earle), 1956–
    Guide to military operations other than war: tactics, techniques, and
  procedures for stability and support operations: domestic and international /
  Keith E. Bonn and Anthony E. Baker.
      p.   cm.
  Includes bibliographical references and index.
  ISBN 0-8117-2939-7
    1. United States—Armed Forces—Operations other than war. I. Title:
Military operations other than war. II. Baker, Anthony E., 1956– III. Title.

UH723.B66 2000
355.3'5—dc21
                                        99-050040

Contents

iii

Acknowledgments

The authors wish to acknowledge the following assistance:

Lt. Col. Richard J. Rinaldo, USA (Ret.), Military Analyst, Joint and Army Doctrine Directorate, U.S. Army TRADOC, for providing advice, support, and—most decisively—access to the official joint and Army doctrinal material on which much of this book is based. His experience and broad understanding of this subject material were instrumental in facilitating the completion of this work.

Lt. Col. Peter S. Vercruysse, USMC, Publications Development Officer, Doctrine Division, Joint Warfighting Center, for patient assistance with joint MOOTW doctrine.

Ambassador William Bishop of Interactions for advice and assistance regarding the requirements and challenges of NGO, PVO, and IO cooperation with MOOTW.

Col. Larry Forster, USA, Col. Mark R. Walsh, USA (Ret.), and Lt. Col. Dan Miltenberger, USA, all of the U.S. Army Peacekeeping Institute, for advice regarding the facilitation of interagency cooperation and encouragement for the completion of this work.

Col. George Oliver, USA, for advice regarding facilitation of interagency cooperation and assistance in contacting key members of the United Nations interagency community.

Ms. Margaret Carey, United Nations NGO Coordinator, for direction and advice regarding NGOs.

Col. Daniel Bolger, USA (Ret.), for advice regarding the content and format of Part III of this book.

Brig. Gen. William J. Lesczczynski, Jr., for sharing his expertise and insights into the conduct of MOOTW during his tenure as Commander, Joint Task Force—Bravo.

Maj. Jeffrey Voigt, USA, for sharing his valuable experience as a brigade S-5 (Civil Military Operations Officer) with the 1st Armored Division during Operation Joint Endeavor in Bosnia in 1997, and for providing important textual references on which this work is based in part.

Captain Clark Lystra, USA, former intelligence officer, 1st Battalion, 1st Special Forces Group (Airborne), for his assistance in developing the Noncombatant Evacuation Operations chapter.

Sergeant 1st Class Jim Peck, USA, operations planner, Joint Task Force 6, Ft. Bliss, Texas, contributed his broad knowledge and extensive expertise to several chapters.

Ms. Fran Doyle and Ms. Karen Lewis, TRADOC Technical Library, Ft. Monroe, Virginia, for their great patience and unsurpassed professionalism in assisting the research process.

The late Wolf Zoepf, Pinneberg, Germany, contributed his military and civil engineering expertise to the dislocated persons camp chapter.

PART I

Overview of Military Operations at the Millennium

In the era of profound change that has followed the end of the Cold War, many nations' armed forces have had to shift their institutional emphasis from fighting to maintain stability to stabilizing to prevent fighting. Soldiers and leaders must expect to participate extensively in operations designed to deter war, resolve conflict, promote peace, and support civil authorities in response to crises. This is not to say that the millennium will bring "world peace" or that a "new age" has dawned in which warfighting skills should be allowed to atrophy in favor of concentration on kinder and gentler missions. The rapidity with which malevolent political leaders can raise armies and cause grievous damage mitigates against such a luxury.

Accordingly, U.S. commanders must remember that their primary mission should *always* be to prepare for, fight, and win America's wars. This is the most rigorous task facing any military establishment and requires nothing less than first priority when training and equipping forces. Indeed, recent experience has proven that the discipline and skills that posture soldiers for victory in war are largely the same ones that facilitate the successful prosecution of *all* operations. The overwhelming majority of the special, or even unique, skills necessary for military operations other than war can be quickly learned by well-trained soldiers. The different—sometimes fundamentally different—attitudes that must be adopted by military participants in today's most common operations can be learned and internalized swiftly and effectively by well-disciplined military personnel.

The purpose of this book is to help military and civilian leaders learn the skills and attitudes essential for success at the tactical and operational levels in these increasingly important and common political–military endeavors.[1]

MOOTWAH, SO-AND-SO, AND OTHER STRANGE-SOUNDING TERMS

Few terminological challenges have given doctrine writers and conceptualizers as many fits and frustrations as the requirement to coin an expression that accurately conveys the idea of "operations that are not meant primarily to kill people and break things—unless they have to." The names currently in vogue just don't fill the bill. Military operations other than war (the acronym is MOOTW, pronounced "moot-wah") can be interpreted as being somewhat euphemistic—to the American public, the images that came out of Mogadishu in October 1993 certainly *looked* like war. The basis of the problem lies not with the understanding of the missions by the soldiers sent

---

[1] This book does not cover maritime or air operations, nor does it cover those missions requiring classified techniques, such as those normally performed by special operations forces (SOF).

to prosecute them but rather with political and public comprehension of the distinction between "war," which is an act between states, and "combat," which is an act between people. Unless and until this distinction becomes commonly understood by the public and the media, military operations other than war will remain a potentially misleading appellation, notwithstanding that it is the joint services' agreed-on title for these types of operations.

Some types of MOOTW were previously called low-intensity conflict (LIC). The LIC terminology came about as an element of the then-current "spectrum of conflict," which was part of America's strategy of deterrence. Although we still have an Assistant Secretary of Defense (Special Operations/Low Intensity Conflict), the most accepted terminology for the operations discussed in this book is MOOTW.

Stability and support operations—a term currently favored by some in the U.S. Army doctrinal community and variously shortened to SO-and-SO or SASO—also creates potential confusion. For example, currently proposed U.S. Army doctrine would classify humanitarian assistance as a "support" operation, whereas the conduct of "humanitarian and civic assistance" missions—part of "nation building"—would be a "stability" operation. As presently structured, the Army's emerging stability and support operations construct might also be at odds conceptually with joint doctrine terminology, which does not differentiate between the two types of operations, but rather lists them all by individual purpose.

This separate listing is somewhat less confusing, as different operations are often conducted concurrently in the same area to achieve the desired results through holistic multinational, joint, and interagency efforts. The operations are as follows:[2]

- Humanitarian Assistance
- Domestic Support Operations
- Military Support to Civil Authorities (MSCA)[3]
- Military Support to Counterdrug Operations (Foreign)[4]

---

[2]Current U.S. joint doctrine also calls for several maritime and air operations that are beyond the scope of this book, namely, Enforcement of Sanctions/Maritime Intercept Operations, Enforcing Exclusion Zones, Ensuring Freedom of Navigation and Overflight, and Protection of Shipping. Recovery Operations, a highly specialized effort to recover the remains of U.S. military personnel or sensitive equipment lost in foreign countries, is also beyond the scope of this book. Strikes and Raids, the last mission listed under this doctrine, is nothing more than the conduct of conventional combat missions on an individual or small-scale basis, and is also beyond the scope of this book.
[3]Includes military support to civilian law enforcement agencies (MSCLEA).
[4]When these are conducted domestically, they fall under the category of MSCLEA.

- Combating Terrorism[5]
- Nation Assistance/Support to Counterinsurgency[6]
- Noncombatant Evacuation Operations
- Peace Operations (Including Peacekeeping and Peace Enforcement)
- Show of Force Operations   `
- Support to Insurgencies

Throughout the remainder of this book, these will simply be referred to collectively as "MOOTW."

---

[5] When these are conducted domestically, they fall under the category of MSCLEA.
[6] Emerging U.S. Army doctrine currently classifies these as distinct missions.

Chapter 1

Characteristics and Principles of MOOTW

CHARACTERISTICS

In MOOTW, political considerations permeate all levels, and the military may not be the primary or lead player. As a result, these operations are governed by highly restrictive rules of engagement (ROE). In war, there is usually one goal, which is to achieve national objectives as quickly as possible and to conclude military operations on terms favorable to the United States and its allies. The purposes of conducting MOOTW, however, may be manifold, with the relative importance or hierarchy of such purposes changing or at times unclear—although helping leaders establish clarity of purpose is a major goal of this book. The Department of Defense (DOD) is often in a support role to another agency, such as the Department of State (DOS), in humanitarian assistance (HA) operations. However, in other types of MOOTW, DOD *is* the lead agency, such as in peace enforcement operations (PEO). MOOTW usually require a great deal of coordination between U.S. agencies and international agencies and may also involve nongovernmental organizations (NGOs) and private voluntary organizations (PVOs). Finally, although most MOOTW are conducted outside of the United States, some may be conducted within the United States in support of civil authorities, consistent with established law and constitutional intent.

Primacy of Political Objectives

Political objectives drive MOOTW at *every level,* and the political objectives may influence military operations and tactics. Two important factors about political primacy stand out.

First, all military personnel should understand the political objectives and the potential impact of inappropriate actions. This understanding helps avoid military actions that may have adverse political effects. It is not uncommon in some MOOTW for junior officers and NCOs to make decisions that have significant political implications.

Second, leaders must remain aware of changes not only in the operational situation but also in political objectives that may warrant a change in military operations. These changes may not always be obvious; precisely because of this, leaders must continuously strive to detect subtle changes that, over time, may disconnect political objectives and military operations. Failure to recognize changes in political objectives early may lead to ineffective or even counterproductive military operations.

Strategic Flexibility
MOOTW contribute to attainment of national security objectives by supporting peacetime engagement, deterrence, and crisis response options. These contributions are discussed below.

Peacetime Engagement
Peacetime engagement activities demonstrate national commitment, lend credibility to alliances, and enhance regional stability while promoting international influence and access. Peacetime engagement activities include periodic and rotational deployments, access and storage agreements, multinational exercises, port visits, foreign military training, foreign community support and military-to-military contacts. Today, many of the organizations key to peacetime engagement, such as Joint Task Force–Bravo in Central America, facilitate the operations of many units conducting MOOTW on an ongoing basis. Given their location and their members' knowledge of the region, forces participating in peacetime engagement activities could be the first committed to additional MOOTW by a combatant commander.

Deterrence
In peacetime, the armed forces of the United States help deter potential aggressors from using violence to achieve their aims. Deterrence can stem from several factors:
- The belief by a potential aggressor that a credible threat of retaliation exists, and that the consequences of retaliation are too severe to warrant the contemplated military action.
- The belief by a potential aggressor that the contemplated action cannot succeed.

Although the threat of nuclear conflict has diminished, proliferation of weapons of mass destruction (WMD) and conventional advanced technology weaponry is continuing. Threats directed against the United States, allies, or other friendly nations—ranging from terrorism to WMD—require the maintenance of a full array of response capabilities. Various MOOTW combat options (such as peace enforcement or strikes and raids) support deterrence by demonstrating national resolve to use force when necessary. Other operations (such as humanitarian assistance and peacekeeping) support deterrence by helping to create a climate of peaceful cooperation, thus promoting stability.

Crisis Response
Military forces must be able to respond rapidly either unilaterally or as part of a multinational effort. Crisis response may include, for example, employment of overwhelming force in peace enforcement, a single strike, or emergency support to civil authorities. The ability of the United States and its allies to respond rapidly with appropriate operational options to potential or actual crises contributes to regional stability. Thus, MOOTW may often be planned and executed under crisis circumstances.

Variable Duration
Many operations may be conducted on short notice and last for a relatively short time (for example, strikes and raids). Other types of MOOTW may last for an extended period to achieve the desired end. While almost always preferable, short-duration operations are not always possible, particularly in situations in which destabilizing conditions have existed for years—or centuries—or when conditions are such that a long-term commitment is required to achieve objectives.

PRINCIPLES
The principles of war, though mainly associated with large-scale combat operations, generally apply to MOOTW, although sometimes in different ways. Strikes and raids, for example, rely on the principles of surprise, offensive, economy of force, and mass to achieve a favorable outcome. However, political considerations and the nature of many military operations require an underpinning of additional principles described in this chapter. MOOTW that involve combat operations require joint force commanders to fully consider principles of war and principles of MOOTW. Although defining mission success may be more difficult in these operations, it is important to do so to keep U.S. forces focused on clear, attainable military objectives. Specifying the criteria for success helps define mission accomplishment and phase transitions.

The political objectives on which military objectives are based may not specifically address the desired military end state. Leaders should therefore translate their political guidance into appropriate military objectives through a rigorous and continuous mission and threat analysis. Leaders must carefully explain to political authorities the implications of political decisions on the capabilities of and risk to military forces. Extensive efforts must be made to avoid misunderstandings stemming from a lack of common terminology.

Changes to initial military objectives may occur because political and military leaders gain a better understanding of the situation, or they may occur because the situation itself changes. Leaders should be aware of shifts in the political objectives, or in the situation itself, that necessitate a change in the military objective. These changes may be very subtle, yet they still require adjustment of the military objectives. If this adjustment is not made, the military objectives may no longer support the political objectives, legitimacy may be undermined, and force security may be compromised.

U.S. military doctrine identifies six principles for the conduct of MOOTW:

- Objective
- Unity of effort
- Security
- Restraint
- Perseverance
- Legitimacy

Objective
Every military operation should be directed toward a clearly defined, decisive, and attainable objective. Leaders must understand the strategic aims, set appropriate objectives, and ensure that these aims and objectives contribute to unity of effort. Inherent in the principle of objective is the need to understand what constitutes mission success and what might cause the operation to be terminated before success is achieved. As an example, excessive U.S. casualties incurred during a peacekeeping operation (PKO) may cause abandonment of the operation.

Unity of Effort
The principle of unity of effort is derived from the principle of unity of command in war. It emphasizes the need to ensure that all means are directed to a common purpose. However, in MOOTW, achieving unity of effort is often complicated by a variety of nonmilitary participants, the lack of definitive

command arrangements among them, and varying views of the objective. This requires that leaders or other designated directors of the operation build and maintain consensus to achieve unity of effort.

While the chain of command for U.S. military forces remains inviolate (flowing from the national command authorities [NCA] through the combatant commander to the subordinate joint force commander [JFC]), command arrangements among coalition partners may be less well defined and not include full command authority. Under such circumstances, commanders must establish procedures for liaison and coordination to achieve unity of effort. Because MOOTW are often conducted at the small unit level, it is important that leaders at all levels understand the informal and formal relationships.

Security

This principle enhances freedom of action by reducing vulnerability to hostile acts, influence, or surprise. Hostile factions must never be permitted to acquire a military, political, or informational advantage.

The inherent right of self-defense against hostile acts or hostile intent applies in all operations. This protection may be exercised against virtually any person, element, or group hostile to the operation—for example, terrorists, or looters after a civil crisis or natural disaster. Leaders should avoid complacency and be ready to counter activity that could bring harm to units or jeopardize the operation. All personnel should stay alert even in a nonhostile operation with little or no perceived risk. Inherent in this responsibility is the need to plan for and posture the necessary capability to quickly transition to combat should circumstances change.

In addition to the right of self-defense, operations security is an important component of this principle. Although there may be no clearly defined threat, the essential elements of U.S. military operations should still be safeguarded. The uncertain nature of the situation inherent in many military operations, coupled with the potential for rapid change, requires that operations security be an integral part of the operation. Operations security planners must consider the effect of media coverage and the possibility that coverage may compromise essential security or disclose critical information.

Security may also involve the protection of civilians or participating agencies and organizations. The perceived neutrality of these protected elements may be a factor in their security. Protection of an NGO or PVO by U.S. military forces may create the perception that the NGO or PVO is pro–United States. Therefore, personnel of some NGOs and PVOs may be reluctant to accept the U.S. military's protection.

Restraint

Appropriate military capability must be applied prudently. A single act could cause significant military and political consequences; therefore, judicious use of force is necessary. Restraint requires the careful balancing of the need for security, the conduct of operations, and the political objective. Excessive force antagonizes the parties involved, thereby damaging the legitimacy of the organization that uses it and possibly enhancing the legitimacy of the opposing party.

Leaders at all levels must take proactive steps to ensure that their personnel know and understand the rules of engagement (ROE) and are quickly informed of changes. Failure to understand and comply with established ROE can result in fratricide, mission failure, and national embarrassment. ROE in MOOTW are generally more restrictive, detailed, and sensitive to political concerns than are those in war, consistent always with the right of self-defense. Restraint is best achieved when ROE issued at the beginning of an operation address most anticipated situations. ROE should be consistently reviewed and revised as necessary. Additionally, ROE should be carefully scrutinized to ensure that the lives and health of military personnel involved in MOOTW are not needlessly endangered. More information on ROE is in chapter 12.

Perseverance

Forces engaged in MOOTW must be prepared for the measured, protracted application of military capability in support of strategic aims. Some military operations may require years to achieve the desired results. The underlying causes of the crisis may be elusive, making it difficult to achieve a decisive resolution. It is important to assess possible responses to a crisis in terms of each option's impact on the achievement of the long-term political objective. This assessment does not preclude decisive military action but frames that action within the larger context of strategic aims. Success in MOOTW often requires patient, resolute, and persistent pursuit of national goals and objectives, for as long as necessary to achieve them. This often involves political, diplomatic, economic, and informational measures to supplement military efforts.

In many cases, due to the *ad hoc* nature of the joint task forces that typically conduct MOOTW, some senior military leaders may be unaware of the full consequences of extended commitment to some missions. Very few civilian leaders appreciate the impact of prolonged military participation in these operations. While perseverance is a virtue for political and military leaders alike, military leaders must tactfully, yet candidly and forcefully,

apprise their superiors of the manifold consequences of protracted commitment of military forces—especially combat forces—to the conduct of
MOOTW. Assessments done within the U.S. Army (principally by the Center for Army Lessons Learned) have found that individual and collective
combat proficiency can drastically deteriorate during the conduct of
MOOTW. The same assessments have also made it clear that egregious personnel losses—through simultaneous rotation to other assignments, end of
enlistments, and so forth—occur in units after a protracted deployment.

Legitimacy

In MOOTW, legitimacy is based on the perception by a specific audience of
the legality, morality, or rightness of a set of actions. This audience may be
the U.S. public, foreign nations, populations in the area of responsi-
bility/joint operations area (AOR/JOA), or the participating forces. Committed forces must sustain the legitimacy of the operation and of the host
government, where applicable. If an operation is perceived as legitimate,
there is a strong impulse to support the action. If an operation is not perceived as legitimate, the action may not be supported and may be actively
resisted. In MOOTW, legitimacy is frequently a decisive element. The pru-
dent use of psychological operations (PSYOPS) and humanitarian and civic
assistance (HCA) programs assists in developing a sense of legitimacy for
the supported government.

Legitimacy may depend on adhering to objectives agreed to by the
international community, ensuring that the action is appropriate to the situation, and dealing fairly with various factions. It may be reinforced by
restraint in the use of force, the type of forces employed, and the disciplined
conduct of the forces involved. The perception of legitimacy by the public
is strengthened if there are obvious national or humanitarian interests at
stake and if there is assurance that American lives are not being needlessly
or carelessly risked.

Another aspect of this principle is the legitimacy bestowed on a government through the perception of the populace it governs. If the populace
perceives that the government has genuine authority to govern and uses
proper agencies for valid purposes, it considers that government legitimate.

Chapter 2

Types of MOOTW

The simplest way to view the various types of stability and support operations encompassed in the term MOOTW is to consider those operations that occur in the United States or support the U.S. *domestic* policies, activities, or environments and those that support policies, activities, and events in the *international* environment, as shown in the accompanying table.

In at least two MOOTW categories, the military is required to provide support in *both* domestic and international environments. Those instances are support to counterdrug efforts and support to U.S. counterterrorism efforts. The primary purpose of both types of support, however, is to protect the domestic tranquility of the United States and its citizens.

MILITARY SUPPORT TO U.S. CIVIL AUTHORITIES

Military operations inside the United States and its territories, though limited in many respects, may include military support to civil authorities (MSCA). Most of this consists of DOD support to civil authorities for domestic emergencies, but it may also include military support to civilian law enforcement agencies (MSCLEA).

Support to Civil Authorities

MSCA operations generally provide temporary support to domestic civil authorities when permitted by law and are normally undertaken when an emergency overtaxes the capabilities of the civil authorities. Support to civil authorities includes diverse missions such as:

- Temporary augmentation of air traffic controllers and postal workers during strikes
- Provision of relief in the aftermath of a natural disaster
- Special support to local and state authorities for missions such as search and rescue

Types of MOOTW and Sample Missions

Primarily Domestic

General Military Support to Civil Authorities
Assistance with government functions during labor strikes
Assistance to states during natural disasters
Assistance to local authorities in search and rescue

Military Assistance to Civil Law Enforcement Agencies
Restoration of law and order (civil disturbances)
Key asset protection
Law enforcement training support
Support to counterdrug operations*
Support for combating domestic terrorism*

Primarily International

Humanitarian Assistance in Crisis Areas
Foreign disaster relief
Refugee/displaced civilian support
Security for those providing aid
Technical assistance and support

Nation Assistance and Counterinsurgency Assistance
Security assistance
Foreign internal defense assistance
Humanitarian/civic assistance (noncrisis)

Noncombatant Evacuation Operations

Peace Operations
Peacekeeping operations
Peace enforcement operations

Show of Force Operations

Support to Insurgencies

*Controlled by U.S. civilian agencies, but has an international operational dimension

Support is constrained in some instances by the Economy Act (31 USC Section 1535), which may require the requesting civil agency to reimburse DOD for the cost of its support. Likewise, the Posse Comitatus Act, *Use of Army and Air Forces as Posse Comitatus* (Title 18, USC Section 1385), prohibits the use of federal military forces to enforce or otherwise execute laws unless expressly authorized by the Constitution or an act of Congress.

Military Support to Civil Law Enforcement Agencies
MSCLEA includes, but is not limited to:
- Military assistance to restore law and order in the wake of civil disturbances
- The Key Asset Protection Program
- Training support to law enforcement agencies
- Support to counterdrug operations
- Support for combating terrorism

In these efforts, the military brings unique and useful capabilities. However, the Constitution of the United States, laws, regulations, policies, and other legal issues all bear on the employment of military forces in domestic operations. *These restraints and constraints—which reinforce the roles of the armed forces of the United States as protector and friend of the people and a bulwark of democracy—must be understood and integrated early in the planning phases of any MSCLEA operation.*

MILITARY SUPPORT TO COUNTERDRUG OPERATIONS
In counterdrug (CD) operations, DOD supports federal, state, and local law enforcement agencies in their efforts to disrupt the transfer of illegal drugs into the United States. The National Defense Authorization Act of 1989 assigned three major counterdrug responsibilities to DOD:
1. Act as the single lead agency for detecting and monitoring aerial and maritime transit of illegal drugs into the United States by emphasizing activities in the cocaine source countries, streamlining activities in the transit zone, and refocusing activities in the United States to concentrate on the cocaine threat at critical border locations;
2. Integrate the command, control, communications, computer, and intelligence assets of the United States that are dedicated to interdicting the movement of illegal drugs into the United States; and
3. Approve and fund state governors' plans for use of the National Guard to support drug interdiction and enforcement agencies.

In addition, the 1993 DOD Authorization Act empowered the DOD to detect, monitor, and communicate the movement of certain surface traffic within 25 miles of the U.S. boundary inside the United States. Other DOD support to the national drug control strategy includes support to law enforcement agencies (federal, state, and local) and cooperative foreign governments by providing intelligence analysts and logistical support personnel; support to interdiction; internal drug prevention and treatment programs; and research and development.

In general, military support to CD operations includes the following:

Interdiction
The ultimate goal of interdiction is to disrupt and/or deter drug smuggling by intercepting and seizing illicit drug shipments en route to or entering the United States. This process is extremely complex because it frequently involves several federal, state, and local agencies and departments with different charters and jurisdictions, operating over vast areas.

Detection and Monitoring
U.S. armed forces' roles in detecting and monitoring the flow of illegal drugs into the United States include:
- Providing platforms, reconnaissance patrols, and sensors for detecting and monitoring suspected traffickers*
- Information processing and fusion activities*
- Communications or dissemination activities*
- Sorting legitimate traffic from that which might be illegal*
- Intercepting potential smugglers*
- Searching potential smugglers*
- Arresting potential smugglers, if they are violating the law*

Other Support
Military support to CD operations also includes institutional and unit training, transfers of equipment to foreign and domestic CD agencies, and activities that support internal development and defuse the power of drug cartels. This latter category includes foreign humanitarian and civic assistance programs and PSYOPS to educate the populace about the evils of drugs and the people and organizations that produce and market them.

---

*Operations significantly restricted within U.S. territory.

COMBATING DOMESTIC TERRORISM
Combating terrorism in the United States involves actions taken to oppose terrorism from all threats. It includes *antiterrorism,* or defensive measures taken to reduce vulnerability to terrorist acts, and *counterterrorism,* or offensive measures taken to prevent, deter, and respond to terrorism.

Antiterrorism
Antiterrorism programs are the foundation for effectively combating terrorism. The basics of such programs include training and defensive measures that strike a balance among the protection desired, the mission, infrastructure, and available manpower and resources. Generally, antiterrorism measures include the following:
- OPSEC
- Individual security for personnel
- Physical security of installations
- Crisis management planning
- Tactical measures to contain or resolve terrorist incidents
- Continuous training and education

Counterterrorism
Counterterrorism operations provide responses that include preemptive, retaliatory, and rescue operations. Domestically, these are generally MSCLEA operations and, as such, are limited to training and equipment transfers. Normally, counterterrorism operations require specially trained personnel capable of mounting swift and effective action and are therefore outside the scope of this book.

HUMANITARIAN ASSISTANCE (HA)
HA operations relieve or reduce the results of natural or man-made disasters or other endemic conditions such as human pain, disease, hunger, or privation *in countries or regions outside the United States.* HA provided by U.S. forces is generally limited in scope and duration; it is intended to supplement the efforts of the host nation civil authorities or agencies, which have the primary responsibility for providing assistance. DOD provides assistance when the relief need is gravely urgent and when the humanitarian emergency dwarfs the ability of normal relief agencies to respond effectively.

The U.S. military can respond rapidly to emergencies or disasters and achieve order in austere locations. U.S. forces can provide logistics; command, control, communications, and computers; and the planning required to initiate and sustain HA operations.

HA operations are directed by U.S. national command authorities (NCA). The NCA also direct the employment of U.S. forces to support HA operations. Usually the DOS or the U.S. ambassador in country is responsible for declaring a foreign disaster that requires HA. Within DOD, the Undersecretary of Defense for Policy has the overall responsibility for developing the military policy for international HA operations.

HA operations may cover a broad range of missions, including:

Relief Missions. Relief missions are conducted to eliminate the suffering of disaster victims. They generally require close coordination and cooperation with international and private civilian authorities; sometimes, military forces are subordinate to a civilian agency. Relief missions can include actions to prevent loss of life and destruction of property; provision of basic sanitation facilities, shelters, and medical care; and distribution of food and medical supplies.

Dislocated Civilian Support Missions. Refugees or dislocated civilian support missions include organization, construction, and administration of dislocated persons camps; provision of subsistence, medical care, and security; and movement to other locations. The term "dislocated civilians" is a generic one that includes several subclassifications. Since these classifications are changeable, it is best to check with a qualified legal adviser regarding the precise terms and differentiations.

Security Missions. Security missions include establishing and maintaining conditions that facilitate the provision of humanitarian assistance by organizations of the international relief community. Delivering humanitarian relief supplies requires the affected country to have secure and serviceable ports and air terminals; when this is not the case initially, U.S. military forces may be called on to establish the appropriate levels of security. Also, secure areas are often needed for the storage of relief material until it can be distributed. Other tasks may involve protecting convoys and personnel delivering emergency aid, protecting shelters for dislocated civilians, and guaranteeing conditions of temporary refuge for threatened persons.

Technical Assistance and Support Missions. These operations include restoration and repair of physical infrastructure, such as communications restoration; relief supply management; high-priority relief supply delivery; provision of emergency medical care; and humanitarian de-mining. Technical assistance may take the form of providing advice and selected training, assessments, manpower, and equipment. Humanitarian de-mining is limited to technical education and training. U.S. forces should not physically take part in the removal of mines unless further directed by competent authority.

NATION ASSISTANCE/SUPPORT TO COUNTERINSURGENCIES
Nation assistance is civil or military assistance (other than HA) rendered to a nation by U.S. forces within that nation's territory during peacetime, crises or emergencies, or war, based on agreements mutually concluded between the United States and that nation. Nation assistance operations support a host nation by promoting sustainable development and growth of responsive institutions. The goal is to promote long-term regional stability. Nation assistance programs often include, but are not limited to, security assistance, foreign internal defense (FID), and humanitarian and civic assistance. All nation assistance actions are integrated through the U.S. ambassador's country plan.

Security Assistance
Security assistance refers to a group of programs by which the United States provides defense articles, military training, and other defense-related services to foreign nations by grant, loan, credit, or cash sales in furtherance of national policies and objectives. Some examples of U.S. security assistance programs are foreign military sales, the Foreign Military Financing Program, the International Military Education and Training Program, the Economic Support Fund, and commercial sales licensed under the Arms Export Control Act.

Foreign Internal Defense
FID programs encompass the total political, economic, informational, and military support provided to another nation to assist its fight against subversion and insurgency. U.S. military support to FID should focus on assisting host-nation personnel to anticipate, preclude, and counter these threats. FID supports host-nation internal defense and development (IDAD) programs. U.S. military involvement in FID has traditionally focused on helping another nation defeat an organized movement attempting to overthrow the government. FID programs may address other threats to a host nation's internal stability, such as civil disorder, illicit drug trafficking, and terrorism. U.S. military support to FID may include training, materiel, advice, or other assistance, including direct support and combat operations as authorized by the NCA, to host-nation forces in executing an IDAD program. FID is principally a special operations forces mission and, as such, is outside the scope of this book.

Humanitarian and Civic Assistance Programs
Humanitarian and civic assistance (HCA) is provided under Title 10 U.S. Code Section 401. This assistance is provided in conjunction with military operations and exercises and must fulfill unit training requirements that incidentally create humanitarian benefit to the local populace. In contrast to

emergency relief conducted under HA operations, HCA programs generally encompass planned activities in the following categories:
- Medical, dental, and veterinary care provided in rural areas of a country
- Construction of rudimentary surface transportation systems
- Well drilling and construction of basic sanitation facilities
- Rudimentary construction and repair of public facilities

NONCOMBATANT EVACUATION OPERATIONS
Noncombatant evacuation operations (NEOs) normally relocate threatened noncombatants from a foreign country. Although principally conducted to evacuate U.S. citizens, NEOs may also include penetrating foreign territory to conduct a selective evacuation of citizens from the host nation, as well as citizens from other countries. NEO methods and timing are significantly influenced by diplomatic considerations. Although they are ideally conducted without opposition, leaders should anticipate opposition and plan the operation accordingly. NEOs are similar to raids in that they involve swift insertion of a force, temporary occupation of objectives, and planned withdrawals. They differ from raids in that the force used is normally limited to that required to protect the evacuees and should be kept to the minimum consistent with mission accomplishment and security of the force.

PEACE OPERATIONS
Peace operations (POs) are military operations to support diplomatic efforts to reach a long-term political settlement. They include the following.

Peacekeeping Operations
Peacekeeping operations (PKOs) are military operations undertaken with the consent of all major parties to a dispute. They are designed to monitor and facilitate implementation of an agreement (cease-fire, truce, and other related agreements) and to support diplomatic efforts to reach a long-term political settlement.

Peace Enforcement Operations
Peace enforcement operations (PEOs) are the application of military force, or the threat of its use, normally pursuant to international authorization, to compel compliance with resolutions or sanctions designed to maintain or restore peace and order. PEOs include intervention operations, as well as operations to restore order, enforce sanctions, forcibly separate belligerents, and establish and supervise exclusion zones for the purpose of establishing an environment for truce or cease-fire. Unlike PKOs, such operations do not require the consent of the states involved or of other parties to the conflict.

Distinctions between PKOs and PEOs

The differences between PKOs and PEOs are characterized by three critical factors—consent, impartiality, and the use of force.

Consent exists when parties to the conflict exhibit willingness to accomplish the goals of the operation as expressed in an international mandate. Consent may vary from grudging acceptance to enthusiastic support—and may shift during the course of an operation. PKOs are conducted when all parties to the conflict have given their consent. PEOs may be conducted without the consent of all parties.

Impartiality means that the PO force *must* treat all sides fairly and even-handedly. The force must carry out its tasks to foster the goals of the mandate, rather than the goals of either of the parties. During PEOs, the force remains impartial by focusing on the behavior of a recalcitrant faction and employing force because of *what* is being done, not because of *who* is doing it.

In PKOs, force is used in self-defense. In PEOs, force is used to compel or coerce compliance with established rules.

SHOW OF FORCE OPERATIONS

Show of force operations, designed to demonstrate U.S. resolve, involve increased visibility of U.S. deployed forces in an attempt to defuse a specific situation that, if allowed to continue, may be detrimental to U.S. interests or national objectives.

Show of force operations are military in nature but often serve both political and military purposes. These operations can influence other governments or politico-military organizations to respect U.S. interests as well as international law.

A show of force involves the appearance of a credible military force to underscore U.S. policy interests or commitment to an alliance or coalition. Political concerns dominate a show of force. The commander of the force coordinates its operations with the country teams affected. A show of force can involve a wide range of military forces, including joint U.S. military or multinational forces.

SUPPORT TO INSURGENCIES

An insurgency is an organized movement aimed at the overthrow of a constituted government through the use of subversion and armed conflict. The U.S. government may support an insurgency against a regime that is threatening U.S. interests. U.S. forces may provide logistical and training support to an insurgency but normally do not conduct combat operations.

PART II

Interagency Cooperation

The integration of political and military objectives into coherent *strategy* has always been essential to success in all types of military operations. The new, rapidly changing global environment—characterized by regional instability, the growth of pluralistic governments, and unconventional threats—requires greater interagency cooperation than ever before. Especially in MOOTW, military actions must be synchronized with those of other agencies of the U.S. government, as well as with multinational forces, nongovernmental and private voluntary organizations (NGOs and PVOs), and intergovernmental and international organizations. These actions must be mutually supporting and should proceed in a logical sequence. To prosecute successful interagency operations, leaders must clearly understand the roles of and relationships among various federal agencies, military headquarters, state and local governments, country teams, and other engaged organizations. Techniques for organizing interagency teams and coordinating their actions are indispensable to success in MOOTW.

Increased involvement of military forces in civil activities at home and abroad is matched, in part, by an increase in situations—primarily overseas—in which civil agencies face emerging post–Cold War realities and military threats. In these new environments, many civilian organizations operate in closer proximity to military forces because their missions may fail without military support or protection.

Unity of effort is made difficult by the agencies' different and sometimes conflicting policies, procedures, and decision-making techniques. To be successful, the interagency process should bring together the interests of multiple agencies, departments, and organizations.

This section provides information to foster better understanding of the complex interagency environment. Although there is only cursory information about interagency cooperation at the strategic level, success at the tactical level ultimately requires a thorough understanding of the intermediate operational level. Therefore, this section focuses on basic techniques and procedures for organizing and coordinating interagency efforts, both domestic and foreign, at the operational and tactical levels.

Chapter 3

Strategic Direction

Although the details of operations at the strategic level are beyond the scope of this book, a basic understanding of the essentials will help leaders at lower levels better understand their duties.

At the national level, the interagency process is grounded within the Constitution and established by law in the National Security Act of 1947. The National Security Council (NSC) is a product of that act. The NSC advises and assists the President in integrating all aspects of national security policy—domestic, foreign, military, intelligence, and economic. Together with supporting interagency working groups, high-level steering groups, executive committees, and task forces, the NSC system provides the foundation for interagency coordination in the development and implementation of national security policy. The NSC staff is the President's personal and principal staff for national security issues. It tracks and directs the development, execution, and implementation of national security policies for the President.

The national command authorities (NCA) establish supported and/or supporting command relationships between combatant commanders when deployment and execution orders are issued. This ensures that tasked combatant commanders receive needed support. The commanders of the geographic combatant commands, supported by the functional combatant commands such as the U.S. Transportation Command and U.S. Space Command, provide forces and resources to accomplish the mission. This command relationship among the combatant commanders lends itself to the interagency process. The supported combatant commander controls and is accountable for military operations within a specified area of responsibility. Supported commanders define the parameters, request the right capabilities, task supporting Department of Defense (DOD) components, coordinate with the appropriate federal agencies, and develop a plan to achieve the common goal. As part of the team effort, supporting commanders provide the requested capabilities to assist the supported commander to accomplish missions requiring additional resources.

DOMESTIC OPERATIONS

Military operations inside the United States and its territories, though limited in many respects, include primarily military support to civil authorities (MSCA). Although sometimes differentiated in official publications, MSCA encompasses DOD support to civil authorities for domestic emergencies resulting from natural or man-made causes, and military support to civilian law enforcement agencies (MSCLEA). MSCLEA—for the purposes of this book, a subtype of MSCA—includes, but is not limited to, military assistance to quell civil disturbances; the Key Asset Protection Program; and interagency assistance, including training support to law enforcement agencies, support to counterdrug operations, and support for combating terrorism.

In all these efforts, the military brings unique and very useful capabilities. *However, the Constitution of the United States, laws, regulations, policies, and other legal issues all bear on the employment of the military in domestic operations.* Despite the increased emphasis on domestic roles for the DOD, the constraints of law and the necessity of maintaining the military's close and friendly relationship to the population of the Republic at large must be recognized and integrated from the outset of these operations.

FOREIGN OPERATIONS

Operations in foreign areas arise as a result of the United States' external relationships and how they bear on the national interest. For the DOD, in the political-military domain, this involves bilateral and multilateral military relationships, treaties, technology transfers, armaments cooperation and control, and humanitarian assistance and peace operations.

Within a theater, the geographic combatant commander plans and implements regional military strategies that require interagency coordination. Coordination between the DOD and other U.S. government agencies may occur through a "country team" or within a combatant command. In some operations, a special representative of the President or special envoy of the United Nations Secretary-General may be involved. The U.S. interagency structure within foreign countries involves the ambassador, the country team system (which includes the Defense Attaché Office and the Security Assistance Office), the American Embassy public affairs officer, the United States Information Service, and geographic combatant commands.

When orders for MOOTW are issued, the NCA establish "supported" and "supporting" command relationships between combatant commanders.

The commanders of the geographic combatant commands, supported by the functional combatant commands or other geographic combatant commanders, provide forces and resources to accomplish the mission. This command relationship among the combatant commanders enables the interagency coordination process.

Chapter 4

Participants in MOOTW

U.S. ARMED FORCES

Increased involvement of military forces in civil activity at home and abroad is matched, in part, by an increase in situations—primarily overseas—in which civil agencies face emerging post–Cold War factors and military threats not previously confronted. With the breakdown of nation-states, there is greater need for developmental, civil assistance, and humanitarian relief organizations to alleviate human suffering. These organizations are, in turn, often drawn closer to military forces by necessity, because their missions may fail without military support or protection.

U.S. military forces that participate in MOOTW include units of all types from the active and reserve components; in fact, Army Reserve and National Guard units play an increasingly important role in support to domestic civil authorities and foreign stability and support operations. This is, in part, reflected in the assignment of an Army Reserve Regional Support Command (RSC) in each Federal Emergency Management Agency (FEMA) region. Additionally, the vast majority of the Army's civil affairs units—key members of the special operations forces (SOF) community in foreign stability and support operations—are in the Army Reserve.

U.S. GOVERNMENT AGENCIES

An increasingly wide variety of governmental agencies interact directly or indirectly with U.S. military forces. Chapter 42 lists the U.S. agencies most often involved in both domestic and foreign operations.

The coordination required with each agency varies significantly with the mission at hand. Generally, in foreign operations, tactical leaders interface with U.S. government agencies through a variety of federal governmental representatives designated by the cabinet secretary responsible for the operation the unit is supporting.

INTERGOVERNMENTAL AND INTERNATIONAL ORGANIZATIONS

Intergovernmental and international organizations have well-defined structures, roles, and responsibilities. They are usually equipped with the resources and expertise to participate in complex interagency operations. Examples of intergovernmental organizations include the North Atlantic Treaty Organization (NATO), the Organization for African Unity (AOU), the Organization of American States (OAS), the Western European Union (WEU), and the Organization on Security and Cooperation in Europe (OSCE). Examples of internationnal organizations include the United Nations and the International Red Cross and Red Crescent Movement.

NGOs AND PVOs

The NCA may determine that it is in the national interest to task U.S. military forces with missions that bring them into close contact with, and may even be in support of, NGOs/PVOs. In such circumstances, it is mutually beneficial to coordinate the activities of all participants. A climate of *cooperation* between NGOs/PVOs and the miliary forces should be the goal. Taskings to support NGOs/PVOs are normally for a short-term purpose due to extraordinary events. In most situations, logistics, communications, and security are those capabilities most needed by the NGOs/PVOs. It is, however, crucial to remember that in such missions the role of the armed forces should be to *enable*—not *perform*—NGO/PVO tasks. Military commanders and other decision makers must also understand that mutually beneficial arrangements between the armed forces and NGOs/PVOs may be critical to the success of the campaign or operation plan.

NGOs/PVOs do not operate within either the military or the governmental hierarchy. Therefore, the relationship between armed forces and NGOs/PVOs is neither supported nor supporting, but rather is a partnership. Where long-term problems precede a deepening crisis, representatives of NGOs/PVOs are frequently on the scene *before* U.S. forces and are often willing to operate in high-risk areas. They will most likely remain after military forces have departed. In general, NGOs/PVOs are flexible and independent and focus on providing grassroots-level primary relief. NGOs/PVOs are involved in such diverse activities as education, technical projects, relief activities, refugee assistance, public policy, and development programs. The sheer number of lives they affect and amount of resources they provide enable the NGO/PVO community to wield a great deal of power within the interagency community.

These organizations play an important role in providing support to host nations. NGOs/PVOs provide assistance to over 250 million people annually. Their combined worldwide contributions total between $9 and $10 billion each year—more than any single nation or international body (such as the UN). Although differences may exist between military forces and civilian agencies, *short-term objectives are frequently very similar.* Discovering this common ground is *essential* to unity of effort.

NGOs/PVOs may range in size and experience from those with multimillion-dollar budgets and decades of global experience in developmental and humanitarian relief to small, newly created organizations dedicated to responding to a particular emergency or disaster. *The professionalism, capability, equipment and other resources, and expertise vary greatly from one NGO/PVO to another.*

The connectivity between NGOs/PVOs and the DOD is currently ad hoc, with no specific statutory linkage. Although their focus remains at the local level and their connections are usually informal, NGOs/PVOs are major players at the interagency table.

Because of their capability to respond quickly and effectively to crisis, the participation of NGOs/PVOs can reduce the quantities and types of civil-military resources that a commander would otherwise have to devote to an operation. Activities and capabilities of NGOs/PVOs must be factored into the commander's assessment of conditions and resources and integrated into the selected course of action. Their extensive involvement, local contacts, and experience in various nations make these organizations valuable sources of information about local and regional governments as well as civilian attitudes toward the operation.

Whereas some NGOs/PVOs will seek the protection afforded by armed forces or the use of military aircraft to move relief supplies to overseas destinations, others may avoid a close affiliation with military forces, preferring autonomous operations. Their rationale may be fear of compromising their position with the local populace or suspicion that military forces intend to take control of, influence, or even prevent their operations. In providing assistance to endangered populations in complex emergencies, humanitarian relief organizations may view the use of military force to support their efforts or to enforce UN mandates as a means of last resort. These organizations view freedom of access as the ideal working environment, in consonance with the basic principles of humanitarian assistance. Certain organizations may even insist on operating *only* on this basis and without armed protection. Military leaders engaged in the preparation of plans for deployment into a humanitarian assistance operation should expect to encounter responses from *some* humanitarian organizations that are influenced by a profound belief in these principles. Other humanitarian assistance organizations enjoy a good, mutually supportive working relationship with governmental and military organizations.

Finally, the plain truth is that although there are some ex-military personnel in NGOs/PVOs, as one military participant in humanitarian relief activities put it, "Perhaps by definition, the individuals who gravitate to that profession are more likely to be people more prone to the Peace Corps than the Marine Corps." [7]

To overcome potential obstacles to effective integration, planners should consult with representatives of NGOs/PVOs, along with the host-country government (if sovereign), to identify local issues and concerns. Leaders should meet with representatives of the humanitarian assistance community to define common objectives and courses of action that are mutually supportive but do not compromise the roles of any of the participants.

The barriers to integrated relations may be further reduced by representation of the NGOs/PVOs at every level of the chain of command. NGO/PVO field-workers are normally experts in their working environment. These workers are guided by the operating principles of their parent organizations, which typically require independence to do the job most effectively.

Leaders must remember that just as they must determine the capacities and roles of NGOs/PVOs, the reverse is also true. And unless they are unusually experienced in interagency operations with U.S. military forces, representatives of NGOs/PVOs may not be deeply knowledgeable of military roles and capabilities. When dealing with NGOs/PVOs, it is wise to explain acronyms and jargon and to go the extra mile to explain the military side of the operation—not in condescension, but in the same cooperative spirit sought from their side. Subjects for special explanation and emphasis may include:

- Capabilities and limitations of military forces
- Varying circumstances that preclude assistance or cooperation
- Types and scope of assistance that are appropriate and authorized by U.S. law
- Lessons learned from previous interagency operations.

---

[7] Observation of a longtime USAID official, cited by Chris Seibel in his book *The U.S. Military/NGO Relationship in Humanitarian Interventions* (Carlisle, Pa. U.S. Army Peacekeeping Institute, U.S. Army War College, 1996), 92.

Chapter 5

Interagency Cooperation

The common thread throughout all MOOTW is the broad range of agencies—many with indispensable practical competencies and major legal responsibilities—that interact with the armed forces. The nature of interagency cooperation demands that leaders consider all elements at their disposal and decide which agencies are best qualified to help achieve the identified ends. This consideration is especially necessary because the security challenges facing the United States today are growing in complexity, requiring the skills and resources of many organizations. The solution to a problem seldom, if ever, resides within the capability of a single agency; plans must be crafted to take advantage of the core competencies of myriad agencies, synchronizing their efforts with military capabilities toward a single objective. When the NCA decide to employ the armed forces of the United States, a set of realistic, attainable military objectives must be determined, and a desired end state identified. These objectives must be developed in consonance with associated diplomatic, economic, and informational objectives.

CHALLENGES TO EFFECTIVE ORGANIZATION

Significant organizational differences exist between the military hierarchy and those of other organizations, particularly at the operational level, where there is seldom a counterpart to the geographic combatant commander. This organizational challenge is compounded by the reality that the overall lead authority in foreign operations is likely to be exercised *not* by the geographic combatant commander but by a U.S. ambassador or other senior civilian, who will provide policy and goals for all U.S. government agencies and military organizations in the operation.

UNUSUAL AND CHANGING ROLES OF THE MILITARY
In MOOTW, the military often plays a *supporting* role to other national agencies. Although the DOD may have little or no choice regarding the agencies engaged in a particular operation or control over the individual agency agendas, understanding how military operations can combine with those of other organizations toward mission accomplishment can provide the key to success.

Each organization brings its own culture, philosophy, goals, practices, and capabilities to interagency operations. This diversity is a *strength* of the interagency process, providing a cross section of expertise, skills, and abilities. In one coordinated forum, leaders must integrate many views, capabilities, and options into a coherent course of action for success.

MEETING THE CHALLENGE
Understand the Nature of Interagency Bureaucracy
There is no overarching national or global interagency doctrine that delineates or dictates the relationships and procedures governing all agencies, departments, and organizations in interagency operations. Nor is there an organization conducting oversight to ensure that the myriad agencies, departments, and organizations have the capability and the tools to work together. The interagency process is often described as "more art than science," whereas military operations tend to depend on structure and doctrine. However, with some commonsense adjustments, some of the techniques, procedures, and systems of military command and control can be meaningfully employed to obtain unity of effort.

Unity of effort can be achieved only through close, continuous interagency and interdepartmental coordination and cooperation, which are necessary to overcome confusion over objectives, inadequate structure or procedures, and bureaucratic or even personal limitations.

To be successful, the interagency process should bring together the interests of multiple agencies, departments, and organizations. This cohesion is even more complex than the multidimensional nature of military combat operations viewed in isolation. When the economic, political and/or diplomatic, and informational instruments of national power are applied, the dimensions of the effort and the number and types of interactions expand significantly. This process, coupled with naturally divergent agency cultures, typically challenges the "results-oriented" military ethos. Nevertheless, by understanding the interagency environment and culture, campaign and operation plans can be crafted more effectively to synchronize the efforts of the various agencies and focus their core competencies synergistically toward the desired end state.

Recognize Agency Strengths and Weaknesses

Core Values. Each agency has core values that it will not compromise. These values form the foundation on which all other functions of the agency grow. In any interaction, all participants must be constantly aware that each agency will continuously cultivate and create external sources of support and will be maneuvering to protect its core values.

Insular Vision. Domestic politics are usually the single most important driver of the various U.S. government agencies' agendas, and these may or may not coincide with international security issues. Sometimes there is fortuitous congruency, but that is not always the case.

Reduction of Uncertainty. Few bureaucracies are built for crisis management. Crisis increases uncertainty and the likelihood that compromises will have to be made. With compromise may come the fear that power, security, or prestige will be sacrificed. Members of organizations often struggle to reduce uncertainty and reduce threats to organizational stability. Information can reduce uncertainty. Thus, *information is the coin of the realm in interagency operations,* as it provides those who possess it a decided advantage in the decision-making process.

Source of Information. NGOs/PVOs and intergovernmental and international organizations on the scene possess considerable information that may be essential to the success of the military operation. Relief workers often have a comprehensive understanding of the needs of the population at the grassroots level. Working closely with indigenous peoples, they understand local culture and practices. As a consequence, the relief community is an important source of information regarding the following:

- Local historical perspective and insights into factors contributing to the situation at hand
- Local cultural practices that will bear on the relationship of military forces to the populace
- Local political structure, political aims of various parties, and the roles of key leaders
- The security situation
- The role and capabilities of the host-nation government

This kind of information is frequently not available through military channels. However, the manner in which information is treated by military forces and the humanitarian assistance community can be sensitive. Handled carefully and sensitively, NGOs/PVOs will be active participants in the interagency team. Ham-handed handling of information can alienate the relief community and create a perception that, contrary to its philosophical ideals, it is considered no more than an intelligence source by the military.

Private Agencies. Private agendas can significantly affect interagency consensus. The goals of an institution may conflict with the private, usually short-term, agendas of its members. Because personality plays such a large part in interagency operations, personal agendas can be significant—often creating an informal hierarchy of the department or agency. All organizations (including the military) have some sort of formal and informal hierarchy, which results in a specific distribution of power, income, and prestige among the members of the organization. Thus, developing an understanding of an organization and of the personalities involved in its informal structure can provide insights into how the organization performs.

Gather the Required Resources

The challenge to commanders at all levels is to recognize what resources may be needed to accomplish the mission, and to integrate them into operations. All efforts must be coordinated and focused, despite philosophical and operational differences between agencies. An atmosphere of *cooperation* must be established. Although some loss of organizational freedom of action is often necessary to attain full cooperation, a zeal for consensus should not compromise the authority, roles, or core competencies of individual agencies.

Before attempting to gain consensus in the interagency arena, it must first be attained in the DOD. The various elements—Office of the Secretary of Defense, the Joint Chiefs of Staff, the Joint Staff, defense agencies and DOD field activities, military departments, and combatant commands—should agree to the ends, ways, and means of an operation before trying to integrate the military instrument of power with other agencies, departments, and organizations. The DOD has a common culture, common procedures, and a hierarchical structure, and the armed forces of the United States possess unique capabilities. These include:

- *Influence:* Domestic and international influence through military-to-military contacts and through the reserves and National Guard.
- *Resources:* The accomplishment of logistical, security, and engineering feats on an unequaled scale.
- *Responsiveness:* A demonstrated ability to organize and project massive resources quickly, to any spot on the globe.
- *Command, control, communications, computers, and intelligence (C^4I):* The unparalleled ability to command, control, communicate, and assimilate intelligence globally, both on the ground and from space.

- *Organizing and planning processes:* The ability to conduct crisis planning and organize crisis response.
- *Training support:* The capability to train large numbers of individuals quickly.
- *Strategic and theater lift:* The capability to rapidly project overwhelming military power anywhere on the globe in support of U.S. national security objectives.

After developing an understanding of other agencies and establishing consensus on the goals of the operation within the DOD, determine the mutual needs between the DOD and each of the other agencies. This can help define the common ground among participating agencies, departments, and organizations. All organizations will strive to look after their interests, follow their policies, and preserve their core values. These must be considered and, to the greatest extent possible, respected, to promote interagency cooperation.

Structuring operations so that each organization relies on others for important support is called *functional interdependence.* This interdependence is the strongest and the most lasting potential bond between agencies, departments, and organizations. For example, NGOs/PVOs often depend on U.S. military forces to most effectively conduct relief operations in high-risk areas. U.S. armed forces can conduct a long-range deployment only with Department of State's (DOS) help in securing overflight and en route basing agreements. These interdependencies can develop over time and lead the way to true interagency cooperation.

Ensuring that all organizations share the responsibility for the job and receive appropriate recognition strengthens these bonds of interdependence. The purpose of such recognition is to wed all the engaged agencies to the process by validating and reinforcing their positive interagency participation.

INTERAGENCY TRAINING AND READINESS

Rehearsal and synchronization exercises involving all potentially-participating players provide an essential forum for anticipation and resolution of policy and procedures for interagency cooperation. Training should focus on identifying and assessing agency capabilities and core competencies, identifying procedural challenges, and achieving unity of effort. To sustain the readiness and coherence of the effort, the training audience should include members of the NGO/PVO coordination sections, liaison sections of U.S. and foreign government agencies, contingency joint task force (JTF) commands, and other agency representatives. Combatant command and JTF exercises should include nonmilitary representatives performing their normal roles, even in hypothetical combat situations. Such exercises greatly enhance operational capabilities and solidify the relationships between civilian organizations and the military.

Increasingly, interagency coordination training is occurring at combatant commands, at senior-level colleges (such as the National Defense University), at the Department of State's Foreign Service Institute, and on the mock battlefields of the combined military training centers.

Chapter 6

Interagency Coordination

Once organizational goals and capabilities have been identified and a viable, functional organization established, the challenge is to *coordinate* their activities. Harnessing the power of disparate organizations with competing priorities and procedures can be a daunting challenge. The following basic steps constitute a systematic approach to interagency coordination during the conduct of MOOTW.

1. DEFINE THE MISSION IN CLEAR AND UNAMBIGUOUS TERMS THAT ARE AGREED TO BY ALL

Differences in assumptions and organizational perspectives can often hamper a clear understanding of the problems inherent to MOOTW. Representatives from each major group of agencies, departments, and organizations—including field offices—should be involved in all levels of planning from the outset. These representatives are especially important to achieve unity of effort during the "problem definition" phase. The early development of options for interagency consideration is necessary and may be facilitated by creating an interagency assessment team capable of rapid deployment to the crisis area to assess the situation.

Within the context of interagency operations, commanders and decision makers should aggressively seek clearly defined, decisive, and attainable objectives, end states, and exit criteria. Successful interagency coordination is essential to achieve these goals and to develop accurate and timely assessments. Such definition allows application of resources of the most appropriate agencies. Not all agencies will necessarily understand or agree to the need for clearly defined objectives with the sense of urgency or specificity of military planners. For example, the DOS may appear to resist defining the objective, since from its perspective, doing so might inhibit the give-and-take necessary to resolve the problems associated with many operations. From the DOS viewpoint, the objective may emerge clearly only in the course of negotiations and may not be established in complete detail at the outset of planning. This illustrates the differences between military and other agencies' cultures.

The interagency environment is complicated by differences in terminology, some of which may have grave impacts. To mitigate this problem, *military planners must anticipate confusion and take measures to clarify and establish common terms with clear and specific usage.* A good start is to provide access to Appendices A (Acronyms) and B (Glossary) of this book. This clarification is particularly important to the establishment of military objectives. Differing operating procedures, bureaucratic cultures, and languages can create similar problems during multinational operations.

2. DEVELOP COURSES OF ACTION OR OPTIONS
Each option should present a significantly different means of achieving the objectives. Military planners should focus their efforts on providing the enabling capabilities that contribute to the attainment of national security policy objectives and are part of the interagency plan of action. Providing too few or clearly impractical options, or recommending the "middle of the road" approach merely for the sake of achieving consensus, is of little service to decision makers. Open debate within the interagency community produces the best options.

Capitalize on Institutional Experience
Several institutional sources are available to help planners more readily formulate and assess proposed courses of action and to reduce the need to learn on the job. Review after-action reports and lessons learned in similar operations using any of the following resources:
- Joint Universal Lessons Learned System
- Center for Army Lessons Learned
- Marine Corps Lessons Learned System
- Air Force Center for Lessons Learned
- Coast Guard Universal Lessons Learned System
- U.S. Army Peacekeeping Institute
- Center for Naval Analyses

Although usually less formal, agencies outside the DOD frequently have their own systems in place to capitalize on operational experience.

Establish Responsibility and Fiscal Accountability
The resources required for a mission must be painstakingly identified, with specific responsibilities assigned to *and accepted by* the agencies that will provide them. To ensure proper reimbursement from other U.S. government agencies for materiel support, careful accounting procedures should be established. Cooperation and synchronization are achieved when interagency coordination allows consideration of all positions. The military planner or commander's voice may be but one among many at the interagency table.

Note that NGOs/PVOs do not operate within either the military or the governmental hierarchy. Therefore, the relationship between the armed forces and NGOs/PVOs is neither supported nor supporting. An *associate* or partner relationship may accurately describe that which exists between military forces and engaged NGOs/PVOs. If such a relationship is formed, the focal point where U.S. military forces provide coordinated support to NGOs/PVOs would be the Civil-Military Operations Center (see page 83 for detailed information on this important tactical coordinating node).

3. PLAN FOR THE TRANSITION OF KEY RESPONSIBILITIES, CAPABILITIES, AND FUNCTIONS
Given the inevitable impact on combat readiness and other aspects of military endeavor, U.S. military support of MOOTW is *never* intended to be permanent. As plans are developed at the operational level, effective transition planning should always be a primary consideration. Particularly during MOOTW, commanders and military planners at this level should anticipate the need to draw down U.S. military support to diminish the impact on the local populace when the transition is made to assistance from other organizations.

4. PLAN FOR MEDIA IMPACT ON INTERAGENCY COORDINATION
Successful national security policy must account for the public's values. As a result, the media can be a powerful force in shaping public attitudes and policy development. The media often have a dramatic influence on the interagency process—whether at the strategic decision-making level of the NSC or in the field as NGOs/PVOs vie for public attention and charitable contributions. Military plans that include interaction with other agencies should anticipate the importance that public affairs and media relations have on the operation and in the interagency process. As early as possible in the planning process, all participating agencies and organizations must establish and agree on procedures for providing media access; issuing and verifying

credentials; and briefing, escorting, and transporting media members and their equipment. Common communication points and public affairs themes should be developed before execution of the plan so that organizations are not perceived by the media as working at cross-purposes with one another. Responsibility for interaction with the media should be established clearly so that, to the extent possible, the media representatives perceive consistent themes from the members of a clearly unified effort.

Chapter 7

Military Support to Civil Authorities

As noted in chapter 2, U.S. military forces are available to support U.S. domestic civil authorities for a variety of tasks. A general distinction is made between general support to civil authorities—for such functions as performance of government operations during large-scale labor disputes and after significant natural disasters—and support to civil law enforcement authorities. The latter type of military support includes restoration of law and order during civil disturbances, protection of key assets, and support to U.S. counterdrug and counterterrorist programs. In both types of military support, U.S. civil authorities have the lead, and their roles are governed by specific legislation.

IMPLEMENTING THE FEDERAL RESPONSE PLAN
Crisis response to natural disasters and civil defense situations inside the United States are implemented through the Federal Response Plan (FRP). The Robert T. Stafford Disaster Relief and Emergency Assistance Act (Disaster Relief Act of 1974, Public Law 93-288, as amended) is the statutory authority for U.S. government domestic disaster assistance. It gives the President the authority to establish a program for disaster preparedness and response, which is delegated to the Federal Emergency Management Agency (FEMA). The act provides procedures for declaring an emergency or major disaster, as well as the type and amount of federal assistance available. There are 28 federal departments and agencies that support the operations of the FRP through execution of their assigned functional responsibilities.

Following a request for assistance from the Governor of the affected state or territory and the determination that local ability to respond has been exceeded, the President implements the FRP by declaring a domestic disaster. With this presidential declaration, the resources of the federal government—through the interagency process—can be focused on restoring normalcy.

The FRP assigns responsibilities to executive departments and agencies in grouped emergency support functions (ESFs), depending on the situation. Agencies are designated as "primary" or "support," based on their core competencies.

DOD policy is set forth in DOD Directive 3025.1, *Military Support to Civil Authorities (MSCA)*. While the Secretary of Defense retains the authority to approve the use of combatant command resources for MSCA, the Secretary of the Army is the DOD executive agent for executing and managing MSCA and responds to the NCA when coordinating with the director of FEMA. Under the FRP, the DOD has the responsibility as "primary agency" for public works and engineering. As a primary agency, the DOD plans, coordinates, and manages the federal response required by this function. The DOD also has specific responsibilities as a "support agency" for all other ESFs.

COORDINATING INTERAGENCY EFFORTS IN DOMESTIC SUPPORT OPERATIONS

Federal assistance to a state or territory is provided under the overall direction of the Federal Coordinating Officer (FCO), appointed by FEMA on behalf of the President after the President has declared a disaster. In coordination with the state, FEMA will send in an emergency response team (ERT) consisting of selected federal agency representatives to assess damage, establish the disaster field office (DFO), and work at the state emergency operations center. All taskings (known as "mission assignments") must be approved by FEMA's FCO for the DOD to be reimbursed for its incremental costs for the mission. When a domestic disaster occurs, FEMA's Catastrophic Disaster Response Group (CDRG) and emergency support team (EST) form at the agency's headquarters. The CDRG is the coordinating group that addresses policy issues and support requirements from the FCO and ESF response elements in the field. The EST is an interagency group composed of representatives from the 10 primary federal agencies (including the DOD) and the FEMA staff to resolve issues.

Combatant Commander for Domestic Support Operations

Acting through the Chairman of the Joint Chiefs of Staff and the designated Director of Military Support (DOMS, the DOD representative on the

Scheme of Interagency Relationships in MSCA

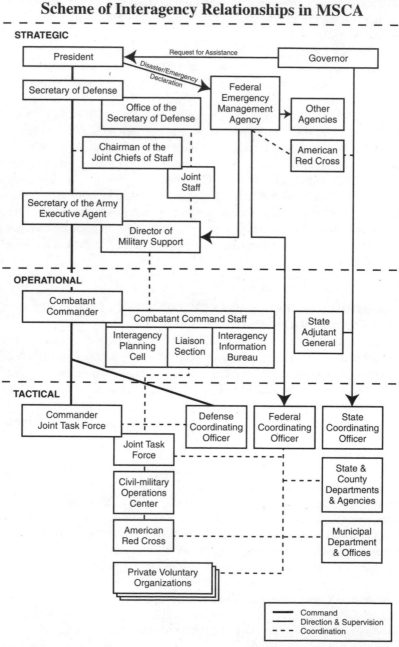

CDRG), the Secretary of Defense approves an order designating one of the following as the supported combatant commander:

- Commander in Chief, U.S. Atlantic Command (USCINCACOM) for the 48 continental states and territorial waters
- Commander in Chief, U.S. Pacific Command (USCINCPAC) for Alaska, Hawaii, or the Pacific territories and territorial waters
- Commander in Chief, U.S. Southern Command (USCINCSOUTH) for Puerto Rico, the U.S. Virgin Islands, and U.S. territorial waters in the Gulf of Mexico

This order also delineates support relationships, directs the U.S. Army Corps of Engineers to begin disaster site support, and directs the Commander in Chief, U.S. Transportation Command (USCINCTRANS) to begin unit or equipment movement as required by the supported combatant commander. Acting through DOMS, the Secretary of the Army tasks and coordinates with the services and other DOD elements (e.g., Defense Logistics Agency), in accordance with support requirements identified by the Department of Health and Human Services (DHHS) or other primary agencies under the FRP and with the mission assigned by FEMA. USCINCACOM and USCINCPAC are the DOD's principal planning agents. They have the responsibility to provide joint planning and execution directives for peacetime assistance rendered by the DOD within their assigned areas of responsibility (AOR).

Defense Coordinating Officer

The supported combatant commander designates a component command as a headquarters to execute the disaster relief operation. This headquarters appoints and deploys a defense coordinating officer (DCO) and, based on the severity of the situation, may also deploy a joint task force. The DCO works with the FCO to integrate JTF efforts in support of the operation. The DCO serves as the on-scene military point of contact for the FCO and principal representatives of other U.S. government agencies participating in the relief operation. *As a practical guide, the DCO and JTF commander are not the same individual because they have different responsibilities and assets.* The separation of these distinct functions allows the commander the flexibility to operate freely in the disaster area, while the DCO focuses on task validation and coordinating DOD response activities in the disaster field office. Within the continental United States (CONUS), USCINCACOM, through Forces Command or a designated continental United States Army (CONUSA) can provide the JTF HQ. The CONUSAs are Army commands with regional boundaries. These headquarters interact on a daily basis with state and local authorities, the FEMA regions, and other federal agencies on a variety of issues that provide a foundation for rapid and smooth transition to support operations during periods of disaster response.

FEMA Role

FEMA provides supporting combatant commanders with interface to federal agencies through Regional Interagency Steering Committees for planning, coordinating, and supporting MSCA efforts. FEMA has adopted the Incident Command System organizational model for the interagency ERT, which includes the functional elements of operations, planning, logistics, and finance and/or administration.

Coordination with State and Local Authorities

DOD interaction with state and local authorities can take the very visible form of MSCA or the more routine involvement of commanders of DOD installations with state, county, and municipal governments. These activities include contingency planning with local governments and field offices of federal agencies and community and social activities.

State or territorial governors are supported in a contingency by the state or territorial Army and Air National Guard under the command of the state or territory Adjutant General. DOD support is generally provided in the form of assistance or augmentation of skills and resources to a federal agency field office or to a state or local agency having responsibility for a particular activity.

Each of the states and territories has an Office of Emergency Services (OES) or an equivalent organization responsible for emergency preparedness planning and assisting the Governor in directing responses to emergencies. The OES coordinates provision of state or territorial assistance to its local governments through a State Coordinating Officer (SCO).

Counterpart relationships to those of DCO, FCO, and SCO are established at lower echelons to facilitate coordination. For example, local DOD installation commanders may work closely with local mayors and commissioners to align capabilities and resources with needs.

DOD support for local environmental operations can begin immediately within the authority delegated to installation commanders. One such example is detection of an oil spill in a harbor. If requested by local authorities, a commander of a DOD installation having the appropriate resources can take immediate action, with coordination of state and federal activities to follow. However, this immediate response by commanders does not take precedence over their primary mission. Commanders should seek guidance through the chain of command regarding continuing assistance whenever DOD resources are committed under immediate response circumstances.

DOD coordination of activities between installations and the local community can include support for public fire and rescue services, public works, police protection, social services, public health, search and rescue operations, and hospitals. Routine interagency coordination between the DOD, the Federal Aviation Administration (FAA), and the municipality takes place on a daily basis when a joint-use military airfield supports commercial aviation serving the municipality.

Additional MSCA Missions
In addition to crisis response roles in civil disasters, DOD assistance may be requested from other agencies as part of a federal response to domestic environmental disasters. Normally, such assistance is provided based on requests from the Environmental Protection Agency (EPA), the U.S. Coast Guard (USCG), or Department of the Interior (DOI) as the lead agency.

Although the DOD response to domestic emergencies is normally coordinated through DOMS, the military may also respond when an interdepartmental memorandum of agreement (MOA) is in effect. For example, the USCG (which in peacetime belongs to the Department of the Treasury) is assured of a rapid response from the U.S. Navy in the deployment of oil containment and recovery equipment to the scene of an oil spill by an interdepartmental MOA. This MOA sets forth procedures for the deployment of equipment and personnel and for the reimbursement of operational costs. Because of this MOA, negotiations at the headquarters level are not required.

ORGANIZING AND COORDINATING MILITARY SUPPORT TO CIVIL LAW ENFORCEMENT AGENCIES (MSCLEA)
Support to Counterdrug Operations
The war on drugs requires extremely complex U.S. governmental interagency coordination. Counterdrug activities of the United States have evolved from independent actions to a more coherent national effort of military and civilian cooperation. Current national strategy aims at demand reduction and treatment, while attacking the drug trade in source countries and interdicting it en route. DOD personnel charged with supporting counterdrug operations must work with more than 30 federal agencies and innumerable state, local, and private authorities—a veritable "alphabet soup" of very different organizations *that generally do not view operations through the same lens as the military.*

Federal Lead/Primary Agencies and Their Responsibilities in Domestic Counterdrug Operations

LEAD/PRIMARY AGENCIES	RESPONSIBILITIES
DEPARTMENT OF DEFENSE (DOD)	DETECTION AND MONITORING OF AERIAL AND MARITIME TRANSIT OF ILLEGAL DRUGS IN SUPPORT OF LAW ENFORCEMENT AGENCIES
DRUG ENFORCEMENT ADMINISTRATION (DEA)	ENFORCING LAWS AND REGULATIONS ON DRUGS AND CONTROLLED SUBSTANCES • Investigating major interstate and international drug law violators • Enforcing regulations on legal manufacture and distribution of controlled substances • Participating in drug intelligence-sharing with other national agencies • Coordinating DEA and international counter-parts' efforts
FEDERAL BUREAU OF INVESTIGATION (FBI)	INVESTIGATING VIOLATIONS OF CRIMINAL LAWS (concurrent with DEA) • Targeting major multijurisdictional trafficking organizations • Goal is dismantling trafficking networks
US ATTORNEYS	PROSECUTING CRIMINALS • Prosecuting violations of federal laws concerning controlled substances, money laundering, drug trafficking, tax evasion, and violent and organized crime • Overseeing OCDETF's activities
US BORDER PATROL	"PRIMARY AGENCY"—LAND INTERDICTION BETWEEN US PORTS OF ENTRY (POEs)
DEPARTMENT OF STATE (DOS) INTERNATIONAL NARCOTICS & LAW ENFORCEMENT AFFAIRS	COORDINATING US INTERNATIONAL SUPPLY REDUCTION STRATEGIES
US CUSTOMS SERVICE	LEAD—INTERDICTION AT US LAND AND SEA POEs (with US Border Patrol as "primary agency" between POEs and US territorial waters) CO-LEAD (with Coast Guard)—AIR INTERDICTION
US COAST GUARD	LEAD—MARITIME INTERDICTION CO-LEAD (with Customs Service)—AIR INTERDICTION

This effort is conducted under the National Narcotics Leadership Act of 1988 (Public Law 100-690), which established the Office of National Drug Control Policy (ONDCP) as the primary agency within the Executive Branch responsible for developing and implementing the National Drug Control Strategy. It does so under the leadership of the Director for National Drug Control Policy. The act unifies the efforts of the various federal and local agencies.

In domestic counterdrug operations, the military role is generally limited to training law enforcement officers and limited detection and monitoring operations. The latter are restricted by executive order to non-U.S. citizens (although certain exemptions exist for operations on federal land such as national parks and military reservations). Also, non-federalized National Guard units may sometimes play a more active role in their capacity as state-controlled assets.

OVERSEAS COUNTERDRUG OPERATIONS

National policy toward counterdrug operations in foreign countries changes often, but barring a radical shift in the strategy, such operations are likely to continue on a regular, if unpredictable basis. Significantly more support may be given to host-nation law enforcement agencies and to other U.S. government agencies when operating in a foreign environment than in the domestic arena. Nevertheless, DOD is *not* the lead agency for these efforts, and interagency organization and coordination are outlined in the accompanying figure.

As noted in chapter 2, counterdrug operations generally include support to interdiction and detection and monitoring missions, although they can also occasionally include support to destruction of drug production sites by host-nation police or military forces.

In interdiction missions in or within the waters of a sovereign foreign nation, close coordination with the Drug Enforcement Administration (DEA) representatives at the embassy will be essential, since they lead the operation and coordinate their activities with the country team. Support rendered often includes mission planning, provision of transportation to the DEA agents and/or host-nation forces to and from the interdiction site, command and control for the operation, and certain categories of logistical support. Because these operations depend on the detection of opportunities for interdiction, they are often conducted on a short-notice basis; the development of detailed checklists and SOPs not only greatly facilitates the conduct of these operations but also ensures that all restrictions and constraints are fully understood and adhered to by military personnel.

Interagency Structure for MSCLEA
(Domestic Counterdrug Support)

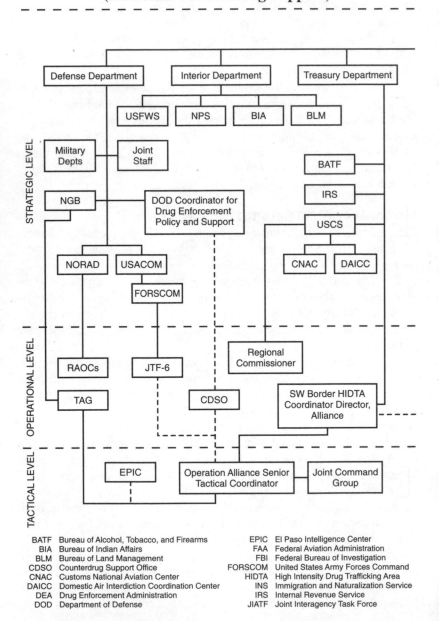

BATF   Bureau of Alcohol, Tobacco, and Firearms   EPIC   El Paso Intelligence Center
BIA   Bureau of Indian Affairs   FAA   Federal Aviation Administration
BLM   Bureau of Land Management   FBI   Federal Bureau of Investigation
CDSO   Counterdrug Support Office   FORSCOM   United States Army Forces Command
CNAC   Customs National Aviation Center   HIDTA   High Intensity Drug Trafficking Area
DAICC   Domestic Air Interdiction Coordination Center   INS   Immigration and Naturalization Service
DEA   Drug Enforcement Administration   IRS   Internal Revenue Service
DOD   Department of Defense   JIATF   Joint Interagency Task Force

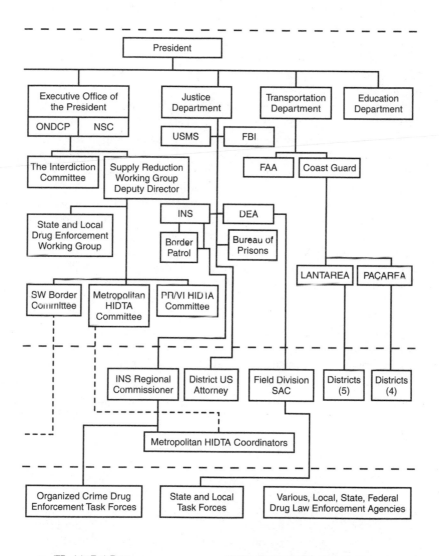

JTF	Joint Task Force
LANTAREA	Atlantic Area
NGB	National Guard Bureau
NORAD	North American Aerospace Defense Command
NPS	National Park Service
NSC	National Security Council
ONDCP	Office of National Drug Control Policy
PACAREA	Pacific Area
PR/VI	Puerto Rico/Virgin Islands

RAOC	Regional Air Operations Center
SAC	Special Agent in Charge
SW	Southwest
TAG	The (State) Adjutant General, Commander of the State's National Guard
USACOM	United States Atlantic Command
USCS	United States Customs Service
USFWS	United States Fish and Wildlife Service
USMS	United States Marshals Service

Military support to detection and monitoring efforts in foreign countries can range from the provision of logistical support and transportation platforms to the intelligence organizations conducting the operations, to intelligence gathering by military assets themselves. Aerial, ground, sea, and space-based sensors can be applied in any combination decided on by the NCA and are often applied with direct U.S. military involvement in the process.

Support to host-nation forces engaged in the destruction of drug production sites can include the provision of planning, command and control, and transportation to host-nation forces and logistical support to the DEA agents who are directly involved in the operation. Close communication with the country team is essential in these operations, as they carry a significantly higher risk than some other counterdrug missions. Mission participants must understand the rules of engagement (ROE) for the mission, and careful consideration must be given to the proximity of landing zones/pick-up zones (LZs/PZs), drop-off sites, and the location of command and control nodes to the sites to be destroyed. These sites can range from simple cornfields in which marijuana is grown between the stalks, to sophisticated processing labs producing heroin or cocaine. Drug producers may forcefully defend their production sites, and U.S. military personnel in the area are not likely to be exempt from automatic weapons fire. Furthermore, U.S. military personnel who are identified as having participated in the support of such operations may become the targets of terrorist or criminal retaliation. At a minimum, personnel so threatened should observe and practice the personal antiterrorism measures described in Part III.

Antiterrorism Operations

The DOD is not the lead agency for combating terrorism but is responsible for:

- Protecting its own personnel, bases, ships, deployed forces, equipment, and installations
- Providing technical assistance or forces when requested by the NCA

The lead agency for combating terrorism domestically is the Department of Justice; the Department of Transportation and/or Federal Aviation Administration has the lead for certain aviation incidents. The U.S. Coast Guard is responsible for reducing the risk of maritime terrorist incidents and for manning the National Terrorism Hotline ([800] 424-8802) for reports of actual or potential domestic terrorism. All other federal agencies possessing resources for responding to terrorism are linked through agency command centers and crisis management groups to ensure effective coordination of the U.S. response.

Civil Disturbance Operations

Civil disturbances are mass acts of violence and disorder that are prejudicial to public law and the maintenance of order. They include riots, mass acts of violence, insurrections, and unlawful obstructions or assemblies. The role of federal military forces is to *assist civil authorities in restoring law and order when the magnitude of the disturbance exceeds the capabilities of local and state authorities.* The President may employ federal military forces to aid local and state authorities to protect the constitutional rights of citizens when a state is unable or unwilling to do so. Federal military forces may also protect federal facilities throughout the United States.

Each instance of military support in these cases is an individually authorized exception to the Posse Comitatus Act's provision that the military will not participate, "except in cases under circumstances expressly authorized by the Constitution or act of Congress" (Title 18, USC Section 1385). Military support is provided in accordance with DOD Directive 3025.12, *Military Assistance for Civil Disturbances (MACDIS),* and the DOD Civil Disturbance Plan GARDEN PLOT. GARDEN PLOT provides guidance and direction to all DOD components that participate in civil disturbance operations that support civil authorities.

State Responsibilities. National Guard units, as state organizations, respond to the Governor in accordance with pertinent state laws. In most cases, the National Guard is the first military responder and usually remains in state status throughout the operation.

Federal Responsibilities. The President may call the National Guard into federal service for civil disturbances. This is normally done only upon the request of the Governor. Such a change of status imposes the limitations of the Posse Comitatus Act and other federal statutes on any federalized Guard units.

Requests for federal military assistance originate with the state, which forwards them to the President.

The U.S. Attorney General is responsible for coordinating and managing all requests for federal MACDIS operations. The Attorney General advises the President whether and when to commit federal military forces. The President orders the employment of federal military forces in domestic civil disturbance operations.

The Attorney General appoints a Senior Civilian Representative of the Attorney General (SCRAG). The SCRAG is responsible for coordinating

Interagency Cooperation in MSCLEA
(Support to Civil Disturbance Operations)

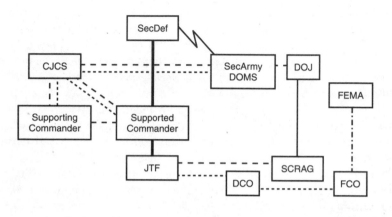

Key

JTF	Joint Task Force	▬▬▬▬	Command Authority
CJCS	Chairman, Joint Chiefs of Staff	─ ─ ─	Crisis Management Coordination
DCO	District Central Office	────────	Crisis Management Tasking
FCO	Federal Coordinating Officer	··········	Consequence Management Coordination
DOJ	Department of Justice		
DOMS	Director of Military Support	─·─·─	Consequence Management Tasking
FEMA	Federal Emergency Management Agency	⊼	Delegation of Executive Agency
SCRAG	Senior Civilian Representative of the Attorney General		

federal civil disturbance operations and assisting state civil authorities. The SCRAG has the authority to request MACDIS support from federal military forces. The SCRAG exercises this authority in coordination with a single-service or JTF commander. *Civilian officials remain in charge of civil disturbance operations.*

Following appropriate approvals, the DOMS coordinates the functions of the military services when federal MACDIS is directed. The DOD executive agent publishes an order, through DOMS, designating USCINCA-COM, USCINCPAC, or USCINCSOUTH as the supported commander for

MACDIS operations; the areas of responsibility are the same as for MSCA humanitarian operations. This order also designates the supporting commanders, services, and agencies. The supported commander determines the organization and forces required to accomplish the civil disturbance mission. The supported commander may establish a JTF to make best use of the forces available for the mission.

Coordination of Civil Disturbance Operations. The task force commander exercises control of all federal military forces, including *federalized* National Guard units committed to assist civil authorities.

Federal forces are *not* placed under command of either state civilians or National Guard commanders in state status; state civilian authorities retain control of their state and local law enforcement agencies (LEAs). However, to coordinate actions, the task force commander establishes liaison with the SCRAG and other appropriate federal, state, and local civil authorities. This liaison can assist LEA officials in determining the types and quantities of military support to be requested; the task force headquarters can facilitate this mission determination by providing civilian LEAs with a detailed listing of the types of missions federal military forces may conduct. Liaisons may also be able to arrange supply of certain logistical resources to the task force.

Continuous coordination between the task force commander and the SCRAG provides the commander with the detailed information required to employ and protect the force effectively. Due to federal restrictions on the collection, retention, and storage of information about U.S. civilians, task force commanders should staff intelligence support missions with the senior intelligence officer and legal counsel prior to approving such missions.

Federal military forces must be employed in tasks or missions appropriate to their organization and training; *they are not employed in ways that violate the legal restrictions in effect.* Certain types of missions are *always* inappropriate for military forces during civil disturbance operations; gathering intelligence on U.S. civilians is one salient mission that can *never* be conducted by U.S. military forces.

Other Missions Related to MACDIS. Other missions are lawful and appropriate.

Generally, they include:

- During the "restoration of order" phase of civil disturbance operations, military forces may be used to disperse unlawful assemblies, patrol disturbed areas to prevent the commission of unlawful acts, and provide quick reaction forces.
- Military forces may assist in the distribution of essential goods and the maintenance of essential services.

- Military forces may establish traffic control points for military traffic, cordon areas, and/or release chemical obscurants.

Requests for the conduct of specific military missions are typically passed through a single state or law enforcement coordinating officer to the SCRAG. Requests validated by the SCRAG are transmitted to the task force commander and the task force headquarters for staffing and coordination. Approved missions are assigned through the military chain of command to the appropriate element or unit for execution. Units and military personnel *do not accept taskings or missions directly from law enforcement or state civilian officials, except in a direct support relationship as approved and ordered through the military chain of command.* This arrangement prevents inappropriate mission execution or misuse of resources. A deployed unit's area of operation should coincide with the jurisdiction or subdivision boundaries of the LEAs it supports. This arrangement facilitates liaison and coordination between law enforcement officials and military chains of command.

LIMITATIONS AND CONSTRAINTS ON THE USE OF U.S. MILITARY FORCES IN DOMESTIC OPERATIONS

In all these efforts, the military brings unique and useful capabilities to the interagency forum. However, operations within the United States are differentiated from other types of military operations. The Constitution of the United States, laws, presidential executive orders, regulations, policies, and other legal restrictions all bear on the employment of the military in domestic operations. These stem from the need to maintain the U.S. Armed Forces in their unique role as protector of the American populace at large and to prevent misuse of the military as a force of internal political repression. Commanders must ensure that competent legal authorities review all domestic operation plans. They should scrutinize each request for conformation with statutory limitations, especially in support to civil law enforcement authorities. Moreover, the Secretary of Defense must *personally* approve any request to assist LEAs that will result in a planned event with the potential for confrontation with named individuals and/or groups or the use of lethal force.

Authorized Activities

Passive activities of military authorities that incidentally aid civilian LEAs are not prohibited. For example, when planning and executing compatible military training and operations, planners *may* consider the needs of civilian law enforcement officials for information when the collection of such information is an *incidental* aspect of training performed for a military purpose.

For example, if a unit is conducting tactical training in a national forest, and there are identified archaeological sites in the training area, military forces *may* apprise law enforcement officials of evidence of vandalism noted during the conduct of training. Planners may *not* plan or create missions or provide training for the *primary* purpose of aiding civilian law enforcement officials. They also may not conduct training or missions to *routinely* collect information about U.S. citizens.

Local law enforcement agents may accompany routinely scheduled training flights as observers to collect law enforcement information. This provision does *not* authorize the use of DOD aircraft to provide point-to-point transportation or training flights for civilian law enforcement officials. This assistance may be provided *only* in accordance with DOD Directive 4515.13-R.

Assistance may *not* include or permit direct participation by a member of the armed forces in the interdiction of a vessel, aircraft, or land vehicle or in search, seizure, arrest, or other similar activity unless such participation is otherwise authorized by law.

Specific Prohibitions
With the exception of members of the Coast Guard and members of the National Guard in state service, military personnel are prohibited under either the Posse Comitatus Act or DOD policy from direct participation in the execution of civil laws in the United States that includes the following:
- Participating in arrest, search and seizure, and stop and frisk activities or domestic interdiction of vessels, aircraft, or vehicles
- Conducting domestic surveillance or pursuit
- Operating as informants, undercover agents, or investigators in civilian legal cases or in any other civilian law enforcement activity

Significant limitations apply under the law to the gathering of information by the military in domestic situations. *Commanders must ensure that all requests for information, both before and during a domestic emergency, comply with applicable laws and are handled in appropriate military channels.*

Commanders must also ensure that intelligence support missions, other than normal liaison with civilian LEAs for force protection, are coordinated with and approved by appropriate authorities delineated by DOD Directive 5240.1, *DOD Intelligence Activities.*

Chapter 8

MOOTW in
Foreign Environments

The Department of State advises and assists the President in foreign policy formulation and execution. However, the Department of Defense is involved in the following related areas:

Bilateral and multilateral military relationships
Treaties involving DOD interests
Technology transfers
Armaments cooperation and control
Humanitarian assistance
Peace operations
Support to counterdrug operations

CAMPAIGN PLANNING
Combatant commanders are responsible for planning and implementing theater and regional military strategies requiring interagency coordination. Coordination between the DOD and other U.S. government agencies may occur in a country team or within a combatant command. In some operations, a special representative of the President or special envoy of the UN Secretary-General may be involved. The combatant commander's regional focus is mirrored at the DOS in its regional bureaus. Similarly, many other U.S. government agencies are regionally organized (e.g., the United States Agency for International Development [USAID]) and the United States Information Agency [USIA]). Within individual countries, the ambassador and country team are the initial focal point.

Campaign Planning within Interagency Operations
The joint campaign plan is based on the commander's concept, which presents a broad vision of the required aim or end state and how operations will be conducted to achieve objectives. Campaign plans enable commanders to help political leaders understand operational requirements for achieving

objectives. Given the systematic military approach to problem solving, it is often the combatant commander who functions as the lead organizer of many operations.

The combatant commander must consider four significant areas:

1. *Ends.* What conditions will achieve the theater strategic objectives?
2. *Ways.* What sequence of actions is most likely to produce these conditions?
3. *Means.* How does the commander apply resources to accomplish this sequence of actions?
4. *Risk.* What is the likely cost or risk to the joint force in performing this sequence of actions?

To frame the campaign plan within interagency operations, the commander must address these four areas in the context of all elements of national power, including political and/or diplomatic, economic, informational, and military. Then, although choices may be limited by circumstances, the combatant commander must determine which agencies are best qualified to wield these elements of power and weld them into a coherent, integrated plan.

Plan Development and Coordination

Combatant commanders frequently develop courses of action with recommendations and considerations originating in one or more U.S. embassies. Each country team can be an invaluable resource; their respective Emergency Action Plans (EAPs) can assist the combatant commanders in identifying options for and constraints on military actions and support activities. More importantly, EAPs incorporate the input of experts with significant experience on the ground. The staffs of geographic combatant commands also consult with the Office of the Secretary of Defense, the Joint Staff, and key interagency offices to coordinate their activities with those of other organizations. Initial concepts of operations may require revision upon consideration of related activities by voluntary and private organizations, particularly with regard to logistics. Such information frequently originates within the country team, which may be in contact with relief organizations in country. Thus, directly or indirectly, refinement of the military mission should be coordinated with other U.S. government agencies and NGOs/PVOs to identify and interpret these messages.

The following example for a comprehensive campaign plan follows the five-paragraph format familiar to U.S. military planners. It is based on one proposed by Professor Arthur E. Dewey of the U.S. Army Peacekeeping Institute and Walter S. Clarke.[8]

---

[8] Arthur E. Dewey and Walter S. Clarke, *The Comprehensive Campaign Plan: A Humanitarian/Political/Military Partnership in "Total Asset" Planning for Complex Humanitarian Emergencies,* 1 May 1997.

Comprehensive Campaign Plan

1. **SITUATION:**
   Describes the threat environment associated with a particular emergency, such as hunger, epidemics, human rights violations, civil strife, etc. Also lists the friendly forces, including all civilian and military resources available to deal with the emergency.

2. **MISSION:**
   A clear, concise, yet inclusive statement of what is to be accomplished. This helps to attenuate the chances of "mission creep," while still facilitating the fine-tuning required as the situation develops. Unlike a combat order—in which the end state is defined in the commander's intent in the Execution paragraph—the mission statement for a campaign should include the end state to further focus the effort. The end state should not be a limit, but rather should be based on the achievement of concrete objectives. These objectives could be the accomplishment of a humanitarian mission or the establishment of a security environment permitting the orderly transfer of responsibility to a successor structure such as a UN transition team, or host nation control.

3. **EXECUTION:**
   Starts with the commander's intent, which is his definition of success in the campaign. Includes the Concept of the Operation, which is a statement of the overarching concept of how the civilian and military forces participating in the campaign will achieve the end state. The main part of the paragraph defines specific tasks to be accomplished by the participating organizations.

4. **OPERATIONAL SUPPORT:**
   Describes precisely how the military and other supporting organizations fit into the overall effort. This paragraph includes—as completely as possible—an enumeration of the tasks that military forces may be called upon to perform in support of the main effort. Such a clarification of potential military tasks can also minimize the confusion and miscalculations associated with these efforts. The term "Operational Support" connotes the military's frequent role as the providers of the "sinew" and security for what may be a most civilian-controlled and -conducted campaign.

5. **COOPERATION AND CONTROL:**
   Describes the unity of civilian and military direction, at all levels. This paragraph *must* specify who is in charge at each level as well.

Chapter 9

Humanitarian Assistance

The chief of mission (i.e., the ambassador) has authority over all elements of the U.S. government in country, except forces assigned to a combatant command. Other key U.S. government organizations in place within most nations include the U.S. Defense Attaché Office (USDAO) and the U.S. Security Assistance Office (SAO)—both part of the country team. In some countries, these two functions may be performed by a single military office. It is important to understand the differences between these agencies in theater interagency coordination.

THE COUNTRY TEAM

The country team system provides the foundation for rapid interagency consultation and action on recommendations from the field and effective execution of U.S. missions, programs, and policies. The country team is often less than adequate for every need. In some cases it may not exist (e.g., Cuba), it may be inoperative due to damage or casualties from natural or man-made disaster, or it may simply be weak or inadequately trained in crisis management. The relationship with military chains of command is frequently ad hoc.

The country team concept encourages agencies to coordinate their plans and operations and keep one another and the ambassador informed of their activities. Although the ambassador is in charge, each agency head has direct communication with—and receives authority directly from—his or her parent organization. A member of the country team who disagrees with the direction of policy may appeal to superiors in Washington. More frequently, a member may receive home agency instructions that conflict with the consensus of the country team. Important issues must sometimes be

Organization of a Typical Country Team

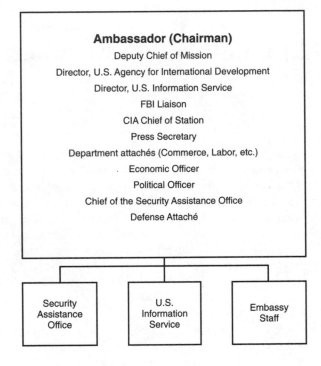

resolved at the national level. The relations of country team members to their home agencies and to one another require that proceedings be consensual.

The Ambassador

The ambassador is the senior representative of the President in foreign nations and is responsible for policy decisions and the activities of U.S. government employees in the country. The ambassador integrates the programs and resources of all U.S. government agencies represented on the country team. As the chief of mission, the ambassador has extraordinary authority and a de facto coordinating mechanism that can be tailored to each crisis as it arises. Ambassadors must interact daily with the Department of State's strategic-level planners and decision makers. Additionally, *the ambassador functions at both the operational and tactical levels,* where recommendations and considerations for crisis action planning are provided directly to the geographic combatant commander and commander of the joint task force. Although forces in the field under a geographic combatant command are exempt from the ambassador's statutory authority, the ambassador's political role is important to the success of military operations involving armed forces.

U.S. Defense Attaché Office

Service attachés constitute the USDAO. The defense attaché (DATT) is normally the senior service attaché assigned to the embassy. Although they keep combatant commanders informed of their activities, DATTs are rated and funded by the Defense Intelligence Agency. These attachés are valuable liaisons to their host-nation counterparts. The attachés also serve the ambassador and coordinate with and represent their respective military departments on service matters. The attachés assist the foreign internal defense (FID) program by exchanging information with the combatant commander's staff on host-nation military, social, economic, and political conditions.

Security Assistance Office

The SAO is the most important FID-related military activity under the supervision of the ambassador. The SAO—which may comprise a military assistance advisory group or liaison group, other military activity, or a single security assistance officer—reports to the U.S. ambassador but is rated by the combatant commander and funded by the Defense Security Assistance Agency. The SAO assists host-nation security forces by planning and administering military aspects of the security assistance (SA) program. The SAO also helps the U.S. country team communicate host-nation assistance needs to policy and budget officials within the U.S. government. In addition, it provides oversight of training and assistance teams temporarily assigned to the host nation. The SAO is forbidden by law from giving *direct* training assistance. Instead, training is normally provided through special teams and organizations assigned to limited tasks for specific periods (e.g., mobile training teams, technical assistance teams, quality assurance teams).

United States Defense Representative (USDR)

The USDR in foreign countries is an additional duty title assigned to a military officer serving in a specifically designated position. The USDR is the in-country focal point for planning, coordinating, and executing support to

U.S. government officials for in-country U.S. defense issues and activities that are not under the mission authority exercised by parent DOD components. The USDR is also the in-country representative of the Secretary of Defense, the Chairman of the Joint Chiefs of Staff, and the geographic combatant commander and is responsible (under the direction of the chief of mission) for providing coordination of administrative and security matters to U.S. government officials for all DOD noncombatant command elements in the foreign country in which the USDR is assigned.

American Embassy Public Affairs Officer and United States Information Service

The public affairs officer is the third senior officer at the embassy. Themes, messages, and press releases prepared by the JTF are normally coordinated with the embassy public affairs officer or U.S. Information Service (USIS) press attaché.

GEOGRAPHIC COMBATANT COMMANDS

Combatant commands and the forces assigned to them are not part of the country team nor technically subject to the authority of the U.S. ambassador. Nonetheless, cooperation and coordination in MOOTW are full and forthcoming.

To bring all elements of national power to theater and regional strategies, as well as to campaign and operation plans, combatant commanders are augmented with representatives from other U.S. government agencies. Frequently, geographic combatant commands are assigned a foreign policy adviser (FPA) or political adviser (POLAD) by the Department of State. This person provides diplomatic considerations and enables informal linkage with embassies in the AOR and with the Department of State. The FPA and/or POLAD supplies information regarding policy goals and objectives of the Department of State that are relevant to the geographic combatant commander's theater strategy.

Other U.S. government agencies may detail liaison personnel to combatant command staffs to improve interagency coordination. For example, representatives of the Director of Central Intelligence may be assigned to staffs of geographic combatant commands to facilitate intelligence support to military operations, to assist in the coordination of intelligence community activities within the combatant commander's AOR, to ensure that intelligence activities remain within policy and legal guidelines, and to anticipate future requirements for support.

BUILDING AN INTERAGENCY FORUM

Interagency forums established early at the operational level enable close relations and constructive dialogue among the engaged agencies. In concert with the Office of the Secretary of Defense and the Joint Staff, staffs of combatant commands should:

- Identify all agencies, departments, and organizations that are (or should be) involved in the operation. This analysis must include identification of the participating NGOs/PVOs, international organizations (IOs), and intergovernmental organizations. In many cases, initial planning and coordination have occurred in Washington, D.C., so the Joint Staff should ensure that the combatant commander and the combatant command staff are made aware of all the agencies to be involved in the mission.

- Establish an authoritative interagency hierarchy and determine the agency of primary responsibility. As previously identified, there may be missions in which the armed forces of the United States perform a supporting role. There may be resistance to the establishment of such an interagency hierarchy, as interagency players may view themselves as "first among equals" at all levels. Nonetheless, commanders should attempt to establish discipline and insert responsibility and rigor so that the process functions effectively. In many cases, the military commander will discover that resistance and disagreement are based on a lack of information or a difference of perception, which can be corrected by ensuring constant communication among all concerned parties. Regardless of the commander's efforts to foster coordination and cooperation, critical issues may arise that need to be forwarded up the chain of command for proper resolution.

- Define the objectives of the response effort. (These should be broadly outlined by the statements of intent of the Chairman of the Joint Chiefs of Staff [CJCS] and the joint force commander [JFC] included in the tasking orders.)

- Define courses of action for both theater military operations and agency activities while striving for operational compatibility.

- Solicit from each agency, department, or organization a clear definition of the role that each plays in the overall operation. In many situations, participating agencies, departments, and organizations may not have representatives either in theater or collocated with the combatant command's staff. In such cases, the combatant commander should request temporary assignment of liaison officers from the participating agencies, departments, and organizations to the combatant command or JTF HQ.

- Identify potential obstacles to the collective effort arising from conflicting departmental or agency priorities. Too often, these obstacles are assumed to have been addressed by another agency, department, or organization. Once identified, if the obstacles cannot be resolved at the JFC's level, they must be promptly forwarded up the chain of command for resolution.
- Identify the resources required for the mission and determine which agencies, departments, or organizations are committed to provide these resources, reducing duplication and increasing coherence in the collective effort. This identification is a critical process by which the expertise of the commander and his staff may contribute decisively in the interagency forum.
- Define the desired end state and exit criteria (e.g., transition from military to civilian control, war to MOOTW).
- Optimize assets to support the longer-term goals of the operation. Military contributions should complement and support the broader, long-range objectives of the international response to a crisis.
- Establish interagency assessment teams that can rapidly deploy to the area to evaluate the situation.
- Implement crisis action planning.

ORGANIZING INTERAGENCY CRISIS RESPONSES
Crisis Action Planning
Crisis action planning by the combatant command staff for operations in which both military and civilian efforts are involved normally consider the following:

- Government officials and agencies of the nation or state
- The Department of State and appropriate embassies
- Officials of U.S. government agencies associated with the U.S. response
- Composition and organization of the combatant command, the JTF, supporting combatant commands, and service and functional component commands, as well as supporting DOD agencies
- Multinational military forces and UN agencies and other intergovernmental and international organizations when they are involved
- Host-nation or local support available
- NGOs/PVOs, and IOs
- Civil contract support

The geographic combatant commander and combatant command staff should establish working relationships with interagency players long before crisis action planning is required. When crisis action planning becomes necessary, the geographic combatant commander (or POLAD) communicates with the appropriate ambassador(s) as part of crisis assessment. The ambassador and country team are often aware of factors and considerations that the geographic combatant commander might apply to develop courses of action, and they are key to bringing together U.S. national resources within the host country.

Crisis Action Organization
The combatant command crisis action organization is activated upon receipt of a CJCS warning or alert order or at the direction of the combatant commander. Activation of other temporary crisis action cells to administer the unique requirements of task force operations may be directed shortly thereafter. These cells support not only functional requirements of the JTF, such as logistics, but also coordination of military and nonmilitary activities. Because there are very few operational-level counterparts to the combatant commander within other agencies, establishment of a temporary framework for interagency coordination is appropriate and is a necessary precondition to effective coordinated operations. When designating a JTF, the combatant commander selects a JTF commander, assigns a joint operations area (JOA), specifies a mission, and provides planning guidance. In coordination with the JTF commander, the combatant commander either allocates forces to the JTF from the service and functional component forces assigned to the combatant command or requests forces from supporting combatant commands.

In contrast to an established combatant commander and JTF commander command structure, NGOs or PVOs in the operational area may not have a defined structure for controlling activities. Further, many of these organizations may be present in the operational area at the invitation and funding of the host country. As such, they may be structured to follow host-nation regulations or restrictions that may hinder military operations. Thus, the staff of the combatant command should anticipate organizational and operational mismatches, primarily by establishing liaisons and coordinating mechanisms as appropriate. These may include the following:

Humanitarian Assistance Coordination Center (HACC). In a humanitarian assistance (HA) operation, the combatant command's crisis action organization may organize as an HACC. The HACC assists with interagency coordination and planning, providing the critical link between the combatant commander and other U.S. government agencies, NGOs/PVOs,

Interagency Coordination for Foreign Humanitarian Assistance

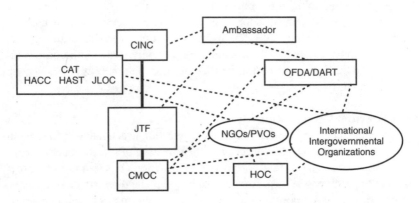

Key

JTF	Joint Task Force	HAST	Humanitarian Assistance Survey Team
CINC	Commander in Chief of a Combatant Command	JLOC	Joint Logistics Operations Center
OFDA/DART	Office of Foreign Disaster Assistance/Disaster Assistance Response Team	HOC	Humanitarian Operations Center
		CMOC	Civil Military Operations Center
CAT	Crisis Action Team	———	Command Authority
HACC	Humanitarian Assistance Coordination Center	- - - - -	Coordination

IOs and intergovernmental organizations that may participate in an HA operation at the strategic level. Normally, the HACC is a temporary body that operates during the early planning and coordination stages of the operation. Once a civil-military operations center (CMOC) or humanitarian operations center (HOC) has been established, the role of the HACC diminishes, and its functions are accomplished through the normal organization of the combatant command's staff and crisis action organization. If a combatant commander chooses to organize an HACC, liaisons from other U.S. government agencies, key NGOs/PVOs, IOs and intergovernmental organizations; and host-country agencies may also be members of the HACC in large-scale HA operations.

Humanitarian Operations Center (HOC). During large-scale HA operations, an HOC may be created through coordination with other participants. Sovereign host nations should provide the primary staff and direction for the HOC. If the sovereign nation is unable to do so or it does not exist, the UN (if engaged) should be considered to direct the HOC. The members of the HOC coordinate the overall relief strategy; identify logistical requirements for NGOs/PVOs, and IOs and intergovernmental organizations; and identify and prioritize HA needs for military support. The HOC does not exercise command and control. Rather, its purpose is to achieve unity of effort through coordination and effective concentration of resources, implemented by the individual organizations in accordance with their own operational practices. It limits or eliminates interference in executing the mission and avoids work at cross-purposes.

Membership of the HOC should include representatives of participating organizations who can speak authoritatively about their own policies, objectives, and practices and who, ideally, can commit their agencies, departments, and organizations to courses of action and expenditure of resources. If the HA operation is a U.S. unilateral effort, a representative of USAID or of the Office of United States Foreign Disaster Assistance (OFDA) will most likely serve as director of the HOC. Other representatives should come from the NGO/PVO community, IOs, intergovernmental organizations, and the government of the affected nation, if appropriate.

A goal of the HOC should be to create an environment in which the host nation, UN, and NGOs/PVOs can assume full responsibility for the security and operations of the humanitarian relief efforts.

Joint Logistics Operations Center (LOC). An LOC functions as the single point of contact for coordinating the flow and distribution of supplies into the operating area, relieving the JTF of as much of this burden as possible. Other actions that the LOC may perform include the following:

- Obtaining authority (from and/or through CINC, J-4, and/or J-5) to negotiate for host-nation support and on-site procurement through the Joint Staff, Office of the Secretary of Defense, and the Department of State
- Determining a lead agency (UN, service, or other agency) for contracting and support negotiation
- Serving as a logistics link to the Joint Staff, the services, the Defense Logistics Agency (DLA), USCINCTRANS, host nations, and other supporting commands and agencies during JTF operations

Liaison Section. As in domestic operations, the liaison section in foreign operations is crucial to interagency coordination. Upon receipt of a

CJCS warning or alert order, or at the direction of the combatant commander, the liaison section is activated. A liaison section assists the combatant commander by providing a single forum for the coordination of military activities among multinational forces and engaged NGOs/PVOs, the local government and indigenous population, and intergovernmental and international organizations. As in domestic operations, military forces, engaged agencies, and, in this case, the host nation should consider assigning liaisons to the combatant command staff in order to maximize information flow and interagency coordination.

Relationships with NGOs/PVOs

Courses of action developed by the combatant command staff should consider and incorporate interagency relationships that the JTF has with other U.S. government agencies, the UN (if engaged), intergovernmental and international organizations, and NGOs/PVOs. These considerations should be forwarded to the Joint Staff for negotiation by the Office of the Secretary of Defense with counterparts at the headquarters level of agencies and organizations. Working through the Joint Staff, geographic combatant commanders may arrange predeployment meetings with U.S. government agencies, intergovernmental organizations, and NGO/PVO agency heads in Washington, D.C., or New York to coordinate activities, identify requirements and capabilities, and establish interagency relationships for the operation. These meetings can be set up through the Joint Staff, the UN, or private agency consortiums such as InterAction. This coordination is another tool used to optimize unity of effort.

Humanitarian Assistance Survey Team (HAST)

Early in the planning for a foreign humanitarian operation, three factors must be assessed:

1. The resources required *immediately* to stabilize the humanitarian crisis (e.g., "stop the dying")
2. The capability of the organizations already operating in the crisis area to meet those needs
3. The resources that the military force must provide until the humanitarian relief organizations can marshal *their* resources

A HAST from a U.S. combatant command can accomplish all these functions.

Prior to the deployment of the main body, the geographic combatant commander may organize and deploy a HAST to do the following:

- Facilitate multiagency participation in humanitarian operations
- Acquire necessary information about the operational area
- Plan for the operation
- Assess existing conditions, available infrastructure, and the capabilities and size of the force required for the mission

To expedite assessments before deployment, the HAST should establish contact with the U.S. Embassy in the affected country to help gain access to the appropriate host-nation officials and other U.S. government agency representatives. The HAST should include representatives from the combatant command J-2, J-3, J-4 (especially transportation and engineer infrastructure planners and contracting and medical personnel), J-5, J-6, legal, chaplain, and civil affairs sections. Based on prior coordination and established associate or partnership working relationships, the HAST may also include key agency NGO/PVO representatives. On arrival in the country, the HAST should complete the following:

- Establish liaison and coordinate assessment efforts with the U.S. Embassy, host-nation and intergovernmental agencies, UN organizations (such as the United Nations Office of the High Commissioner for Refugees [UNHCR]), supported commanders or their representatives, and other national teams and relief agencies.
- Define coordinating relationships and lines of authority among military, embassy, and USAID personnel, and make these relationships known to all appropriate parties. This is an important preliminary step for identifying specific support arrangements required for the collective logistical effort and for coordination with NGOs/PVOs, IOs, and intergovernmental organizations.
- Initiate liaison with the USAID/OFDA Disaster Assistance Response Team (DART). This organization, consisting of specialists trained in a variety of disaster relief skills, assists with U.S. government response to disasters. Also establish liaison with the UN Department of Humanitarian Affairs (UNDHA) and UN Development Programme (UNDP), if deployed. The DART and UN elements are equipped to calculate the food, water, shelter, and health services required for the humanitarian relief effort, as well as the sources of these requirements. Integration of these calculations into the HAST assessment can reduce the potential for duplication of effort and ensure more accurate estimates of required support.

Sample Organization of a DART

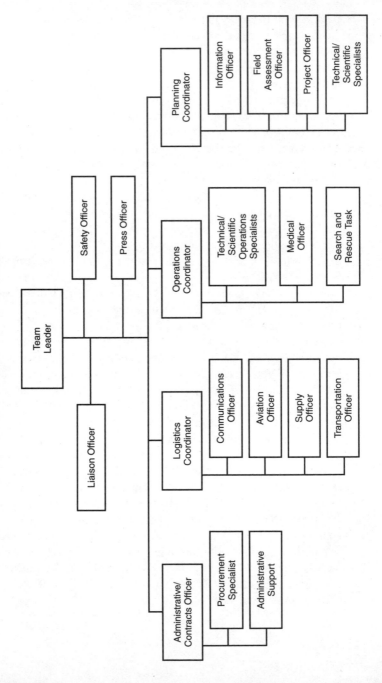

Chapter 10

Peace Operations

Although U.S. forces have long been involved in peace operations, such as the 46-year-long peace enforcement effort on the Korean Peninsula and the 16-year-old peacekeeping operation in the Sinai Desert, events of the post–Cold War era indicate that U.S. forces will conduct such operations with even greater frequency.

PEACEKEEPING OPERATIONS (PKOs)
The main function of units conducting PKOs is to establish a presence that inhibits hostile actions by the disputing parties and bolsters multilateral confidence in the peace process. PKOs support the continuation of diplomatic efforts to achieve long-term political settlements and normalized, peaceful relations. The United States may participate in PKOs as the lead nation, as a contingent, or by providing military observers.

Fundamentals of Peacekeeping
Fundamentals of PKOs include:
- *Firmness.* Peacekeepers must evince a firmness of purpose and unwavering solidarity in matters of principle and integrity.
- *Impartiality.* Even the perception of partiality will compromise a PK force's effectiveness. The actions of the PK force must be absolutely impartial to preserve all parties' consent for the operation.
- *Clarity of intention.* To maintain trust and understanding, keep all parties to the agreement informed regarding what the PK force is trying to achieve.
- *Anticipation.* Foresee and deter or preclude incidents likely to provoke violations of the accords.

- *Consent.* Respect the host nation's laws and culture to maintain all parties' consent to the operation.
- *Integration.* This can be achieved in at least two ways. National contingents can perform certain functions forcewide (e.g., the Slobovian contingent is responsible for logistics, and the Druidian contingent is responsible for communications). Another integrating method is to create, train, and deploy a reserve composed of individuals from all PK contingents, to demonstrate solidarity and share the risk.
- *Freedom of movement.* Mobility—for support and performance of all requisite missions—must be maintained at all times to prevent compartmentalization of the effort, with corollary perceptions of impartiality or uneven effort.

Multilateral Coordination

Coordination between PK military forces and IOs, NGOs, and PVOs is an important feature of PKOs. U.S. military personnel may perform a wide variety of functions in support of PKOs. They may be detailed to serve on a multinational staff or in a group of military observers. The United States may also participate in PKOs by providing PK forces. These may include ground, air, maritime, space, and special operations forces. The force size, contribution, and organization vary with the mission, mandate, and threat in the operational area. PK missions usually involve observing, monitoring or supervising, and assisting parties to a dispute.

Generally, the organization of a PK force headquarters is structured around common military staff functions, such as administration, intelligence, operations, logistics, communications, and civil affairs. The commander also has a personal staff and a civilian staff. In UN-sponsored operations, national contingents perform under operational control of the UN force commander. The geographic combatant commander exercises combatant command (command authority) over U.S. forces assigned to PKOs in his or her area of responsibility. The U.S. contingent commander, who is the senior U.S. officer, provides the command link between U.S. PK units and the geographic combatant commander. The force commander's directives provide numerous details about command and control, responsibilities, tasks, methods, force identification, media relations, and other details of PK force operations.

The political mandate, terms of reference (TOR), and status-of-forces agreement (SOFA) are important sources of information for mission analysis and planning. Additionally, commanders and staffs may gain valuable insights by reviewing lessons learned from previous PKO or training exercises. Information is critical to a PK force, not only for mission success but

Sample Chain of Command for a PKO

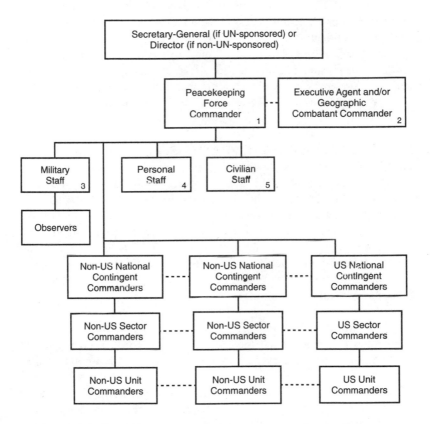

1. May or may not be US command

2. Will always be US command

3. Normally consists of a Chief of Staff, a Deputy Chief of Staff, and an operations staff

4. Normally consists of a military assistant, political adviser, legal adviser, public affairs officer, interpreter(s), and liaison officers from the armed forces of the parties in the conflict

5. Provided by the UN Secretariat for UN-sponsored operations

—————— Peacekeeping Operational Control Combatant Command (command authority)

- - - - - - Coordination/Liaison (as requried)

also to protect the force. Information is collected in generally the same way as in other military operations.

Force protection is a high priority for a deployed PK force. Rules of engagement (ROE) are also an essential element of force protection and provide for appropriate action to protect the force. Although the UN sometimes designates multinational reserves, the U.S. contingent commander also designates a U.S. reserve. The U.S. contingent reserve should be sufficiently armed, trained, equipped, and funded; advantageously located; and mobile. PKOs require contingency planning for disasters, evacuation, and handling of displaced persons and refugees, as well as hostile action.

PEACE ENFORCEMENT OPERATIONS (PEOs)

In PEOs, the "enemy" is the dispute or antagonism, not the belligerent parties to a dispute. Although PEOs may require combat, they may have more restrictive ROE than most situations. Conflict, violence, disorder, a high level of mistrust, and possibly even chaos, rather than peace, are all common characteristics of the PEO environment. Consent of the parties to the dispute is *not* a requirement, although some parties may extend it. Although there may be some restrictions on weapons and targeting, peace enforcers generally have full combat capabilities, depending on the political mandate, ROE, and tactical situation.

Fundamental Principles

Fundamentals that help guide the conduct of successful PEOs include:

- *Success.* Measure success by the absence of fighting, not military victory.
- *Impartiality.* Impartiality will definitely help achieve a lasting peace, but it is not as central to the process as it is in PKOs. Some parties may break the terms of the armistice or cease-fire more often or more flagrantly than others and make impartiality impossible.
- *Restraint in the use of force.* Use nonlethal force whenever and wherever possible, but remember that military operations alone cannot be the basis of a lasting peace.
- *Methods of coercion.* Force, up to and including lethal force, may be necessary to convince the parties that a politically embraced peace is more attractive than continuation of the conflict.
- *The presence of civilians.* Commanders must be extremely sensitive to the presence of civilians in combat zones and must avoid collateral damage and civilian casualties to a unique degree. These measures

are critical to the success of the political peacemaking process; the old shibboleth "We had to destroy this city to save it" must be avoided.

• *Varying multinational commitment.* For political, cultural, financial, and other reasons, some partners in the PE force may not be as committed to the operation as others. Multinational force commanders must craft their operations to simultaneously sustain multinational solidarity and mission effectiveness throughout the range of potentially necessary operations.

Assignment of PEO Missions
Accurate intelligence and comprehensive mission analysis are the basis for determining the structure and composition of the force. The U.S. commander has the authority to employ the force's full range of combat capabilities to achieve mission objectives and protect the force. Peace enforcement missions may include enforcement of sanctions and exclusion zones, protection of humanitarian assistance efforts, operations to restore order, and forcible separation of belligerent parties or parties to a dispute.

Peace Enforcement Operations
For both unilateral and multinational operations, U.S. forces will probably be structured as a joint task force (JTF). The composition of the JTF will depend on the mission, the political objectives, and the threat. For multinational operations, PE forces may operate under either a "lead nation" or a parallel command and control arrangement. In a lead nation arrangement, one nation's commander directs or leads the multinational partners because that nation is providing the preponderance of the force and command and control structure. Such an arrangement is conducive to unity of command and direction of effort. In a parallel system, the PE force commander is chosen by the sponsoring international organization, and the ad hoc staff consists of members from all participating nations. Although this arrangement does not provide the same unity and cohesion of effort as the lead nation system, it does promote continued commitment to the operation by all participants.

U.S. PEO forces are normally employed in accordance with a detailed military campaign or operation plan, which *includes the desired end state and a plan to shift responsibilities to a PK force.* A corresponding political-military interagency plan supports successful mission achievement and smooth transition. Mission-termination objectives, determined in accordance with the political goals and desired end state (and, in UN operations, found in the mandate), ideally set conditions for maintaining or restoring peace and a long-term settlement of the dispute.

PEO Intelligence

Intelligence is developed to support PEOs using the same process used in other combat operations, but information similar to that required in PKOs is also sought. In PEOs, fire support is constrained by more restrictive ROE, necessary to minimize collateral damage. Logistics planning and support in PEOs are the same as in other combat operations but include considerations for PKOs and the possible transition to other MOOTW. Integrating information operations, PSYOPS, and civil-military operations is also key to effectively conducting PEOs.

Rules of Engagement

Well-conceived, clearly stated, and thoroughly disseminated ROE can make the difference between success and failure in peace operations. ROE in PEOs are usually less restrictive than in PKOs, but more restrictive than in other combat operations. Too many ambiguous situations may arise for ROE to specifically address each and every one; for this reason, all members of the PE force must not only understand the ROE themselves but also comprehend the rationale behind them. To ensure a mobile, survivable force, both engineer and chemical protection forces provide essential support during peace operations. Employment planning for PEOs is the same as for combat operations, since these may occur. See chapter 12 for more information on ROE.

INTERAGENCY COORDINATION

Other agencies, particularly the Department of State (DOS), will be deeply involved in peace operations. Commanders must ensure that military activities are closely integrated with the activities of other agencies to optimize the effectiveness of the total effort. Emphasis should be placed on early establishment of liaison among the various agencies. The establishment of interagency coordinating centers, such as civil-military operations centers (CMOCs), is one means of fostering unity of effort in achieving the objectives of the operation. If available, a country team may facilitate coordination at the host-nation level.

Often, peace operations are conducted in environments characterized by adverse humanitarian conditions such as human suffering, disease, violations of human rights, civil wars, or privation. Commanders must coordinate their efforts not only with the sponsoring organization, other militaries, and the host nation but also with a legion of NGOs/PVOs and other agencies involved in relieving adverse humanitarian conditions. All participants must understand the intent, methods, and local disposition of the NGOs/PVOs and foster a spirit of cooperation and common interest. They may help commanders and staffs to better accomplish the mission because of their familiarity with the culture, language, and sensitivities of a populace. However, caution is necessary to prevent any perception by the populace or the parties to the dispute that these organizations are part of an intelligence-gathering mechanism. Their purpose is to address humanitarian requirements, and their primary source of security is their neutrality. Commanders will also find that the cultures of some of these organizations differ markedly from military culture, and there may be a strong desire on their part to maintain a wide distance from military activities.

Although the two types of peace operations—PKOs and PEOs—are clearly defined, the distinctions between them are not always easy to discern or maintain in the field. "Gray areas" may arise due to the dynamic political and military environments in which these operations are conducted. Commanders and staffs must remain prepared for transition to other operations, such as offensive or defensive ones, or even to conduct humanitarian assistance missions. Further, even within an otherwise clear PKO, the conditions within certain sectors might change, forcing local operational changes within an otherwise static overall situation. Especially close political-military coordination and communications are essential for continuing operations successfully in such situations.

MULTINATIONAL COOPERATION

Several factors are essential for success when peace operations are conducted in cooperation with other nations.

- *Respect and Professionalism.* Respect for multinational partners' ideas and culture and maintenance of a demeanor of military professionalism help establish a basis for cooperation and unity of effort.
- *Mission Assignment.* Missions assigned by the force commander must be appropriate to each partner's capabilities and national direction. Multinational partners should be integrated into the planning process, thus ensuring unity of effort. Language requirements and linguistic support are important considerations.
- *Management of Resources.* Multinational partners may seek assistance with logistic support. Establish agreements for exchangeable or

transferable commodities before operations begin, and further develop and refine them throughout the operation. Legal support is important in formulating and interpreting these agreements.

- *Harmony.* Establish personal relationships and an effective rapport among members of a multinational force at all command levels; such relationships can contribute significantly to the success of the operation.

Chapter 11

MOOTW at the Tactical Level: The Joint Task Force

When it is necessary to engage the military instrument of national power for any type of MOOTW, a combatant commander usually in charge of the operation designates a JTF to conduct the military operation. The combatant commander develops the mission statement and concept of operations based on the direction of the NCA and the Chairman of the Joint Chiefs of Staff. Input from the Department of State, USAID's Office of Foreign Disaster Assistance (OFDA), and other U.S. government agencies, coupled with METT-TC (mission, enemy, time, terrain–troops available, civil considerations) in the joint operations area (JOA), inevitably affects the mission statement.

Components establish a force list (personnel, equipment, and supplies) and associated movement requirements to support the operation. In coordination with the JTF commander, the combatant commander determines the military forces and other national means required to accomplish the mission, allocates or requests the military forces, and determines the command relationships for the JTF.

ORGANIZING A JTF

The JTF concept provides organizational flexibility, is task-organized, reflects the mission's requirements and the unique and necessary capabilities of the service and functional components, and facilitates rapid deployment and phased introduction of forces. A JTF is normally designated when the mission has a specific limited objective and does not require overall centralized control of logistics. The mission assigned to a JTF requires not only the execution of responsibilities involving two or more military departments but also, increasingly, the support of all types of agencies. Generally, a JTF is dissolved when the purpose for which it was created has been achieved.

The JTF organization resembles a traditional military organization, with a commander, command element, and the forces required to execute the mission. The primary purpose of the JTF headquarters (HQ) is command, control, synchronization, and administration of the forces assigned to the JTF.

PLANNING FOR THE JTF MISSION

During interagency operations, the JTF HQ provides the basis for a unified effort, centralized direction, and decentralized execution. The unique aspects of the interagency process require the personnel of the JTF HQ to be especially flexible, responsive, and cognizant of the capabilities of not only the JTF's components but those of other agencies as well. The JTF HQ is the operational focal point for interagency coordination. Accordingly, the JTF commander may find it necessary to expand the JTF staff to accommodate additional requirements.

Creating Assessment Teams

A valuable tool in the mission analysis process is the deployment of a JTF assessment team to the projected JOA. The JTF assessment team is similar in composition to the humanitarian assistance survey team (HAST) and, if given early warning of pending operations, may be able to conduct assessment in association with the HAST. If so, staffing requirements will be reduced. Typical team members include the JTF commander, J-2, J-3, J-4, J-5, J-6, key logistics staff personnel (including transportation and engineer planners and contracting personnel), medical personnel, legal officer, chaplain, civil affairs officer, a member of the USAID/OFDA DART scheduled to work with the JTF (if a humanitarian mission), and other staff members necessary to commence the interagency planning process. Special operations force personnel possessing unique cultural, language, and technical skills are usually extremely useful and should be requested through the combatant commander.

The assessment team helps clarify details of the mission (i.e., the concept of the operation), the type of force required to accomplish it, the optimal sequence of force deployment, availability of in-country assets, and ongoing operations by organizations other than U.S. military forces.

Coordinating Operations

Other types of operations (e.g., development or humanitarian relief operations) may be in progress prior to arrival of the JTF in the JOA. The desired end state, essential tasks, and exit criteria must be clearly expressed to the media to gain and maintain public support. NGOs/PVOs and other inter-governmental and international organizations are often conducting operations well before the arrival of military forces and will be there long after the U.S. military departs. What is done by the military in the meantime has a distinct influence on long-term goals and the ability to achieve them. The ranking U.S. military commander may be the only official in the crisis area whose goals and responsibilities include unifying the efforts of all agencies. In humanitarian assistance operations, a JTF's mission cannot successfully conclude until in-place organizations are operating effectively. Therefore, successful interaction between organizations is imperative.

In peace operations, coordination is required with a host of international, regional, and regional security organizations. While this is accomplished at the strategic level by the U.S. NCA, the participating U.S. JTF commander is likely to be required to send representatives to mission planning and coordination meetings.

Identifying *the* Priority Task
Determine the single most important task that will stabilize the situation (e.g., establishing secure convoy routes). Communicate this to the combatant commander as well as to the ambassador. To reach this "bottom-line" determination, seek not only military staff input but also that of key agency representatives.

Reviewing the Regional Strategy
In further analyzing the mission, consider the regional strategy for the projected JOA. The Department of State, UN, and other intergovernmental and international organizations can provide this information with an appreciation for how the regional strategy affects the countries involved in projected operations. This information helps legitimize the mission and assists in emphasizing end-state and force requirements.

Establishing Political Relationships
When the JTF deploys, the JTF commander must quickly establish a relationship with the U.S. ambassador, the country team, and either the U.S. agency representatives in country for foreign operations or the federal coordinating officer (FCO) for domestic disaster relief operations. If not initiated at the national level in advance, these relationships should be negotiated with the U.S. Embassy upon arrival. If time and the situation permit, it is important that the JTF commander and key staff members meet with the

NSC working group in Washington, D.C., prior to deployment. It may also be useful to meet with the regional and functional elements of the Office of the Secretary of Defense, Joint Staff representatives, the appropriate regional bureau at the Department of State, and appropriate officials from the embassies of the nations involved. Establishing an effective working relationship with the ambassador will help in any foreign interagency endeavor.

In cases of cross-border operations in which more than one country is involved, each U.S. mission may have a different perspective of the operation. Intelligence and information relationships between the JTF commander, local and state authorities, the country team, and U.S. government agency representatives must be established at the earliest stages of planning. *Commanders should recognize local and organizational sensitivities to counterintelligence units and their operations.* The JTF commander should consult with appropriate ambassadors and country teams to coordinate actions and determine areas of concern, ensuring that the combatant commander and the Chairman of the Joint Chiefs of Staff are informed of all consultations so that the Joint Staff can properly coordinate with the Department of State.

Establishing JTF HQ
Whether afloat or ashore, the location of the JTF HQ is very important. Not only should it be defensible, but it should be positioned to facilitate coordination with representatives of the political and private sectors, the media, and other military elements of an operation. It needs a sufficient power source and communication lines to support operations and should provide a location for a possible Special Compartmented Information Facility (SCIF) and a collateral storage of intelligence information. Coordination at all levels is a requirement. Proximity to the American Embassy or U.S. Diplomatic Mission may provide the potential to enhance military operational capability.

ORGANIZATIONAL TOOLS FOR THE JTF COMMANDER
Commanders should establish control structures to provide coherence to the activities of all elements in the JOA. In addition to military operations, this structure should address political, civil, administrative, legal, and humanitarian activities, as well as the activities of media groups that may be involved. Commanders should ultimately consider how their actions and those of engaged organizations contribute toward the desired end state.

Executive Steering Group (ESG)
The ESG may be composed of key leaders and staff from the JTF, the embassy, NGOs/PVOs present in the JOA, and other organizations as

appropriate. In the absence of a similar forum, the ESG can facilitate the exchange of information about operational policies, as well as the resolution of difficulties arising among the various organizations. The ESG plays a policy role and is charged with interpreting and coordinating theater aspects of strategic combat support and combat service support.

Civil-Military Operations Center (CMOC)

Conceptually, the CMOC is the nexus of coordination and planning for military forces, U.S. government agencies, civilian authorities, participating NGOs/PVOs/IOs, and representatives of the population. Although not a new concept, the CMOC has been effectively employed as a means to coordinate civil and military operations and plays an executive role (as opposed to the policy role of the ESG). The organization of the CMOC is theater- and mission-dependent. During large-scale HA operations, if an HOC is formed by the host country or the UN, the CMOC becomes the focal point for coordination between the military and civilian agencies involved in the operation. A commander at any echelon may establish a CMOC to facilitate coordination with other agencies, departments, organizations, and the host nation. In fact, more than one CMOC may be established in an AOR or JOA, and each is tailored for mission accomplishment.

Purposes of a CMOC. The JTF commander may form a CMOC as the action cell to perform the following activities:

- Carry out the JTF commander's decisions regarding civil-military operations
- Perform liaison and coordination between military units and other agencies, departments, and organizations to meet the needs of the populace
- Provide a venue for partnership between military and other engaged organizations
- Receive, validate, and coordinate requests for support from NGOs/PVOs, ISOs, and intergovernmental organizations

Civilian and Multinational Military Representation in the CMOC. The JTF commander should invite representatives of other agencies to participate, including the following:

- Liaisons from service and functional components, as well as representatives from the supporting infrastructure, such as port and airfield managers or their proxies
- USAID/OFDA DART representatives
- DOS, country team, and other U.S. government representatives
- Military liaison personnel from participating countries

Sample Organization of a CMOC

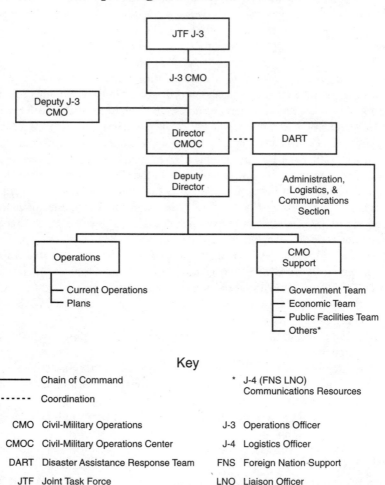

Key

————	Chain of Command	* J-4 (FNS LNO)
- - - - - -	Coordination	Communications Resources

CMO	Civil-Military Operations	J-3	Operations Officer
CMOC	Civil-Military Operations Center	J-4	Logistics Officer
DART	Disaster Assistance Response Team	FNS	Foreign Nation Support
JTF	Joint Task Force	LNO	Liaison Officer

- Host-country or local government representatives
- Representatives of intergovernmental and international organizations (e.g., UNHCR and ICRC)
- Representatives from NGOs/PVOs
- Political representatives

Political representatives may provide the JTF commander with the means of satisfying operational requirements, resulting in consistency of military and political actions. Additionally, the CMOC forum appeals to NGOs/PVOs because it provides direction for their efforts when and where most needed. The JTF commander cannot *direct* interagency cooperation among engaged agencies, but the provision of JTF resources and capabilities, such as protection, logistical support, information, communication, and other services, often leads to greater cooperation.

Activities in the CMOC. The key functions of a JTF CMOC include:

- Continuous coordination of JTF operations with those of other agencies
- Identification of mission requirements and organizations that can fulfill them; validated requests go to the appropriate JTF or agency representative for action
- Validation and coordination of requests from NGOs/PVOs/IOs for routine and emergency military support, and coordination of requests *to* them for their support
- Coordination with the DART deployed to the scene by USAID/OFDA
- Formation of ad hoc mission planning groups to address complex military missions that support NGO/PVO requirements
- Formation of follow-on assessment groups
- Coordination of public affairs issues
- Submission of situation reports regarding JTF operations, security, and other information to participants in the collective effort
- Formation and coordination of port and airfield committee meetings for space and access-related issues
- Facilitation of the creation and organization of a logistics distribution system for food, water, and medical relief efforts

As an active member of the CMOC, the JTF public affairs officer (PAO) is responsible for ensuring that member agencies agree on messages and press releases and for developing a group consensus in response to media queries.

Liaison Teams

Commanders designate liaison officers (LNOs) as the focal point for communication with external agencies and the host-nation government. Supported agencies usually need a much clearer understanding of the military planning process than might otherwise be possible; often, the best solution is direct liaison. LNOs are normally assigned to the office of the JTF's chief of staff and work closely with the operations officer to resolve interagency problems. Experience indicates that ready transportation, relevant language qualifications, and reliable communications are essential.

Members of the DART are uniquely qualified to address both sides of the civil-military relationship. They understand the NGO/PVO/IO culture and language, as well as military involvement in humanitarian assistance. A JTF-DART liaison relationship should be sought during coordination between the geographic combatant command staff and the Joint Staff. It is extremely important that LNOs be conversant in the languages spoken in the area, be familiar with the culture, and possess a solid knowledge of the doctrine, capabilities, procedures, and culture of their own organizations. Civil affairs or coalition support teams may be available to serve as LNOs. The use of contracted interpreters to augment liaison teams may be another option, although in some cases, their loyalties may affect reliability.

OTHER JTF INTERAGENCY CONSIDERATIONS
Intelligence Support and Control
The combatant command's staff should request and support the deployment of a national intelligence support team (NIST) to help ensure JTF connectivity with the theater joint intelligence center (JIC) and national intelligence agencies. The interagency support provided by a NIST allows access to agency-unique information and analysis. It affords a link to national-level databases and other information that is normally beyond the capacity of the JTF. Participating agencies retain control of their members deployed with the NIST, but the NIST operates under the staff supervision of the JTF J-2.

The JIC is the primary intelligence organization providing support to joint operations in theater. It is responsible for producing and providing the intelligence required to support the joint force commander and staff, components, task forces, and elements; it also coordinates support from other intelligence organizations.

The joint intelligence support element (JISE) is the JTF commander's primary intelligence apparatus. The JISE may constitute a new entity, or it may be little more than the combatant command's JIC, or elements thereof, moving forward.

Intelligence must also be shared among all command elements supporting the JTF and combatant command (including USTRANSCOM elements providing strategic lift capabilities).

JTF intelligence operations require redundant communications capabilities to properly support various complex requirements. Joint intelligence planners normally prepare a detailed intelligence architecture to support all components during the course of each unique operation. Standard JTF intelligence operations require Joint Worldwide Integrated Communications Systems (JWICS) capability to provide the JTF commander with secure video teleconferencing and data capabilities. JWICS also provides a secure data path for the Joint Deployable Intelligence Support System (JDISS). The JDISS provides secure intelligence data and image processing. Each service also links its own intelligence systems to support its specific requirements.

Personnel in the JISE face unique challenges in providing support to the JTF commander. Traditional sources of classified military information have to be melded with unclassified information from open sources and local human intelligence (HUMINT). This effort is complicated by sensitivities of certain nonmilitary interagency partners to the basic *concept* of military intelligence.

Consideration must be given to control of sensitive or classified military information in forums such as the CMOC, where representatives of other U.S. government agencies, NGOs/PVOs, and IOs will be present. Procedures for control and disclosure of classified information practiced by the DOD normally do not exist within other agencies. This omission may result in the inadvertent or intentional passage of sensitive information to individuals not cleared for access to such information.

The combatant commander is responsible for controlling the release of classified military information within the JOA in accordance with MCM 176-92, *Delegation of Authority to Commanders of Unified Commands to Disclose Classified Military Information to Foreign Governments and International Organizations*. In the absence of other guidance, J-2s should share only information that is mission essential, affects lower-level operations, and is perishable. When required, authority to downgrade classification or to sanitize information should be provided to the appropriate operational echelon. Any U.S. classified information released to a non-U.S. force or organization must be properly marked to indicate that it is releasable.

Most organizations cannot afford more than a minimal level of security protection for classified information given to them by the United States. Therefore, it is likely that any information they are provided will be disclosed to unauthorized individuals.

Force Protection

Depending on METT-TC, JTF operations may require significant force protection support. An operational force protection package may be deployed in early-arrival echelons to quickly develop the local situation for the JTF commander. Force protection teams can consist of counterintelligence personnel, interrogators, interpreters, and other specially trained personnel. Force protection teams normally have mobile communications and may use the Theater Rapid Reaction Intelligence Package system to communicate critical data to the JTF.

Logistical Support

The level of the logistical effort conducted by local government or civilian agencies has a bearing on deployment and sustainment of the JTF. Moreover, the JTF commander may be asked to assume all or part of the burden of logistics after arrival. The supported combatant commander's LOC links the JTF with the Joint Staff, the services, the Defense Logistics Agency (DLA), USTRANSCOM, and other supporting commands and agencies.

As U.S. military force structure continues to be drawn down, contracting with U.S. or local civilian agencies to augment military support capabilities with local supplies, services, and real estate requirements becomes more important, particularly for JTFs. Another contracting avenue is the Logistics Civil Augmentation Program (LOGCAP), which provides civilian contractual assistance in peace to meet crisis or wartime support requirements worldwide. LOGCAP can provide myriad specialty contract services, such as well drilling, laundry, power generation, portable toilets, cranes, plumbing, construction, lighting, and port support.

The JTF must establish movement priorities between JTF requirements and those of other U.S. government agencies, the country team, coalition or UN forces, and NGOs/PVOs. The Joint Movement Center (JMC) is the primary organization for coordinating movements to support joint operations in theater. Close communications should be established with all elements to ensure that their movement requirements are fully understood by the JTF to enable effective planning and security for materiel movement.

Coordination is essential for optimal use of NGO/PVO resources; such employment reduces military support requirements in many humanitarian operations. In addition, it helps avoid saturation of one sector at the expense of another and strengthens unity of effort.

Meteorological and Oceanographic (METOC) Support

Environmental and geophysical conditions cause natural disasters (typhoons, hurricanes, floods, droughts, earthquakes, tidal waves), can adversely affect the response to these disasters, and can influence the course of operations of all types. To best anticipate these effects, the JTF commander must have access to accurate advance knowledge of METOC conditions.

The combatant command senior METOC officer should coordinate for the deployment of METOC support to provide accurate weather and oceanographic data. Component commands provide METOC personnel and resources.

The Joint METOC Forecast Unit (JMFU) is the primary organization providing forecasting support to joint operations in theater. The JMFU is assisted by service METOC centers. The JMFU is responsible for producing and providing the METOC information required to support the joint force commander and staff, components, task forces, and elements, and it coordinates support from other METOC organizations.

The JMFU and component METOC personnel perform observation and forecasting services, maintaining a constant vigil for the operational consequences of weather and oceanographic conditions. The JMFU and component METOC personnel have access to weather satellite imagery and data, accurate forecast models of atmospheric and oceanographic conditions, and National Oceanographic and Atmospheric Administration (NOAA) capabilities, and they can exploit international weather and oceanographic databases.

Legal Support

Legal advisers should possess a comprehensive understanding of the regulations and laws applicable to military forces and all other participating agencies. Legal advisers must be active participants in the interagency process to obtain the working knowledge necessary for the identification and resolution of legal issues confronting the commander.

Legal advisers can help resolve some of the toughest interagency issues involving the following:

- Domestic legal authority for DOD participation and support
- International law
- Dislocated civilians
- Immunity and asylum
- Claims
- Investigations
- War crimes and related issues
- Arrests and detentions
- Intelligence law
- Budget and fiscal matters
- Contracting
- Environmental restrictions
- Limitations on employment of U.S. military forces
- Rules of engagement (ROE)

Rules of Engagement

ROE and requests for changes to ROE can quickly escalate to the presidential level. Maximum coordination and understanding among all participants is crucial to a well-informed and timely decision at the national level. In multinational operations, for such purposes as peacekeeping operations or humanitarian assistance missions, a preplanned set of ROE becomes critical. The CJCS standing ROE (CJCS Instruction 3121.01, *Standing Rules of Engagement for U.S. Forces,* 1 October 1994) serves as a coordination tool with U.S. allies for the development of multinational ROE. ROE and revisions to ROE must be communicated to NGOs/PVOs, IOs, and intergovernmental organizations when these rules affect their operations. Sample ROEs are in chapter 12.

Media Affairs

In building an atmosphere of trust and cooperation with the media, the United States must speak with one voice—both politically and militarily—and at the same time, see that partners' voices are heard. Media considerations for the JTF commander include the following:

- Establish a Joint Information Bureau (JIB).
- Include a public affairs representative during all stages of planning for the operation.
- Coordinate with the combatant commander, the DOD, the ambassador, and the country team in JTF interaction with the media.
- Coordinate with the embassy through its PAO and civil information officer, if present, and with the host-nation Ministry of Information.
- Provide representatives of NGOs/PVOs with access to the media through the JIB's facilities.
- Allow a representative from the JIB to be present at command meetings and briefings and to attend CMOC or similar civil-military organization meetings.
- Assemble the JTF public affairs section, including a dedicated JIB representative from engaged agencies, if possible.
- Invite assignment of a spokesperson from the humanitarian relief community to assist in media briefings when the JIB is created.
- Establish a civil information program, coordinated among a civil affairs command, the joint psychological operations task force (JPOTF), the USIS officer, the host country, and other appropriate agencies.

Space Support

Support from space is essential during joint operations and unified actions, especially when infrastructure in the JOA is damaged or nonexistent. Space systems can provide reliable communications, weather data, terrain information, mapping support, and precise navigation data. Such support is provided by a variety of sources and must be coordinated among agencies. The JTF commander should consider establishing a space operations cell consisting of members from U.S. Space Command's joint space support team, the NIST, the Defense Mapping Agency, and the Defense Information Support Agency. This will ensure the JTF commander has direct access to the major resources necessary to provide multiagency space support.

PART III

Tactics, Techniques, and Procedures for MOOTW

This part covers tactics, techniques, and procedures for the tasks most commonly associated with the execution of MOOTW. It does *not* include the many tasks associated with MOOTW which are also commonly associated with combat operations. Other books, such as Stackpole's *Combat Leader's Field Guide, 12th Edition,* address them.

Throughout this part, we repeatedly use the term "METT-TC." METT-TC is the military abbreviation of the seven key factors used to assess a military situation and plan an operation. The factors are: Mission, Enemy, Terrain (including weather), Troops available, Time, and Civilian considerations.

The accompanying figure relates the list of MOOTW missions to the tactical tasks covered in the following chapters.

MOOTW Missions and Tasks

Mission	Know and Use ROE	Establish and Operate an OP	Establish and Operate a Chkpt	React to Bomb Threat/Car Bomb	Conduct Cordon and Search	Search a Building	Process Confiscated Documents	Evaluate a Civilian Infrastructure	Populace and Resource Control	React to Civil Disturbance	Control Civilian Movement	Control Dislocated Civilians	Establish and Operate a DC Camp (DCs)	Conduct a Show of Force
Military Spt to Counterdrug Opns	X													
Combating Terrorism	X	X	X	X		X								
Humanitarian Assistance	X							X	X		X	X	X	
Domestic Spt Opns (MSCA)								X				X	X	
Domestic Spt Opns (MSCLEA)	X	X		X						X				
Nation Assistance/Support to Counterinsurgency	X								X					X
Noncombatant Evacuation Operations	X		X	X		X						X	X	
Peace Ops (PK & PE)	X	X	X	X	X	X	X	X	X	X	X	X	X	X
Show of Force Operations	X													X
Support to Insurgencies	X													

MOOTW Missions and Tasks (Continued)

	Deliver Supplies/Humanitarian Aid	Medical Care to Noncombatants	Protect Noncombatants/Facilities	Apprehend/Detain Noncombatants	Identify and Process Detainees	Monitor Prisoner Exchange	Interdict Smuggling Operations	Interact with Media Representatives	Disarm Belligerents	Establish an Operating Base	Escort and Defend a Convoy	Evacuate Noncombatants (NEO)	Employ Personal Antiterrorism Measures	Conduct Negotiations
Military Spt to Counterdrug Opns				X				X	X				X	
Combating Terrorism			X	X	X			X			X	X	X	
Humanitarian Assistance	X	X							X	X	X			
Domestic Spt Opns (MSCA)	X	X								X				
Domestic Spt Opns (MSCLEA)							X*			X			X	
Nation Assistance/Support to Counterinsurgency		X	X	X	X			X			X			
Noncombatant Evacuation Operations	X									X		X	X	
Peace Opns (PK & PE)	X	X	X	X	X	X	X	X	X	X	X	X	X	X
Show of Force Operations														
Support to Insurgencies		X		X										

* Legal limitations exist when this task is conducted inside the U.S.

Chapter 12

Know and Use
Rules of Engagement

In MOOTW, well-crafted rules of engagement (ROE) can make the difference between success and failure. ROE are directives that delineate the circumstances and limitations under which U.S. forces initiate and/or continue engagement with antagonists. The ROE discussed in this chapter pertain only to ground forces.

In MOOTW, ROE define when and how force may be used. ROE may reflect the law of armed conflict and operational considerations but principally address restraints on the use of force. ROE are also the primary means by which commanders convey legal, political, diplomatic, and military guidance to the military force.

DEVELOPING ROE

ROE are developed by military commanders, but they *must* reflect the direction and strategy of political leaders. This process must balance mission accomplishment with political considerations while ensuring protection of the force. Restraint remains a guiding principle and should pervade ROE development. The staff judge advocate (SJA) or JTF legal adviser should review all ROE.

When formulating ROE, it is unlikely that commanders can anticipate every conceivable situation that will confront the soldiers of the MOOTW force. Just as with any operational directive, commanders must include a clear statement of their intent within ROE, so that their subordinates in the field may use their disciplined initiative and judgment to conduct operations accordingly. An "intent" statement in the ROE is therefore highly appropriate.

PREPARING UNITS FOR OPERATIONS UNDER ROE

ROE for MOOTW are often quite different from those under which units operate while training for or conducting combat operations. Rehearsing and war-gaming ROE in a variety of scenarios will help soldiers and leaders better understand the ROE.

If possible, integrate challenging ROE scenarios into predeployment tactical training, down to the individual level. Having each soldier carry ROE cards on his or her person, or even requiring rote memorization of ROE, may be helpful but will be far more effective when supplemented by personal, live experience in training, with the manifold challenges of conduct under the ROE. Leaders at all levels should personally ensure that their subordinates understand the ROE in detail appropriate to their levels of responsibilities and two levels higher, in the event that unexpected situations or casualties place them in charge.

ROE are best understood within the context of the mission. Good ROE are not pie-in-the-sky limitations dreamed up by some distant, detached "do-gooder," but rather the realistic, serious, appropriate constraints on the enormously lethal capabilities available to modern forces. They should be explained to soldiers as such and are best conveyed as "things we have to do to get the job done." When possible, connections with the principles of land warfare—which must be observed in any situation—can and should be emphasized in training. Similarly, just as soldiers are trained to observe the law of land warfare even in the face of flagrant violations by the enemy, they must be trained to observe the ROE despite strenuous provocations by antagonistic factions. In combat under any circumstances, atrocities breed atrocities, and one need look no further than the actions of the now-disbanded Canadian Airborne Regiment in Somalia in 1993 to see the possibilities for and counterproductive consequences of unconstrained violence in MOOTW.

ROE should *always* be included in OPLANs and OPORDs and should address all means of combat power potentially available to the unit. For example, indirect fire support ROE are as important as individual or crew-served weapons ROE.

EMPLOYING ROE

ROE in multinational operations can create unique challenges. Commanders must be aware that there will most likely be differing national interpretations of the ROE. Close coordination of ROE with multinational partners will help preclude problems stemming from conflicting or differing interpretations.

Commanders should be firm and determined when executing ROE in peace operations. If the peace operations force is seen by potential antagonists to lack confidence, its soldiers and leaders may be further challenged, resulting in an unnecessarily high level of response or an escalation in the overall level of violence. Commanders should thoroughly plan the manner in which force is to be used and rehearse anticipated actions. Finally, ROE must be impartially applied in PK. In PE, this guideline may not fully apply. Even in PE, however, use of force without prejudice remains important.

CHANGING ROE

ROE vary in different operations and sometimes change during peace operations. The ROE must be consistent at all levels of command. Nothing in the ROE should negate a commander's obligation to take all necessary and appropriate action to protect the force. Additionally, the ROE in peace operations may establish guidance for situations such as the search and detention of inhabitants or their property, the authority of local security patrols, the prevention of black-market operations, the surrender of hostile personnel, and the protection of contractor personnel and equipment in support of U.S. operations.

Commanders at all levels must know how to request changes to ROE. ROE are developed with political considerations in mind and are approved at a high level of authority. However, the requirement to change the ROE may result from immediate tactical emergencies at the local level; introduction of combat forces from a hostile nation; attacks by antagonistic factions using sophisticated weapon systems, including nuclear, biological, or chemical (NBC) weapons; or incidents resulting in loss of life. Commanders should anticipate these situations and proactively request changes through appropriate channels.

SAMPLE ROE

These are actual unclassified ROE and instructions for use of force and weapons policy provided to familiarize commanders and their staffs with the types of rules and instructions and various formats and means of dissemination used by U.S. ground forces in recent operations. The selected operations are Operation Restore Hope, the UN-sanctioned humanitarian relief and enforcement operation conducted in Somalia in 1992 and 1993, and Operation Provide Comfort, a UN-sanctioned humanitarian protection operation conducted in northern Iraq in 1991.

ROE for Operation Restore Hope

1. Situation. Basic OPLAN/OPORD.
2. Mission. Basic OPLAN/OPORD.
3. Execution.
   a. Concept of the Operation.
      (1) If you are operating as a unit, squad, or other formation, follow the orders of your leaders.
      (2) Nothing in these rules negates your inherent right to use reasonable force to defend yourself against dangerous personal attack.
      (3) These rules of self-protection and rules of engagement are not intended to infringe upon your right of self-defense. These rules are intended to prevent indiscriminate use of force or other violations of law or regulation.
      (4) Commanders will instruct their personnel on their mission. This includes the importance of proper conduct and regard for the local population and the need to respect private property and public facilities. The Posse Comitatus Act does not apply in an overseas area. Expect that all missions will have the inherent task of force security and protection.
      (5) ROE cards will be distributed to each deploying soldier (see the figure at the end of this chapter).
   b. Rules of Self-Protection for All Soldiers.
      (1) U.S. forces will protect themselves from threats of death or serious bodily harm. Deadly force may be used to defend your life, the life of another U.S. soldier, or the life of persons in areas under U.S. control. You are authorized to use deadly force in self-defense when—
         (a) You are fired upon.
         (b) Armed elements, mobs, and/or rioters threaten human life.
         (c) There is a clear demonstration of hostile intent in your presence.
      (2) Hostile intent of opposing forces can be determined by unit leaders or individual soldiers if their leaders are not present. Hostile intent is the threat of imminent use of force against U.S. forces or other persons in those areas under the control of U.S. forces. Factors you may consider include—
         (a) Weapons: Are they present? What types?
         (b) Size of the opposing force.
         (c) If weapons are present, the manner in which they are displayed; that is, are they being aimed? Are the weapons part of a firing position?
         (d) How did the opposing force respond to the U.S. forces?
         (e) How does the force act toward unarmed civilians?
         (f) Other aggressive actions.
      (3) You may detain persons threatening or using force that would cause death, serious bodily harm, or interference with mission accomplishment. You may detain persons who commit criminal acts in areas under U.S. control. Detainees should be given to military police as soon as possible for evacuation to central collection points (see paragraph e below).

c. Rules of Engagement. The relief property, foodstuffs, medical supplies, building materials, and other end items belong to the relief agencies distributing the supplies until they are actually distributed to the populace. Your mission includes safe transit of these materials to the populace.

(1) Deadly force may be used only when—

    (a) Fired upon.

    (b) Clear evidence of hostile intent exists (see above for factors to consider to determine hostile intent).

    (c) Armed elements, mobs, and/or rioters threaten human life, sensitive equipment and aircraft, and open and free passage of relief supplies.

(2) In situations where deadly force is not appropriate, use the minimum force necessary to accomplish the mission.

(3) Patrols are authorized to provide relief supplies, U.S. forces, and other persons in those areas under the control of U.S. forces. Patrols may use deadly force if fired upon or if they encounter opposing forces that evidence a hostile intent. Nondeadly force or a show of force should be used if the security of U.S. forces is not compromised by doing so. A graduated show of force includes—

    (a) An order to disband or disperse.

    (b) Show of force/threat of force by U.S. forces that is greater than the force threatened by the opposing force.

    (c) Warning shots aimed to prevent harm to either innocent civilians or the opposing force.

    (d) Other means of nondeadly force. If this show of force does not cause the opposing force to abandon its hostile intent, consider if deadly force is appropriate.

(4) Use of barbed wire fences is authorized.

(5) Unattended means of force (for example, mines, booby traps, trip guns) are not authorized.

(6) If U.S. forces are attacked or threatened by unarmed hostile elements, mobs, and/or rioters, U.S. forces will use the minimum amount of force reasonably necessary to overcome the threat. A graduated response to unarmed hostile elements may be used. Such a response can include—

    (a) Verbal warnings to demonstrators in their native language.

    (b) Shows of force, including the use of riot control formations.

    (c) Warning shots fired over the heads of the hostile elements.

    (d) Other reasonable uses of force, to include deadly force when the element demonstrates a hostile intent, which are necessary and proportional to the threat.

(7) All weapons systems may be employed throughout the area of operations unless otherwise prohibited. The use of weapons systems must be appropriate and proportional, considering the threat.

(8) U.S. forces will not endanger or exploit the property of the local population without their explicit approval. Use of civilian property can usually be compensated by contract or other form of payment. Property that has been used for the purpose of hindering our mission will be

confiscated. Weapons may be confiscated and demilitarized if they are used to interfere with the mission of U.S. forces (see rule 10 below).

(9) Operations will not be conducted outside of the landmass, airspace, and territorial seas of Somalia. However, any USCENTCOM force conducting a search and rescue mission shall use force as necessary and intrude into the landmass, airspace, or territorial sea of any county necessary to recover friendly forces.

(10) Crew-served weapons are considered a threat to U.S. forces and the relief effort whether or not the crew demonstrates hostile intent. Commanders are authorized to use all necessary force to confiscate and demilitarize crew-served weapons in their area of operations.

(a) If an armed individual or weapons crew demonstrates hostile intentions, they may be engaged with deadly force.

(b) If an armed individual or weapons crew commits criminal acts but does not demonstrate hostile intentions, U.S. forces will use the minimum amount of necessary force to detain them.

(c) Crew-served weapons are any weapon system that requires more than one individual to operate. Crew-served weapons include, but are not limited to tanks, artillery pieces, antiaircraft guns, mortars, and machine guns.

(11) Within those areas under the control of U.S. forces, armed individuals may be considered a threat to U.S. forces and the relief effort, whether or not the individuals demonstrate hostile intent. Commanders are authorized to use all necessary force to disarm and demilitarize groups or individuals in those areas under the control of U.S. forces. Absent a hostile or criminal act, individuals and associated vehicles will be released after any weapons are removed/demilitarized.

d. Use of Riot Control Agents (RCAs). Use of RCAs requires the approval of CJTF. When authorized, RCAs may be used for purposes including, but not limited to—

(1) Riot control in the division area of operations, including the dispersal of civilians who obstruct roadways or otherwise impede distribution operations after lesser means have failed to result in dispersal.

(2) Riot control in detainee holding areas or camps in and around material distribution or storage areas.

(3) Protection of convoys from civil disturbances, terrorists, or paramilitary groups.

e. Detention of Personnel. Personnel who interfere with the accomplishment of the mission or who use or threaten deadly force against U.S. forces, U.S. or relief material distribution sites, or convoys may be detained. Persons who commit criminal acts in areas under the control of U.S. forces may likewise be detained.

(1) Detained personnel will be treated with respect and dignity.

(2) Detained personnel will be evacuated to a designated location for turnover to military police.

(3) Troops should understand that any use of the feet in detaining, handling or searching Somali civilians is one of the most insulting forms of provocation.

(4) Service Support. Basic OPLAN/OPORD.

(5) Command and Signal. Basic OPLAN/OPORD.

ROE for Operation Provide Comfort

1. All military operations will be conducted in accordance with the laws of war.
2. The use of armed force will be utilized as a measure of last resort only.
3. Nothing in these rules negates or otherwise overrides a commander's obligation to take all necessary and appropriate actions for his unit's self-defense.
4. U.S. forces will not fire unless fired upon unless there is clear evidence of hostile intent.

   Hostile Intent—The threat of imminent use of force by an Iraqi force or other foreign force, terrorist group, or individuals against the United States, U.S. forces, U.S. citizens, or Kurdish or other refugees located above the 38th parallel or otherwise located within a U.S. or allied safe haven refugee area. When the on-scene commander determines, based on convincing evidence, that hostile intent is present, the right exists to use proportional force to deter or neutralize the threat.

   Hostile Act—Includes armed force directly to preclude or impede the missions and/or duties of U.S. or allied forces.
5. Response to hostile fire directly threatening U.S. or allied care shall be rapid and directed at the source of hostile fire using only the force necessary to eliminate the threat. Other foreign forces (such as reconnaissance aircraft) that have shown an active integration with the attacking force may be engaged. Use the minimum amount of force necessary to control the situation.
6. You may fire into Iraqi territory in response to hostile fire.
7. You may fire into another nation's territory in response to hostile fire only if the cognizant government is unable or unwilling to stop that force's hostile acts effectively or promptly.
8. Surface-to-air missiles will engage hostile aircraft flying north of the 36th parallel.
9. Surface-to-air missiles will engage hostile aircraft south of the 36th parallel only when they demonstrate hostile intent or commit hostile acts. Except in cases of self-defense, authorization for such engagements rests with the designated air defense commander. Warning bursts may be fired ahead of foreign aircraft to deter hostile acts.
10. In the event U.S. forces are attacked or threatened by unarmed hostile elements, mobs, or rioters, the responsibility for the protection of U.S. forces rests with the U.S. commanding officer. The on-scene commander will employ the following measures to overcome the threat:
    a. Warning to demonstrators.
    b. Show of force, including the use of riot control formations.
    c. Warning shots fired over the heads of hostile elements.
    d. Other reasonable use of force necessary under the circumstances and proportional to the threat.
11. Use the following guidelines when applying these rules:
    a. Use of force only to protect lives.
    b. Use of minimum force necessary.
    c. Pursuit will not be taken to retaliate; however, immediate pursuit may begin and continue for as long as there is an immediate threat to U.S. forces. In the absence of JCS approval, U.S. forces should not pursue any hostile force into another nation's territory.
    d. If necessary and proportional, use all available weapons to deter, neutralize, or destroy the threat as required.

Rules of Engagement
Joint Task Force for Somalia Relief Operations
Ground Forces

Nothing in these rules of engagement limits your right to take appropriate action to defend yourself and your unit.

1. You have the right to use force to defend yourself against attacks or threats of attack.

2. Hostile fire may be returned effectively and promptly to stop a hostile act.

3. When US forces are attacked by unarmed hostile elements, mobs, and/or rioters, US forces should use the minimum force necessary under the circumstances and proportional to the threat.

4. You may not seize the property of others to accomplish your mission.

5. Detention of civilians is authorized for security reasons or in self-defense.

Remember

The United States is not at war.

Treat all persons with dignity and respect.

Use minimum force to carry out the mission.

Always be prepared to act in self-defense.

Sample ROE Card

Chapter 13

Establish and Operate
an Observation Post

One of the most common and important missions for a platoon in stability and support operations is the establishment and operation of an observation post (OP). Because of widely varying conditions, the techniques and requirements of this mission differ significantly from the establishment of an OP for most tactical missions. Generally, OPs are manned by platoons (with a squad or other subelement on relief at all times), but they are sometimes manned by smaller elements. In the case of a squad OP, the tasks are the same, with the organization of the personnel being adapted to fit the situation.

ESTABLISHING THE OP

Reconnoiter the area to be observed and select a site that affords the most unobstructed view of all observation areas. The site should also afford access by covered and concealed routes and must facilitate all-around security. Once the site is selected, occupy the site and begin work according to a prioritized sequence. Security and protection tasks receive the highest priority; observation tasks should begin as soon as possible, or at least by the time required by higher headquarters; comfort measures receive lowest priority.

Physical Characteristics

Illumination (e.g., floodlights), painting, and other physical characteristics may be dictated by terms of agreements in effect regarding the operation; otherwise, the OP should generally be as inconspicuous as possible. Similarly, to the extent possible, barrier materials, early warning pyrotechnics, and other devices should be emplaced as required for the protection of the OP force. Overhead cover should be constructed for protecting weather-sensitive equipment. Each observation position should be equipped with a clearly marked map indicating the sector to be observed from that particular point; markings should include easily recognizable day and night points

Observation Post

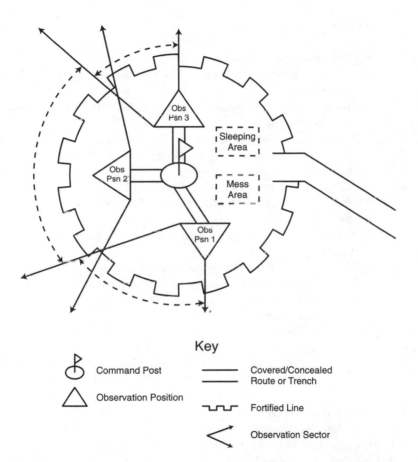

of reference, azimuths to each, and so forth. Establish wire communications between each observation position and the OP command post if the OP commander and his observers cannot see one another or are beyond voice range. A sand table may be useful for briefing platoon members and facilitating subsequent reliefs. Finally, comfort measures, such as the construction of covered sleeping quarters, eating areas, physical training or recreation areas (if personnel are to remain at the OP when not on duty), and so forth are built last.

Equipment

Depending on the mission, equipment required to operate an OP may include any or all of the following:

Observation Devices

- Binoculars
- Telescopes
- Crew-served weapon sights
- Thermal, light intensification, or other devices for conditions of limited visibility
- Electronic target acquisition devices (e.g., GSR, PEWS, REMBASS, Q36 Radar)
- Range finders, lasers, and/or other optical (e.g., coincidence) devices
- Television, videotape, still photo automatic cameras, with appropriate lenses
- Compasses and protractors
- Maps or sector sketches for each observation position

Communications

- Radios, including receivers for commercial broadcasts of information relevant to the situation
- Telephones, both wire and cellular, as appropriate
- Tape recorders, for recording incoming or monitored messages (per commander's permission)
- Duty logs and clipboards

Other Equipment

- Electrical generators, as needed
- Sufficient Class I, III, and V supplies for three days' operations without resupply

OPERATING THE OP

Determining Observation Sectors

If the area to be observed is too much for one soldier to scan constantly—and most will be—then the platoon leader/OP commander must divide the sector identified in the mission statement into subsectors. Each subsector must be observed from at least one observation position, and, if possible, the sectors should overlap, much like fields of fire. If the operation evolves into an offensive or defensive one, these sectors of observation may well *become* fields of fire. The platoon leader/OP commander ensures that a sector sketch is developed for each subsector, posted on a map, and passed on to the next relief. All details should be posted on the master sketch and map in the OP command post.

Conducting Observation

Observers should actually observe their sectors for no more than 30 minutes at a time; therefore, it is wise to occupy each observation position with two soldiers, so they can alternately conduct observation duties. When night vision devices are in use, rotation should probably be more frequent. One soldier observes the designated sector, while the other performs close security duties, improves the position, and takes brief rests—but never sleeps—at the position, ready to assume duties from his or her partner. Talking about issues not related directly to the mission at hand should not be permitted, to minimize distractions.

Generally, the following should be recorded and/or reported, per mission requirements:

- Movement of any military elements
- Shooting (heard and/or seen), explosions, hostile acts, threats (communicated or perpetrated)
- Improvement of positions by belligerent parties
- Unauthorized (or unscheduled) aircraft overflights
- Violations of other agreements in effect, such as the movement of armored vehicles too close to a neutral zone
- Unusual civilian traffic or activities, such as abnormally light participation in agricultural chores or other indicators of belligerent activities or preparation nearby
- Unusual animal activities, such as the absence of birds singing where and when they normally do, or other indicators of human presence when and where there normally are none

Entries in the OP journal must be legible, clear, detailed, and accurate. The written journals at OPs can become documents at the center of international controversy. To the greatest extent possible, recorders should be selected for their ability to write legibly and intelligently.

Determining the Composition and Duties of Reliefs

Considering the following, the OP commander determines the duration and composition of each relief. (No relief should exceed four hours, if possible.)

- Nature of observation (i.e., continuous or periodic)
- Area to be observed
- Hours of peak activity in the observation area
- Type and complexity of equipment to be employed
- Effects of fatigue and weather on observation
- Local security requirements

The platoon sergeant determines the composition of each relief. An NCO should be in charge of each relief, and unit integrity should be maintained to the greatest extent possible. One effective way to approach the performance of duties at OPs may be to treat them as guard duty, with inspections, knowledge of duty requirements, and observation of general and special orders required. This may help the chain of command and the soldiers better understand their responsibilities in the early phases of OP operation.

A sample relief on an OP with three observation positions might be organized this way:

Commander of the Relief: Squad leader

Observation Position #1: Alfa Team leader plus one soldier from Alfa Team

Observation Position #2: Senior specialist (E-4), Bravo Team, plus one soldier from Bravo Team

Observation Position #3: Senior specialist (E-4), Alfa Team, plus one soldier from Alfa Team

Security Team (at entrance to OP): Bravo Team leader, plus one soldier from Bravo Team

The remaining soldiers from each team (assuming an 11-soldier squad at full strength) can be trained and employed as relief radio operators or recorders in the OP command post. Sometimes, platoons on OPs may be augmented by outside individuals. These may include crews for TOWs, operating their sights as surveillance devices; crews for ground surveillance radars or seismic anti-intrusion devices or other intelligence personnel; snipers or designated marksmen; fire support coordinators; allied personnel—especially those who speak the local language; or representatives of neutral nations or PVOs/NGOs. To the greatest extent possible, they should be integrated into the reliefs and rotated on observation duties. This will help develop rapport and cohesion and will also help the commander of each relief establish his authority and better regulate his relief's activities.

Transition of Responsibilities at OPs

Whether exchanging responsibilities between two reliefs of the same platoon or handing over the OP to a platoon from a different unit altogether, the routine is similar. The commander of the outgoing relief briefs the commander of the incoming relief on all significant events during his unit's watch, using the OP journal as a guide. He verifies that all equipment is accounted for and functional, that all communications are intact and working, and that all guard post ammunition not in sealed containers is completely accounted for. In the event that an SOP has been developed for execution of responsibilities at an OP, the commander of the incoming relief becomes thoroughly familiar with it before assuming responsibilities, and the platoon leader/OP commander ensures that he understands it.

Instituting Emergency Procedures

The platoon leader/OP commander issues an evacuation/extraction or reinforcement order and conducts rehearsals for the platoon. These should be coordinated with participating or controlling higher headquarters and supporting units and/or agencies. The platoon leader/OP commander must be prepared to request a quick reaction force (QRF) from higher headquarters and must know how to employ it or operate in coordination with it upon its arrival.

If the QRF is an element of the platoon itself, the platoon leader/OP commander ensures that it maintains communications with the commander of the OP at all times. The QRF deploys with all capabilities necessary to effectively counter the threat, while reducing risk to itself and the remainder of the force. The QRF enters the confrontation area in a visible and unprovocative manner, taking no action that could be interpreted as partial or antagonistic to a particular faction. If large enough, the QRF maintains an overwatch force to facilitate extraction; this force must not become decisively engaged unless the safety of personnel in the confrontation area requires it. The QRF uses only such force as is necessary or allowed under the ROE to accomplish the mission or evacuate the OP.

Chapter 14

Establish and
Operate a Checkpoint

In MOOTW, units often monitor and control traffic through a unit area of responsibility by establishing and operating checkpoints. There are two types of checkpoints: hasty and deliberate. The type depends on the conditions at the time the checkpoint is emplaced, but both are operated in the same fashion, to the same standards.

Current U.S. military literature often mentions that, during the conduct of MOOTW, relatively junior soldiers and leaders often make decisions with international import. Actions at checkpoints are among the most visible and important performed at the platoon level—nowhere will their roles as "ambassadors" be more subject to scrutiny by media representatives, local inhabitants, higher headquarters, and NGO/PVO personnel. For all these reasons, this is one of the most important missions a platoon can be called on to perform.

PREPARING AND ESTABLISHING A HASTY CHECKPOINT
"Hasty" checkpoints are those established with little warning—usually because of rapid developments in the situation.

Organize the Unit
Leaders organize the unit into five basic elements (the exact number of each varies with METT-TC):
1. Security elements
2. Sentries
3. Search teams
4. Reserve
5. Command element

Equipment, Transportation, and Other Resources

If necessary, procure transportation for personnel and equipment essential for the establishment and operation of the checkpoint. At a minimum, equipment must include:

- Multilingual signage as follows:
  - "Warning! Prepare to stop. Have ID ready." (Apply U.S. or multinational coalition/alliance/UN insignia as appropriate.)
  - Contraband warning sign, including definition and summary of possible consequences (e.g., arrest, confiscation) or opportunities for turning it in.
  - "Halt! Follow orders of sentry."
  - "Vehicle search area."
  - "Drivers and passengers dismount here."
  - "Open doors and hoods/trunks."
  - "Personnel search area."
  - "First Aid Post." (Be prepared to use Red Crescent in areas inhabited by Muslims.)
  - "Detention/Holding Area."
- Barrier material in sufficient quantities to mark entries to the checkpoint and search areas, at a minimum.
- Search aids, including mirrors, lights, metal detectors, and so forth.
- Communications devices sufficient to maintain contact between security posts, main search area, and command post.
- Tracer ammunition for warning shots.

At least one person possessing adequate language skills must be present at the checkpoint. Additionally, if feasible, female personnel should be present to conduct searches of women and children passing through the checkpoint. If military women are not available, then host-nation or, if they are willing and able, NGO/PVO women may be used for this delicate and important task.

Since there is rarely time to arrange for heavy antivehicular obstacles at a hasty checkpoint, armored vehicles or, at a minimum, heavy antiarmor weapons—possibly prominently displayed (another METT-TC and ROE decision)—are often helpful to deter or prevent vehicle charge-throughs. If the threat warrants it, these systems may be retained throughout the course of checkpoint operation.

Reconnoiter the Site

If the site has not been precisely designated by higher headquarters, select a location that is beyond small arms range of buildings, particularly occupied homes. If possible, the site should be defensible and afford good fields of observation for the unit conducting checkpoint activities. It should be relatively level, but with good drainage. The site must have room for a vehicle and personnel search area off to one side or, if a two-way checkpoint, off to both sides of the road.

Identify possible routes for bypassing the checkpoint. These should be blocked with barrier materials when they become available, and manned if possible. Identify dominating terrain that might be used by belligerents to influence actions at the checkpoint. (These might make good locations for OPs later.) Lastly, note the presence (or absence) of belligerent factions, obstacles (especially mines), and host-nation police and the volume of traffic through the area.

Briefback/Rehearse Actions at the Checkpoint

The establishment of a hasty checkpoint is an intrinsically rapid process. Although highly desirable (as for all missions across the range of military operations), rehearsals may not be feasible. Nevertheless, due to the potentially extremely sensitive nature of checkpoint operations, leaders must ensure that, at a minimum, their soldiers demonstrate minimum proficiency by briefing back the following:

- Specific limitations on the use of lethal force (e.g., to halt a charging vehicle or a fleeing person)
- Specific authority to search vehicles and personnel
- Authorized search methods and specific procedures
- Methods of stopping vehicles and questioning personnel
- Authority and techniques for apprehension and detention of civilian personnel
- Authority for, types of, and extent to which humanitarian aid may be rendered to noncombatants

Establish the Site

A hasty checkpoint must be functional within 15 minutes of the unit's arrival on site. The most important measure is to post security teams 50 to 100 meters from the site, with advance observation posts on the side or sides from which traffic is to be controlled. If earlier warning is desirable, security teams may be posted further out; if hostilities are likely, they should be supportable by crew-served weapons (essentially, this is a METT-TC decision). Other key actions involved in establishing a checkpoint include:

- Post sentries and erect signs.
- Emplace barriers.

- Prepare special equipment as necessary.
- Notify higher headquarters that the site is ready for operation.

PREPARING AND ESTABLISHING A DELIBERATE CHECKPOINT
Organize the Unit
Units operating deliberate checkpoints are organized in a fashion similar to that of hasty checkpoints but are further organized into reliefs. If possible, use integral elements for the teams (e.g., fire teams, squads). This facilitates continuity and promotes teamwork. If this is not possible, then attempt to preserve team integrity throughout the duration of the checkpoint mission.

Reconnoiter the Site
Conduct a thorough reconnaissance of the site, looking for the same things as for a hasty checkpoint. Since there will be more time available, it may be possible to bring engineers along for a more detailed analysis of the roadway and a more precise estimate of barrier materials necessary for construction of the checkpoint. Also, assess the availability of electrical power, telephone communications to civil authorities, water, sewage, and garbage disposal. Determine the checkpoint's proximity to any buffer zones, ceasefire lines, areas of separation, factional boundaries, significant cultural sites, or other potential "danger areas." Apprise higher headquarters of problems, and render specific recommendations for mission accomplishment.

Equipment, Transportation, and Other Resources
If necessary, procure transportation for personnel and equipment essential for the establishment and operation of the checkpoint. At a minimum, equipment must include:
- Multinational signage as listed for hasty checkpoints
- Pole barricade, sliding gate, or other movable barrier constructed to physically block a roadway
- Barrier materials to:
  — Channel pedestrian traffic into the checkpoint
  — Protect against dismounted attack
  — Construct anti-crash obstacles to force vehicles to slow down (e.g., concrete blocks, cement-filled 55-gallon drums, "caltrops" to explode tires)
  — Secure search and detention areas
  — Block bypass route
- If required or allowed by ROE or other directives, lights to illuminate:

Checkpoint

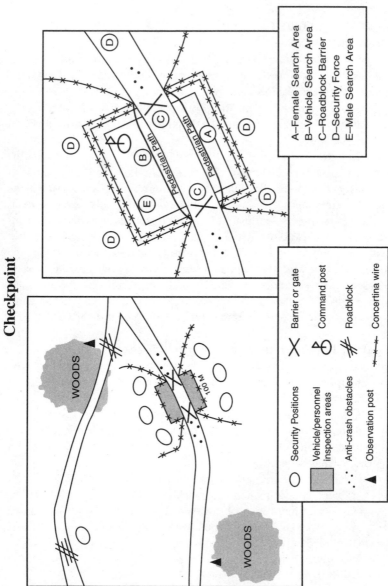

A—Female Search Area
B—Vehicle Search Area
C—Roadblock Barrier
D—Security Force
E—Male Search Area

X	Barrier or gate
⚐	Command post
⚟	Roadblock
✕✕✕	Concertina wire

Security Positions

Vehicle/personnel inspection areas

Anti-crash obstacles

Observation post

> — All signage
> — Speed obstacles
> — Search areas
> — Detention areas
> — Barricades at bypasses
> — Guard shacks and command post
- A generator sufficient to power lights and other mission-essential appliances
- Search aids, including mirrors, lights, and metal detectors
- Security aids, including restraints for detainees
- Weapons sufficient to defend the checkpoint and, if civil disturbances or demonstrations are likely, shotguns and riot batons, in addition to conventional small arms
- Communications devices sufficient to maintain contact between security posts, main search area, and command post (For security purposes, install wire communications, and use radios as alternative means; for addressing crowds, a public address system or bullhorn is useful.)

Coordinate for the following support resources:
- Engineer assets to improve site
- Military working dogs to assist with searches
- Host-nation authorities for liaison or sensitive operations
- Female search personnel, as per hasty checkpoints
- Medical treatment and evacuation teams
- Civil affairs teams to facilitate relations with host-nation authorities and advise on civil-military issues
- Translators
- PSYOPS products to encourage the maintenance of good order at the checkpoint
- Mechanics to assist with comprehensive vehicle inspections
- Explosive ordnance disposal personnel
- Intelligence personnel to interrogate blacklisted/graylisted personnel

Just as with hasty checkpoints, armored vehicles or heavy antiarmor weapons can be helpful in deterring or preventing vehicle charge-throughs until heavy antivehicle obstacles can be emplaced. If the threat warrants, these systems may be retained throughout the course of checkpoint operations.

Rehearse Actions at the Checkpoint
By definition, there will be time to rehearse the actions necessary for operating a deliberate checkpoint. Using performance-oriented training techniques,

ensure that all members of the unit are proficient in their duties; at a minimum, rehearse them in the tasks listed for briefback in the section on hasty checkpoints. If time permits, rehearse emergency actions at the checkpoint, including defense, halting a speeding vehicle, and discovery of a car bomb.

Establish the Site
Post security teams at the site before the arrival of other elements. If earlier warning is desirable, security teams may be posted further out; if hostilities are likely, they should be supportable by crew-served weapons (essentially, this is a METT-TC decision). Other key actions include:
- Emplace barriers; a deliberate checkpoint should be constructed so that it may be converted to a roadblock almost immediately upon order from higher headquarters.
- Post sentries and erect signs.
- Prepare special equipment as necessary.
- Have engineers build blast berms in vehicle search areas; emplace heavy obstacles as required, including bars to potential bypass routes.
- Notify higher headquarters that the site is ready for operation.

OPERATING A CHECKPOINT
Inspect soldiers of each relief before they assume checkpoint duties. Each soldier must be in proper uniform with all required equipment; each soldier must also demonstrate complete facility with pertinent ROE and checkpoint policies/SOPs.

Structure the checkpoint so that only the minimum number of personnel necessary is not behind or under cover. If allowable by the ROE, site automatic weapons to cover the entire checkpoint as overwatch for checkpoint personnel.

Conduct Vehicle Searches
Each time a vehicle approaches, follow this pattern and sequence:
1. Security reports approach, including any special information (e.g., approach too fast, occupants appear to be armed, vehicle fits blacklist description).
2. Sentry moves into position to signal driver to halt vehicle.
3. Sentry allows vehicle to pass forward to checkpoint barrier on signal from the commander of the relief. Generally, no more than one vehicle at a time may enter the checkpoint. All others must remain at least 50 meters from the checkpoint.

4. Designated sentry inquires about the purpose of the driver's and passengers' travel.
5. Sentry (sometimes accompanied by host-nation civil authorities) checks ID, registration, trip authorization, and so forth.
6. At least two sentries cover the vehicle; one covers the driver, the other the passengers. Larger vehicles with more passengers may require additional personnel to adequately cover all passengers.
7. While papers are being examined, one sentry visually examines the inside of the vehicle (through the glass or open apertures) for suspicious objects, contraband, or attempts to hide contents.
8. Commander of the relief decides to allow vehicle to pass.
9. Sentry signals driver to proceed.

According to U.S. Army Training Circular 7-98-1 (June 1997), the following table depicts typical vehicular search planning times.

Vehicle Search Times and Rates		
TYPE OF SEARCH	MINUTES/SECONDS PER VEHICLE	RATE (VEHICLES/HOUR/LANE)
None	—	600 – 800
Vehicle ID decal	:06 – :09	400 – 600
Driver ID	:09 – :18	200 – 400
Visual observation of vehicle interior	:12 – :24	150 – 300
Basic physical search of vehicle interior	:24 – 1:12	50 – 150
Comprehensive vehicle search	2:30 – 5:00	12 – 24

If a vehicle is to be comprehensively searched, a sentry signals the driver to pull into the search area. The driver and passenger are directed to get out of the vehicle, and the search is conducted using at least one mechanic and, if a bomb is likely, with explosive ordnance disposal (EOD) personnel present. Follow these procedures:

- Have the driver open all doors, hood, and trunk.
- Check all identification papers against the black/graylist from S-2.
- Have all personnel face away from the security element.
- Start at one side of the engine compartment and work to the other side of the compartment.
- Look for new wires.
- Use mirrors to inspect hard-to-see areas.
- Pay special attention to sun visors and glove compartments.
- Look under seats and feel seat backs for packages.
- Feel headliner for packages.
- Feel door panels for packages.
- Inspect area behind rear seat for packages or wires.
- Inspect under dashboard.
- Look under carpet for wires.
- Never touch wires or switches.
- Give suspicious objects to EOD personnel.
- Look at and under spare tire.
- Inspect all luggage and packages.
- Be suspicious of innocent-looking items (e.g., newspapers, envelopes).
- Inspect bumpers, wheels, and covers.
- Inspect complete chassis with mirrors.
- Inspect spare gas tank closely.

Conduct Personnel Searches

Comprehensive personnel searches should be conducted, whenever possible, in the presence of host-nation authorities and always with a translator present. Follow these procedures:

- Feel along clothing, paying extra attention to armpits and lower back.
- Check boots, hats, and other clothing that could easily contain contraband.
- If using a metal detector, direct the magnetic field over the whole body of the person being searched.
- Search all personnel away from the vehicle.
- Conduct searches in a concealed position behind cover.
- Provide security for the element conducting the search.
- Segregate searched from nonsearched individuals.
- Have the person stand facing a wall, lean over at a 45-degree angle with the feet spread, one hand behind the head.

- If a wall is not available, have the person lie on the ground with arms outstretched and legs crossed.
- If available, have a woman search the women and female children. In many situations, this will be mandated by higher headquarters or by pertinent international agreements.

Discovery of Contraband or Bombs

Upon discovery of contraband during the search process, the searcher should announce it clearly so that the other search team personnel on duty are aware of the find. The NCOIC then informs the possessor that he or she will be detained for questioning and that the contraband items are being confiscated. The detainees should be moved to the detention area until the arrival of military or civil host-nation police. The vehicle should be moved out of the search area but kept under observation until it, too, is turned over. It is necessary to complete the search of the person or vehicle even after contraband has been found; smugglers commonly "hide" small or less significant contraband in places likely to be searched early, in the hope that it will throw the searchers "off the scent" of more important items hidden elsewhere.

If a bomb—or something appearing to be a bomb—is discovered, clear the search area and alert EOD personnel. Halt all search activities until the situation is resolved. Immediately notify higher headquarters of developments in the situation.

Attempts to Crash Through the Checkpoint

Security teams must immediately report vehicles approaching at high speed and failing to heed signs warning of a checkpoint ahead. Sentries should always be especially cautious about the approach of a vehicle with only a driver.

If verbal and hand or arm signals fail to halt the vehicle, the sentry verbally alerts checkpoint personnel of an imminent crash-through attempt. All checkpoint personnel immediately occupy protective positions and prepare to fire warning shots. If feasible, the first shots should be aimed into the ground in front of the vehicle, then into the headlights or engine compartment. Use tracer ammunition if available.

If the vehicle does not stop and appears able to breach the obstacles, the checkpoint commander orders the use of antivehicular munitions. These may range from light antitank weapons (LAWs) and M203 grenade launchers (using high-explosive/dual-purpose [HEDP] rounds) to Dragons, TOWs, Bradley Fighting Vehicle 25mm guns, or tank main guns, if available. Protection of checkpoint personnel is paramount.

If the vehicle stops, crashes into the barrier, or is engaged and occupants survive, they should be ordered to get out and move away from the vehicle. If the driver is injured and unable to comply, the checkpoint commander keeps all personnel in protective positions in the event of a delayed action device.

All traffic through the checkpoint is halted.

The checkpoint commander, security team, medics, and EOD personnel (if immediately available) move to the vehicle. Medics administer first aid while the vehicle is quickly inspected. Surviving passengers and driver are detained. The checkpoint commander reports the incident to higher headquarters. The NCOIC directs preparation of witness statements and supervises maintenance of continued security.

The checkpoint commander determines when to allow more traffic to pass.

MAINTAINING/IMPROVING THE CHECKPOINT

Like most military facilities, checkpoints can be continually improved. Some improvements include permanent or semi-permanent facilities for search areas, a command post, a guard shack, a detention facility, soldier living quarters, latrines, PT or recreation area for checkpoint personnel, barricades, and security positions.

Chapter 15

React to
Bomb Threat or Car Bomb

Bombs are the weapon of choice for factions attempting to undermine the credibility or discourage the presence of a force attempting to stabilize a situation. Such bombs are most commonly used against personnel in an urban or fixed/semipermanent installation environment and may be used with or without advance warning. Soldiers must be educated and warned about the hazards presented by bombs, and procedures for employing explosive ordnance disposal (EOD) teams must be developed and rehearsed if bombing is a possibility.

PREVENTION MEASURES

Bombing can often be prevented. Security measures should include the establishment of checkpoints where units conduct invasive and noninvasive searches of personnel and vehicles. Invasive searches should be conducted by qualified personnel, that is, soldiers trained to recognize bombs and places in which they are commonly hidden. Such searches should be conducted in a brisk, nonhostile, professional fashion, much like preboarding security checks at most airports in the United States. Noninvasive searches—which can be used as either a substitute for or a complement to invasive searches, depending on METT-TC—can be conducted using appropriately trained military working dogs and X-ray devices. Metal detectors are usually not adequate to protect against bombs, as there are many ways to construct devastating bombs without using significant quantities of metal. Other prevention measures include:

- Irregularly scheduled, unannounced inspections of storage or other infrequently trafficked areas
- Training programs that sensitize soldiers about the threat of bombs and educate them to recognize and report suspicious objects in their duty areas

- The use of parking areas for nonmilitary vehicles that are well away from occupied buildings or other facilities
- Outdoor obstacles providing vehicle crash-through protection
- Arming sentries or checkpoint personnel with weapons capable of destroying a vehicle attempting to crash through a barrier

ACTIONS UPON RECEIPT OF A BOMB THREAT
Evaluate Authenticity
Commanders must consider the authenticity of a bomb threat before ordering action. Persons receiving bomb threats should be trained to record the details of the bomb's location, alleged time of detonation, and description of the device; if this information is not volunteered by the caller, the person receiving the call must ask for it or otherwise attempt to ascertain it. To the extent allowed by military law, recording devices can be employed to completely capture all details of the threat. If such measures are not possible, receivers should note the caller's gender, accent (if any), and apparent stress level; background noises; the quality of the audio connection; whether the caller seems to be reading a text or extemporizing; and the duration of the call.

Upon rapidly ascertaining all possible information about the bomb threat—including available background intelligence—commanders also evaluate any potential advantages that might accrue to the different factions through the evacuation of the threatened facility or actual detonation of the alleged device.

Evacuate and Isolate the Area
If possible, the area threatened is evacuated in an orderly and safe fashion; occupants must be alert for unusual or out-of-place items in their areas and must take their personal items with them. Simultaneously, the area is isolated or cordoned through the use of roadblocks, barricades, or barriers. The size of the perimeter established depends on the suspected size and type of explosives that may be used.

Search the Area
Search teams, preferably including EOD personnel and/or appropriate military working dogs, thoroughly inspect the threatened area. Control parties supervise the search teams, communicating without the use of radios, since radio signals may inadvertently detonate certain types of command-detonated bombs. Control teams record areas searched, note observations of unusual items, and report to the on-site commander. Even if one or more

bombs are found and removed or neutralized, the search continues until all areas have been cleared; warning of one bomb while planting several is a favorite technique of some terrorists.

Actions upon Discovery of Bomb

Sometimes, a bomb is discovered without warning, particularly if a unit has an effective prevention program. The actions regarding evacuation, isolation, and search are similar to those described earlier.

Chapter 16

Cordon and Search

This mission requires superb discipline, assiduous attention to ROE and other constraints, and sensitivity to cultural factors. Units conduct cordon and search operations to comb out and apprehend wanted war criminals or other blacklisted personnel or to confiscate contraband. Either way, this mission involves two potentially incendiary processes, namely, temporarily limiting the freedom of movement of innocent noncombatants, and searching buildings, possibly including occupied dwellings.

The potential for seriously negative consequences is clear, as these actions will never be popular with those who have to endure them. At best, if the unit demonstrates a high degree of professionalism and fully exploits the potential of PSYOPS, they may be *tolerated*, but no one likes to be surrounded and rousted out of their homes or places of business while their personal property is searched by foreigners. Disciplined, efficient performance of all tasks can minimize the chances for problems during this mission.

PREPARING FOR CORDON AND SEARCH
Reconnoiter the Objective
Conduct an area reconnaissance to ascertain the size and exact location of the area to be searched; from this, the trace of the cordon can be determined. Special considerations must be given to the following:

- Total circumference of the cordon line
- Obstacles or fortifications
- Early warning systems, including human mechanisms, such as lookouts or neighborhood information chains (e.g., banging on drums, garbage cans), and mechanical devices

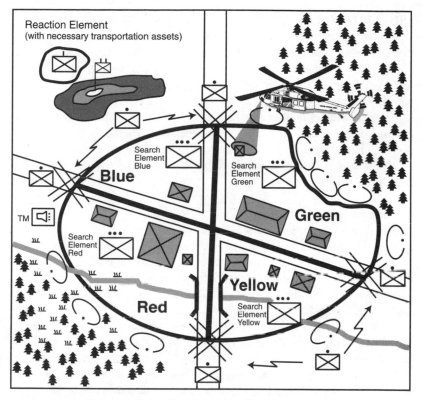

Organizing the Area to Be Searched & Establishing the Cordon

- Presence of subterranean avenues of egress, such as sewers and tunnels
- Clandestine routes (e.g., holes in walls, alleys)

Always keep "eyes on" the objective. Leave a surveillance team in place with communications equipment to provide real-time updates of significant activities in the objective area.

Organize the Objective Area

Divide the objective area into zones and assign one to each search element. If time is limited, designate multiple areas for each search team, and prioritize according to intelligence and commanders' estimates.

ORGANIZING FOR THE CORDON AND SEARCH

Determine the extent of the cordon required for the search. This determination is no simple reckoning of the physical size of the objective; the cordon must seal off all possible routes of egress, including subterranean, pedestrian, vehicular, and possibly aerial—if the factions being targeted have helicopters or vertical/short take-off and landing (V/STOL) aircraft.

A double-layer cordon may be required. Similar to the ancient Roman *circumvallation* and *contravallation,* this technique establishes an inner cordon to control egress from the objective area and an outer cordon to prevent arrival of disruptive or even hostile elements in the objective area during the search (METT-TC dependent).

Cordon Element

Organizing a cordon element requires extensive mission tailoring of the units within a battalion. At a minimum, the cordon element must be of sufficient size to provide overlapping physical observation of all avenues of egress. Its soldiers may also have to be prepared to conduct civil disturbance operations. The following assets or subelements should be considered (METT-TC dependent):

Checkpoint/Roadblock Teams. These may be relatively small if the search will only be of brief duration; otherwise, these teams' composition will have to allow for rotation of personnel if extended operations occur.

Patrols. Patrols (preferably with a mobility advantage over dismounted escapees) are required to monitor potential escape routes and apprehend persons as they attempt to flee.

Blocking Teams. In some cases, it may be necessary to deploy dismounted units to physically block avenues of escape that provide concealment, such as woods or swamps.

Aerial Surveillance Teams. Aerial observation, using Army aviation, unmanned aerial vehicles (UAVs), or any other platforms that can provide real-time information to the commander about activities in the objective area, is extremely useful.

Engineers. Engineers can quickly emplace obstacles to block attempted egress.

PSYOPS Team. Crowds may gather at points along the cordon, and PSYOPS elements can help defuse potentially explosive situations with loudspeaker announcements, posters, leaflets, and the like.

Air Defense Team. An air defense element is needed to prevent aerial exit of the objective area (METT-TC and ROE dependent).

Typical Cordon Element

HQ

Patrols[1]

Blocking Teams[1]

Checkpoint/ Roadblock Teams[1]

TM — Aerial Surveillance Team[2]

TM PSYOPS Team

TM Air Defense Team[3]

[1] Number and composition of teams METT-TC dependent

[2] If available and weather-dependent. UAVs may be substituted

[3] METT-TC dependent

Search Element

The search element should be of sufficient size to conduct the search in a rapid yet thorough fashion. To a significant extent, this is a "bigger is better" situation: more searchers means a faster search and less time spent in the objective area, which means less chance for the development of the manifold problems that a cordon and search can cause or exacerbate.

The search element should comprise the following assets or subelements:

Search Teams. These teams conduct the actual search. The number of teams is METT-TC dependent.

Entry Teams. Entry teams clear and secure entry to buildings. The number of teams is METT-TC dependent.

Engineer Teams. Engineer or EOD teams are needed for clearing obstacles, handling explosives, and disposing of booby traps.

Typical Search Element

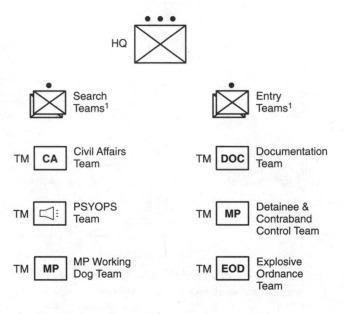

HQ

Search Teams[1]

Entry Teams[1]

TM | CA | Civil Affairs Team

TM | DOC | Documentation Team

TM | PSYOPS Team

TM | MP | Detainee & Contraband Control Team

TM | MP | MP Working Dog Team

TM | EOD | Explosive Ordnance Team

[1] Number of teams METT-TC dependent

MP Teams. Military police working dogs are used to detect contraband, hidden persons, or explosives.

Documentation Team. The documentation team checks papers and verifies identities. This team should include host-nation authorities, interpreters, and/or civil affairs (CA) personnel.

Detainee/Contraband Control Team. This team takes charge of detainees or contraband materials discovered by the search teams. Military police are best suited to this task.

PSYOPS Team. The PSYOPS team is used to reassure the local populace of the legitimacy and purpose of the search and to apologize for the inconvenience (METT-TC dependent).

Civil Affairs Team. The CA team coordinates with host-nation authorities.

Reaction Element

If intelligence indicates that the potential exists for a mass breakout attempt, a robust, highly mobile reaction capability should be retained to reinforce the points of attempted penetration, assist in the apprehension of detainees, and conduct civil disturbance operations if necessary. It should be kept out of sight until it is needed, to avoid unnecessary provocation, but if the situation is tense from the beginning, it is sometimes wise to use the reaction element to conduct a demonstration.

Supplies and Other Resources

Procure sufficient barrier materials to block avenues of egress. These may range from engineer or "police line" tape to barbed wire and antivehicular obstacles.

Establish a radio net incorporating all participating units. To prevent confusion, each unit conducting a cordon and search operation should have its own net whenever possible. Host-nation authorities should be included on this net.

Coordinate for transportation assets into the objective area so that the cordon can be established swiftly and simultaneously. Also, retain sufficient transportation assets on "standby" to remove detainees or contraband. These may be ground or aerial assets (helicopters, V/STOL aircraft, or, if the objective is near an airstrip, air-land assets).

Video and still cameras are needed for recording entry and search procedures. Appropriate containers for contraband (plastic bags for vegetable substances, boxes for ordnance) are also required. Generally, these should be available to the search teams during the conduct of the search.

Authorization and Specific Information

Leaders must obtain explicit authorization for the search from the legitimate authority in the objective area. Other explicitly understood information must include:

- Specific instructions for apprehending and detaining nonmilitary personnel
- Specific details—by category or individual item—of contraband to be confiscated
- Constraints of the general ROE as they apply to this specific situation

Legal Review

Ensure that the search, apprehension, and detention authorizations and blacklists have been reviewed by competent legal authority.

Rehearsals

Due to the sensitivity of *every* aspect of a cordon and search operation, they all must be realistically and thoroughly rehearsed. If possible, use civilians (possibly from supportive NGOs/PVOs) to rehearse search procedures. Rehearse PSYOPS and, if possible, test them with a host-nation audience to evaluate and verify their effectiveness; at a minimum, check with host-nation authorities and CA personnel to ensure that they have a high probability of achieving the desired effects.

ESTABLISHING THE CORDON

If possible, move the cordon element to its debarkation sites during hours of limited visibility. Debark the cordon element from its transportation beyond hearing range of the population in the objective area. Move as quickly as possible to seal the objective area. If available, aerial reconnaissance assets should arrive on station immediately after the establishment of the cordon. The reaction force moves into overwatch position or remains out of sight in a nearby assembly area (METT-TC dependent). Report establishment of the cordon to higher headquarters.

CONDUCTING THE SEARCH

One of the initial steps in conducting search operations is to use PSYOPS teams and/or host-nation authorities to announce the purpose of and authority for the search. PSYOPS continue throughout the operation.

The following techniques can be used to conduct the search, depending on the conditions:

- Assemble the noncombatant inhabitants in one location and place them under guard to immobilize them, or
- Restrict inhabitants to their households or places of business, or
- Order heads of households and businesses to remain in place and assemble all others in a central location.

When as many inhabitants as possible have been secured, commence the search. (See chapter 17, "Search a Building.") The search should be conducted as quickly as possible, consonant with force protection considerations.

The cordon element denies egress to any person not authorized to leave the area and apprehends those who attempt to break the cordon. Use incrementally ascending force in accordance with the ROE and other pertinent restrictions. The cordon element also denies entry to any unauthorized personnel—generally, the only persons authorized entry are inhabitants returning to their dwellings.

The reaction element moves in to preclude escalation of any disturbances; request reinforcement from higher headquarters early if the situation continues to develop negatively.

Videotape or otherwise record as much of the search operation as possible. Film of contraband discoveries or apprehensions is the most important. Another priority subject for filming is the transfer of custody of contraband or detained personnel to host-nation or other appropriate authorities. As always, obtain a written, signed receipt. If appropriate, use PSYOPS and CA teams to thank the population for their cooperation, and reiterate the purpose—and results—of the search. Finally, report to higher headquarters.

Chapter 17

Search a Building

Frequently conducted during MOOTW, building searches can be very sensitive operations. Booby traps, structural flaws resulting from decrepitude or fire damage, and other dangers can lurk in any building. Not only might contraband be found and confiscated, but noncombatants might be apprehended and detained—sometimes directly from their residences. Few actions can evoke more outrage within a community or faction, so these operations must be conducted as carefully, sensitively, and efficiently as possible.

PREPARING TO SEARCH
Organize for the Search
Organize the unit as follows:
- Command element to command and control the operation.
- Entry team to create and secure an entry, by force if necessary. It clears each room ahead of search teams.
- Search teams to conduct the search. Military police and host-nation authorities can be helpful in assisting other soldiers to conduct searches.
- Security team to secure the area around the building.
- Support element to handle detainees and contraband, provide equipment needed for the search, and provide medical care to persons injured in the course of the search. PSYOPS and CA personnel can be employed on this team to calm the nearby population and explain the purpose of the search (if permissible). EOD personnel should be on hand to deal with explosive booby traps.

If possible, reconnoiter the building to be searched. Build a mockup or find a suitably similar building and conduct rehearsals.

Procure Equipment and Resources for the Search
The following equipment can be useful during a building search:
- Metal or wooden ram to break in door or window
- Explosives (if authorized) for forcible entry
- Personnel restraints for uncooperative detainees
- Bullhorn or public-address system
- Boxes or plastic bags for contraband, if practical
- Tags for identifying detainees, contraband, or other seized material
- Paint for marking a building after the search is complete
- Chalk for marking doors after rooms have been cleared
- Ladders and/or ropes for ascending to upper floors or roof
- Barriers (e.g., sawhorses, road cones) to help keep onlookers back
- Signs to indicate "Search in Progress," with appropriate U.S., coalition, or UN insignia
- Blueprints or other plans to buildings to be searched (especially if they are extensive facilities)
- Still or video cameras to record the circumstances of discovery and/or seizure
- Electrical plans and sewer diagrams (if these exist at all, they are procured by CA units from host-nation authorities)

CONDUCTING THE SEARCH
Gain Entry
Security teams cordon the building, erecting barricades and emplacing signs. Civilians are warned away from the building by the PSYOPS team and host-nation authorities. Security team personnel prevent people from exiting the building through back doors or windows and watch for items that may be tossed out.

The unit leader approaches the building, escorted by a representative of the host-nation's civil authorities, a translator, or both. He knocks on the door, announces the source of authority for the search; and requests compliance from the inhabitants. If the door is answered and there is no resistance to entry, the entry team secures the entrance and the search teams begin work. The support element takes charge of the inhabitants, except for the one who is requested to accompany the search team to open doors, explain idiosyncrasies of the building, and so forth. If the door is not answered, the entry team establishes an entry point that is both unexpected and will be difficult to use for unrestricted access after the search is

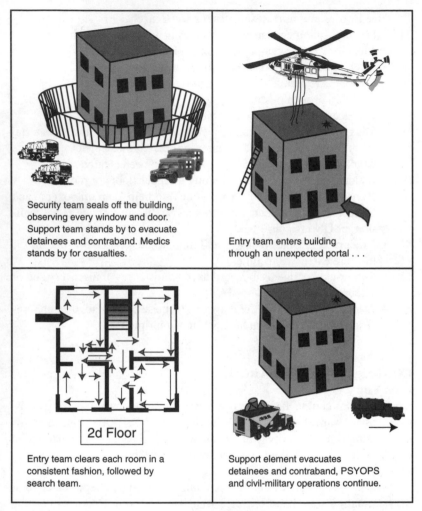

Security team seals off the building, observing every window and door. Support team stands by to evacuate detainees and contraband. Medics stands by for casualties.

Entry team enters building through an unexpected portal . . .

2d Floor

Entry team clears each room in a consistent fashion, followed by search team.

Support element evacuates detainees and contraband, PSYOPS and civil-military operations continue.

Search a Building

concluded. (This is actually done in consideration of the owners of the building, so that their dwelling or business is not easily entered, or looted.) Consider using second-story windows, trapdoors in the roof, and the like. Use the minimum force necessary to gain entry to the building—using explosives or causing gross damage in any other way should be a last resort. Check with higher headquarters first.

The entry team searches for dangerous devices in the first room upon entry. The first soldier in provides security at the entry point. The second one in checks for hidden people, weapons, booby traps, or other dangerous devices. When this search is complete, he announces clearance of room to the unit leader and remains at the entry point for security.

Search the Building

Search one floor at a time in a consistent fashion, (e.g., follow walls to the left). Announce entry into each room, and search it for designated contraband. The point man checks for trip wires and booby traps on the door. The team enters the room using high-man/low-man technique, tracking the search areas with their weapons. Personnel scan assigned areas of each room (e.g., left side/right side) in all three dimensions.

The search is also conducted in three dimensions. Check for false ceilings and trapdoors, in closets, under furniture and carpets, and so forth. Search for specific items to avoid wasting time and effort. For example, if the team is looking for crew-served weapons, there is no need to search small drawers or cabinets.

Actions on Discovery. If officially listed or unauthorized people are discovered, have civil police or translators determine their identity. Search them using standard body search techniques; whenever possible, have females search women or girls. If female soldiers or civil police are not available, female members of NGOs/PVOs are sometimes willing to assist in this task. Some international agreements/ROE forbid men to search women; check with higher headquarters for permission if there is any question.

Confiscate contraband and explain why it is being confiscated. Affix and fill out detainee tags; at a minimum, indicate the date and time of discovery and basic details of the apprehension. Transfer detainees to the support element until they are picked up by civil police, MPs, CA, or military intelligence (MI) personnel.

Contraband that is discovered should be placed in a bag or box and tagged. Mark the tag with the date and time of discovery, the quantity of items, serial numbers (if any), and a brief description of the circumstances. If the confiscated item might be personal or business property, offer a receipt to the person responsible for the building.

Check weapons and other equipment for booby traps before picking them up. EOD teams may be necessary for this task.

Continue the search, even if contraband has already been found. It is a common technique to hide small quantities or minor items in likely places, in the hope that the search will end with their discovery.

Booby Traps. Upon discovery of an identified or suspected booby trap (e.g., trip wire, explosive device), immediately summon the EOD team or, if not available, engineers. Notify civil authorities and higher headquarters. Take a picture, if possible, and have the "guide" witness the discovery—get him or her to sign a statement if possible.

The security team moves onlookers back to a safe distance; use public-address systems or bullhorns to announce the possibility of explosions due to booby traps. If the EOD team has to detonate the device to make the building safe, this pre-announcement will help defuse or prevent subsequent accusations of vandalism or purposeful destruction. Above all, suspend all search activities in the building until the device has been rendered safe.

After the Search Is Complete

If nothing was found, use CA and PSYOPS personnel and host-nation authorities to apologize for the search or conduct other appropriate civil-military operations. If the search resulted in the apprehension of wanted criminals or other listed elements or netted significant contraband, PSYOPS personnel can be used to explain the results of the search to justify the operation to local inhabitants.

Chapter 18

Process Confiscated Documents and Equipment

Whether seized in a building search, turned in as part of a disarmament effort, or confiscated from detainees, contraband and documents and equipment of informational value must often be handled by forces conducting MOOTW. In many cases, the simplest and most effective means of accomplishing the mission is to immediately transfer the materials to the military or civil agency to receive them. However, circumstances sometimes force units to conduct this mission themselves.

Although usually a fairly routine process, this can become a highly contentious and potentially sensitive endeavor. Just as when seizing and processing controlled materials in U.S. legal actions, leaders must adhere strictly to applicable guidelines and principles of custody. International law, local laws or customs, and the stipulations of international agreements often vary from the much more familiar U.S. rules; be careful to learn the differences, and follow them meticulously.

PREPARING FOR PROCESSING
Establish Procedures
Ensure that all procedures are in accordance with applicable regulations, international agreements, and ROE. Use procedures already established by higher headquarters or have all procedures developed by the unit reviewed by higher headquarters and, if possible, the staff judge advocate.

Equipment
Equipment needed to process and handle confiscated equipment includes:
- Boxes, plastic bags, or other appropriate containers

- Scales, rulers, and measuring containers appropriate for the material being processed
- Still and/or video cameras for recording images of the contraband
- Tags with ties or other means of attachment to the contraband
- Receipts (if possible, in the local language as well as English) for certain confiscated materials

Support
Coordinate to have EOD personnel or engineers on call to check for suspected booby traps and for transportation of materials to appropriate authorities. Designate a secure facility for storing materials until they are transferred to appropriate authorities.

Train and Rehearse
All soldiers must understand specifically what is considered contraband. Soldiers who search for or handle contraband should learn the words in the local language for the specific items the unit is searching for; this can ease the search process and sometimes allows useful information to be gathered when hearing conversations among local inhabitants.

Practice restraint and impartiality in the seizure of materials. Place loose or small items in boxes or plastic bags that can be sealed and tagged. Tags used to identify materials must include the date and time of seizure, a description of the items, and the quantity of items or estimated weight or volume (for liquids, vegetable matter, chemicals, and the like).

PROCESSING MATERIALS
As soon as the contraband is located, use a camera to record the discovery *in situ* (exactly as it has been found). Box or bag the items (if practical), and tag them. Count, measure, or weigh the contraband, and record the results on the tag, as well as the date and time and the circumstances of seizure.

If the confiscated items are not clearly contraband (e.g., privately owned weapon or suspected—but not confirmed—illegal substances), provide a receipt to the losing party. If materials are confiscated during a search of a detainee's personal clothing, annotate the detainee tag with all the pertinent information about the seizure.

If there is any suspicion that the materials may be booby-trapped or otherwise unsafe to move, request EOD or engineer support. Render objects that are beyond the unit's capacity to move inoperable, but do not destroy them unless destruction is specifically ordered or authorized. Emplace security until appropriate transportation is available. Produce a report detailing all materials seized (including serial numbers, if applicable) and forward a copy to higher headquarters.

Store all materials in a secure facility until they are transferred to appropriate authorities. Keep a record of who has access to the materials and who handles them, in a fashion similar to establishing the "chain of custody" in legal proceedings.

Chapter 19

Evaluate Civilian Infrastructure

Often, even before the arrival of a task force, civil affairs (CA) teams have been in the area, compiling significant amounts of detailed information. This information is usually available in a report called a Civil Affairs Area Study (CAAS). These reports are living documents that must be updated in accordance with information obtained by all units during the course of operations.

There are also various other area studies written by special operations forces (SOF) that have operated in the task force area of responsibility (AOR). While informative, they are not normally as current as a CAAS. Requests for these studies should be made through operations (S-3/G-3/J-3) channels to the first special operations cell in the chain of command.

The Civil Military Operations Center (CMOC) is the organization at the joint task force (JTF) level responsible for designing and managing a civilian infrastructure database. The CA forces assigned to operate in the AOR are the proponent organization for this task. Daily situation reports (SITREPS) and after-action reports (AARS), as well as information from a variety of other sources—such as NGOs and PVOs— are collated at the CMOC. Various bulletins for distribution to unit commanders at all levels and locations in theater are produced from this database.

CONTRIBUTING TO THE CMOC DATABASE
At battalion level and above, units conducting MOOTW collect and organize information for use in evaluating civilian infrastructures. Usually, this effort is led and coordinated by the S-2, with assistance from the S-3 and S-5. To align the information collection effort with the databases assembled and maintained at the CMOC, units should collect data according to the categories used in the CAAS (see the sample CAAS).

One of the most useful methods of arraying data on a civilian infrastructure is by depicting it geographically on a color-coded overlay. For example, overlays could be used to depict the status of public works

Civil Affairs Area Study (CAAS)

Transportation Nets
    Roads *(type, condition, width)*
    Airfields *(type of surface, length of runways, suitability for commonly used aircraft, controlled/uncontrolled, facilities)*
    Port facilities *(size; services; access to inland and coastal waterways; suitability for commonly used ships)*
    Rail facilities and lines *(gauge(s), terminals, conditions of track, rolling stock and locomotives)*
    Historic foot routes
Health and Medical
    Clinics
    Hospitals
    Health-related NGOs or PVOs active in the area
    Locations of medically trained civilians
Public Works
    Water sources, lines, and treatment facilities
    Power sources, grids, and relay facilities
    Fuel sources, natural gas lines, and petroleum-based fuelling points
    Waste disposal
    Key structures that could be used for warehousing or habitation
Communications
    Wired telephone and telegraph lines and centers
    Non-wired (cellular) telephone towers, microwave relays, or ham radio operators
    Mass media *(radio stations, television stations, newspapers)*
Public Administration
    Fire departments *(equipment; capabilities; full-time or part-time)*
    Police stations and detention areas and prisons *(equipment, training levels, uniforms)*
    Schools
    Military/paramilitary locations *(facilities, fortifications, uniforms)*
    Governmental and administrative centers
    Political headquarters *(parties and campaign/poster themes)*
Agriculture
    Farming areas by type *(grain, vegetable, cattle, poultry, aquaculture)*
    Markets
    Stock yards and production facilities
    Dislocated civilians
    Locations of camps or enclaves *(capacities, facilities, security)*
    Potential areas for camps or enclaves *(proximity to water, roads, power, population centers)*
Demographics
    Ethnicities
    Religions
    Clans

throughout the AOR; the overlay specifically concerning potable water could display those areas that have adequate potable water sources in green, those to which a water supply is being established or replenished in yellow, and those areas still without the prospect of self-support in red.

Data may be collected by a combination of means. Periodic reports may be required, and patrols should always be debriefed by S-2/S-3/S-5 representatives to gain as much information as possible about developments in civilian infrastructure in the AOR. Modification of conventional SALUTE (size, activity, location, unit, time, and equipment) reports to include CAAS information from units during operations can be an especially timely and efficient way of collecting pertinent data.

In addition to maintaining a database at battalion and brigade headquarters and forwarding information to the CMOC, horizontal distribution of information is beneficial. Staff officers should exchange information with adjacent units at the same time they forward it to higher headquarters or to the CMOC.

Whether or not there is a CA element supporting the unit, the S-5 must have a close working relationship with the CMOC. Prioritization for requests of assistance by NGOs/PVOs is based in part on the data.

Chapter 20

Enforce Populace and Resource Control Measures

The neo-nationalism of the post–Cold War era and the breakup of the former Soviet Empire have resulted in significant violence against ethnic and religious minorities living in enclaves among the majority population. Protecting these minorities, and ensuring that they receive essential humanitarian supplies, is often a primary mission of forces conducting MOOTW. Even forces conducting support operations can find themselves in situations in which they must protect groups that would otherwise be deprived of humanitarian assistance, whether by a more dominant clan or sect, or by overtly antagonistic factions.

Populace and resource control (PRC) missions are conducted to accomplish the following:
- Provide security for and humanitarian assistance to the populace, NGOs, PVOs, and CA forces operating in the unit's AOR.
- Deny personnel who might be used as soldiers and war materiel to belligerent factions.
- Mobilize the local population and resources for humanitarian and civic assistance actions.
- Detect the use and reduce the effectiveness of those working as agents for the antagonistic factions.

Clearly, PRC operations generally must be conducted with the active support of host-nation civilian authorities. Whenever possible, these civilian authorities must be included in the planning and conduct of PRC operations. Involving host-nation authorities not only provides additional legitimacy to other military activities but also enhances the authorities' image with their own population and places them in the role of friends and protectors of *all* the people.

This can become problematic if those very authorities, which may represent only or mainly the majority factions, divert humanitarian aid from minority factions that are not in favor with the government. If this is the case, notify higher headquarters and intervening PVOs/NGOs of specific incidents. This must be done to avoid the appearance of aiding or abetting prejudicial policies and hence creating an atmosphere of hostility against the peacekeeping forces among the deprived factions.

PLANNING PRC MEASURES

Using intelligence, host-nation, and NGO/PVO resources, determine the locations of minority or nonaligned faction population or unit concentrations. Evaluate the adequacy of existing means of separation and humanitarian assistance. Be especially aware of reports of the following:

- Diversion of humanitarian aid (e.g., hijacking, mysterious "disappearances")
- Forcible expropriation of aid *after* it has been delivered to minority or nonaligned factions
- Black-marketeering of goods to charge money to rightful recipients

Identify areas in which the population might be sympathetic to the dominant factions; assess the integrity of local civil authorities in the delivery of goods to intended recipients; and coordinate for integration of the following into the PRC plan:

- CA units to interface with the local authorities
- PSYOPS units to persuade and inform the populace about key issues
- Army aviation or unmanned aerial vehicles (UAVs) for broad-area reconnaissance

Above all, develop a plan to restrict the movement of belligerent factions through the area and to prevent black-marketeering, smuggling, and diversion or theft of humanitarian supplies. Integrate checkpoints, OPs, patrols (mounted and dismounted), and overflights. Also, develop policies to assist in these operations.

CONTROLLING A POPULACE AND RESOURCES

Populace control measures can include:

- Curfews
- Geographic movement restrictions (checkpoints/safe zones or corridors)
- Travel permits
- Registration or ID cards

Resource control measures include:
- Licensing of commercial activities
- Ration controls (to curb-black marketeering)
- Amnesty programs (for the turn-in of stolen or black-market goods)
- Reward programs for important information
- Inspection of suspected contraband/black-market goods storage facilities

Whenever possible, curfews should be enforced by, or in conjunction with, host-nation authorities. The theater CMOC normally provides the means to issue and control personal IDs and travel documents. Licensing is normally done in conjunction with local authorities and is coordinated with CA assets. Ration control measures and amnesty programs are most likely handled by NGO/ PVO personnel. Inspections of facilities follow the SOFA and ROE.

Integrate PSYOPS

PSYOPS resources can be used to accomplish the following:
- Communicate the importance of ending support to belligerent factions (i.e., this will end the conflict).
- Inform the population of what constitutes controlled items and contraband.
- Explain to the population the reasons for the institution of curfews, licensing requirements, safe conduct lanes, and amnesty programs.
- Convince the population that its support will minimize future inconveniences and that the control measures are temporary.
- Encourage identification to the local authorities of violators and/or agents of the belligerent factions .

Integrate CA Activities

CA units have the capability to ensure that the CAAS is as current as possible. In addition, they can assist in coordinating efforts with host-nation authorities and NGOs/PVOs. CA unit members have often established especially favorable relationships with host-nation VIPs; these can be of great value in conducting PRC. Additionally, CA units can help:
- Assess the movement of civilians within the AOR.
- Assess the distribution of HA for fairness, equity, and compliance with guidance.
- Establish checkpoints for search and seizure of contraband and prohibited quantities of controlled items, as well as apprehend black-

listed and/or graylisted personnel for transfer to MI or coalition authorities.
- Conduct mounted and dismounted patrols to check for caches of contraband, illegal quantities of controlled items, and evidence of smuggling routes.

As with all MOOTW tasks, report all PRC discoveries and apprehensions to higher headquarters and the CMOC, and exchange information with adjacent units.

Chapter 21

React to Civil Disturbance

Factions opposed to the conduct or implications of stability and support operations often resist or attempt to prevent mission accomplishment. In addition to military action and terrorism, one of the courses of action most often exercised by such factions is to conduct civil disturbances. These activities generally play to western audiences' sympathies better than overt military violence and can be extremely effective in undermining the political will of the nations attempting to stabilize the situation.

Military forces must not allow themselves to be provoked to overreaction when responding to civil disturbances; in many cases, this is precisely what the organizers of the demonstrations want most. There are few greater propaganda victories than images of civilians bloodied at the hands of military forces.

U.S. military forces are legally bound by the specific restrictions and principles of the Posse Comitatus Act in their involvement with civil disturbances within the United States. Generally, such forces (not including nonfederalized National Guard units) may not be used in lieu of duly appointed law enforcement officers without specific presidential or congressional approval and direction. This law prevents the abuse of the armed forces by the executive branch and reinforces the role of the armed forces as the protectors of the people and their freedoms, not the oppressors.

In foreign situations, especially when conducting MOOTW, U.S. military forces may be the solution of choice, however. Often, the host-nation's law enforcement infrastructure has broken down or become otherwise ineffective, and U.S. and multinational forces are called on to react to civil disturbances.

In quelling or containing civil disturbances, soldiers must strictly adhere to ROE and all pertinent agreements. Under no circumstances can soldiers or leaders allow themselves to be unduly provoked. No other military mission requires more discipline or direct leader involvement for success.

Experience in the Balkans during Operation Joint Endeavor resulted in a technique that has achieved considerable success and can be summed with the acronym IDAM.

Isolate—in time and space—the trouble spot from outside influence or interaction. Establish hasty checkpoints or roadblocks at all points of ingress and egress and OPs to observe activities throughout the area.

Dominate the situation through force presence and control of information resources. Conduct show of force operations (see chapter 25) to awe the crowd; conduct information operations to maintain information dominance; employ PSYOPS assets to calm the crowd or discourage violence.

Maintain common situational awareness through the use of aerial platforms, including reconnaissance and attack helicopters, UAVs, and ground sensors. Integrate with reports from human intelligence sources, checkpoints, OPs, and NGO/PVO offices in the area. Disseminate information periodically and whenever there is a significant change in the operation.

Multidimensional, multiecheloned actions are key. For example, while combat elements engage in operations to discourage, contain, and resolve the actions in the streets, employ CA teams to negotiate political solutions, (e.g., to convince faction leaders to keep the demonstration quiet, to end the disturbance, or to convince radio stations to stop broadcasting inflammatory programs). Simultaneously, request PVOs/NGOs or other intermediaries to appeal to faction leaders by reminding them of possible consequences of violent actions (e.g., withdrawal or curtailment of NGO/PVO support).

PREPARING FOR CIVIL DISTURBANCE OPERATIONS
Assemble Equipment and Munitions
Key elements of equipment for civil disturbance operations include:
- Bayonets (for all soldiers armed with the M16A2)
- Face shields
- Shotguns with buckshot
- CS or other approved riot agents
- Bullhorn or public-address system
- Barriers for marking crowd limits (with multilingual signs)—sawhorse types or concertina (METT-TC and ROE dependent)
- Videotape cameras
- Restraints for apprehending suspected criminals

Coordinate for Support

Coordinate to have available:

- MI personnel to assist with identification of crowd leaders or covert direction of crowd activities
- CA elements and/or translators to communicate with crowd leaders and conduct liaison with civil authorities
- PSYOPS units to conduct mass communications with the crowd
- MPs for apprehending and evacuating criminal suspects
- Medical units for treating friendly casualties and others as directed
- NGO/PVO representatives to help attenuate the causes of the disturbances
- PAO representatives to escort and brief media representatives
- Transportation for detainees

Use Designated Marksmen

If allowed by ROE, snipers or soldiers who are especially good shots may be selected to serve as designated marksmen. They are used to provide the commander with another option in the incremental use of force; they can respond to isolated gunfire by eliminating the source with minimal chances of collateral danger. Specially equipped sniper weapons should be used if available; if not, standard-issue rifles can suffice. Be sure to use weapons equipped with properly zeroed night sights for conditions of limited visibility.

Rehearse Formations

Riot control formations must present a formidable, disciplined appearance to quell a crowd. To the greatest extent possible, conduct training under conditions that closely approximate those they will encounter in a civil disturbance. For example, have them heckled and verbally abused by role-players dressed as the crowd would dress. Rehearse actions with and without protective masks.

The capability to outlast or "face down" a crowd is often absolutely essential for controlling a civil disturbance. Train to high standards of personal discipline; it is a fact of military life in most Western armies today that soldiers are not used to standing in one position for long periods, especially in uncomfortable conditions (rain, heat, cold); therefore, this type of discipline must be instilled during training.

Transitions between formations and activities must appear seamless to the crowd. All soldiers must understand ROE and must be trained to near-perfection in these drills, to avoid any perception of disorganization to the crowd.

Controlling Civil Disturbances

U.S. joint doctrine prescribes the following principles of reaction to civil disturbances:

- Be flexible and change tactics as necessary to meet the situation.
- Rehearse to ensure success.
- Remember that the appearance of being able to do damage is often more effective than actually having to resort to force.
- Control the situation by positioning personnel and presenting the image of having and maintaining full control, even if the situation deteriorates.
- Provide all-round defense of assigned sectors of observation and fire and be able to observe and fire 360 degrees around the control force.
- Use speed in deployment, arrest, apprehension, and reaction to change.
- Use surprise to keep the crowd off balance.

Incremental Application of Force

Adherence to the principle of incrementally applied and appropriate force is paramount when reacting to civil disturbances. The commander must first determine the scope and severity of the disturbance; liaison with local authorities can accomplish this, and a liaison team should be left in place throughout the operation. Leaders confer with MI, MP, PSYOPS, and neutral observers (if any) for additional information regarding past patterns, crowd mood, presence of known agitators, and so forth. Next, the leaders reconnoiter the disturbance to judge for themselves.

In priority of force, the following actions may be taken:

- Defuse or deter the disturbance using CA, PSYOPS, and/or NGO/PVO resources. Continue to employ these techniques throughout the situation, unless people's lives or limbs are threatened.
- Passively contain the disturbance (e.g., erect barriers with signs bearing appropriate instructions).
- Employ aerial platforms to monitor the situation and report.
- Post sentries at entrances to threatened facilities.
- Establish checkpoints at routes of ingress and egress.
- Establish OPs to keep the area under observation.
- Move civilian occupants to safest areas.*
- Establish small security posts to visually monitor the situation, while the main force remains hidden close by. *Weapons should have magazines locked, but there should be no rounds in the chamber.

- If major violence appears imminent, conduct a show of force. Move the main force into position to deter movement of the crowd into areas to be protected.* Leave an exit in the direction the crowd is to move.
- Fix bayonets, scabbards on.
- Fix bayonets, scabbards off.
- Mask and employ riot agents (if permitted by ROE)*
- Request reinforcement if the situation could be contained by the appearance of additional forces or if the commander believes that further escalation will result in mission failure (e.g., the crowd is armed and could overwhelm the force on site).
- Engage with designated marksmen, if there are appropriate targets.
- Load weapons. Warn the crowd of the specific consequences of further escalation.
- Engage with shotguns.
- General engagement. Due to their devastating and potentially collateral effects, fully automatic weapons are rarely appropriate for use in civil disturbance situations.

---

*To the greatest extent possible, rotate small units or individuals into these high-stress positions.

Chapter 22

Control Civilian Movement

Units conducting MOOTW often face the challenge of keeping main supply routes and other road nets open for military traffic. One of the most common problems encountered can stem from civilian pedestrian and vehicular traffic on those critical routes. Especially heavy traffic may consist of refugees from a disease-stricken area, a natural disaster site, belligerent action, or a combination of any of these. Other than these especially serious circumstances, challenges can also result from the routine traffic of legitimate commerce or other mundane activities. Whatever the source or degree of civilian movement, it must not be allowed to interfere with mission-essential military traffic. Nor should military traffic unduly constrain legitimate civilian movement, lest those constraints cause unnecessary tension in the areas of operations.

RECONNOITERING THE AREA AND ROUTES
Ascertain which military or other friendly forces' facilities are in the area, and consider these "controlled areas" that civilians must be discouraged from visiting or transiting. Establish routes by which civilians may move without transiting these controlled areas. These routes must be able to accommodate normal civilian traffic and, preferably, any anticipated surges in traffic volume. Anticipate the "magnet effect," by which civilians seeking to avoid danger or to receive relief may cluster around military facilities.

Using normal route reconnaissance techniques, determine which routes are essential and suitable for use by military traffic. Using hasty checkpoints, determine the volume of normal traffic on routes under consideration. Determine the location of roadblocks and permanent checkpoints necessary to eliminate civilian traffic on essential routes for periods of exclusive use by friendly military elements. Designate alternative routes to accommodate diverted civilian traffic.

ESTABLISHING A ROUTE NET

Establish security for controlled areas, and designate escorts for civilians who must transit them. Notify local civilian authorities of controlled areas, routes of civilian traffic, and routes on which military traffic will be traveling often. Encourage area civilians to remain in their communities, using CA and PSYOPS teams whenever available.

Visibly mark routes to be used by military traffic; notify all pertinent headquarters and civilian officials. Clear obstacles such as mines or barricades from essential primary or alternative routes. Repair or upgrade routes as required; some projects may be eligible for classification as civic actions, and others may be completed by local civilian contractors.

In consonance with higher authorities, establish a pass system to facilitate the movement of nonmilitary forces through controlled areas or over a controlled road net.

CONTROLLING CIVILIAN MOVEMENT

When units must have priority use of a route, such as when dispatching a quick reaction force (QRF), delivering emergency humanitarian aid, or evacuating casualties from a disaster, activate or establish the roadblocks, checkpoints, and detours necessary to clear essential routes while still providing for civilian traffic to the greatest extent possible. Notify pertinent headquarters and civilian authorities of the measures taken and the expected duration of the closures and diversions.

Chapter 23

Control and Move Dislocated Civilians

Units often encounter civilians—sometimes in masses—who have been dislocated from their indigenous region by war, natural disaster, famine, disease, or political or religious persecution. Also, the parameters of some treaties or other agreements can result in migrations of peoples to new locations. Movement of dislocated civilians (DCs) must be controlled: in addition to the tragic human dimension of such phenomena, these migrations can become extremely dangerous and jeopardize military mission accomplishment.

Generally, the purposes of all DC operations include:

- Protecting civilians from the dangers of combat operations
- Preventing and controlling the outbreak of disease among DCs, which could threaten the health of military forces
- Relieving human suffering as far as practicable
- Centralizing the masses of DCs
- Facilitating military mission accomplishment

DETERMINING THE DIMENSIONS OF THE DISLOCATION

Upon learning of a migration of DCs in the friendly area of responsibility, dispatch a patrol to determine the location, numbers, and demographic composition of the group. To the extent feasible by METT-TC, tailor the patrol to include civil affairs and medical personnel. Specifically, acquire the following information:

- Total number, sex, and age of the DCs
- Number of families, if possible
- Condition of DCs including clothing, shelter, food, water, and medical aid required

- Proximity to belligerent factions or ethnic or religious rivals
- Terrain factors, including proximity to minefields, unexploded ordnance, and suitable roads

After the patrol leader confirms (in accord with instructions or, in the absence of instructions, with higher headquarters) that there are no restrictions against rendering humanitarian aid to the group, and if the patrol leader determines that it would involve only an acceptable amount of risk to the patrol, the patrol renders such humanitarian assistance as is possible. The patrol leader must make no promises, commitments, or guarantees other than those directed by higher authorities.

GAINING CONTROL OF THE DISLOCATED CIVILIANS

The commander determines the immediate requirements of the situation and notifies higher headquarters. The commander also initiates coordination with appropriate NGOs, PVOs, or other civilian agencies.

There are basically two nodes used in the process of gaining control of DCs; these are through the use of civilian collection points or temporary assembly or holding areas.

Civilian Collection Points

The purpose of the civilian collection point (CCP) is to establish control and direction over the movement of the civilian populace. A CCP is temporary for small numbers of DCs until they can return to their homes or, if the tactical situation requires, move to a safer area.

CCPs are established as close to the source of the dislocation as possible. Since it is a temporary measure, screening is rapid. It may include screening for intelligence information and emergency assistance. Screening must facilitate segregation of belligerents from DCs.

Assembly Areas

An assembly area is a temporary holding area for civilians before their return to their homes or movement to a more secure area. Assembly areas are usually located in a secure, stable environment and may include buildings such as schools, churches, hotels, and warehouses. A consideration in selecting a specific area should include the ability to provide overnight accommodations for several days. Here, more detailed screening or segregation of the different categories of DCs takes place. Local civilians may operate an assembly area under the supervision of tactical or support troops or CA personnel.

If the DCs are in danger of attack or injury by one or more of the belligerent factions, a security element must isolate the area by patrols or roadblocks.

Using all available resources, such as local intermediaries, translators, and CA teams, the commander advises the DCs of the available options, which may include:

- That the necessary humanitarian assistance will exceed unit capabilities over a protracted period.
- That the protection provided at the current location is not absolute and cannot be maintained.
- That the unit does not possess the transportation assets to move the entire group, except to avoid immediate danger.
- That NGOs, PVOs, or other civilian agencies may make transportation available, but that resources may not be adequate for moving the entire group. The leaders of the DCs must prioritize and organize them for transportation.
- That the unit may be able to escort the DCs to safety.
- That the unit may be able to provide maps of safe routes to desired or appropriate destinations for the DCs.

MOVING DISLOCATED CIVILIANS

If transportation for the DCs is arranged, conduct movement in a fashion similar to any convoy. If some or all of the DCs are to move on independently, control their movement in the same fashion used for all civilian movement, but be prepared, based on METT-TC, to add an escort element to prevent both violence from rival factions and straggling.

Chapter 24

Establish and Operate a Camp for Dislocated Civilians

This delicate, difficult mission is one for which tactical units must be carefully organized and prepared. Experience since the 1980s has shown that these missions can be rewarding or can be extremely taxing on the discipline of participating units. Under some circumstances, operating a DC camp can be an ungratifying and even bitter experience. Nevertheless, as the United States and other nations grapple with the problems of large-scale migration of populations, this will be a mission that, if anything, becomes more common in the years to come.

Units establish DC camps when large groups of civilians must be quartered pending decisions about their ultimate destinations. Host-nation personnel usually direct the administration and operation of a camp, but it is not uncommon for U.S. units to do this, too. CA units provide technical advice, support, and assistance, depending on the requirements. They may also furnish additional detachments and functional teams or specialists to resolve public health, public welfare, or public safety problems at a particular camp.

ESTABLISHING A DC CAMP
Location
If possible, DCs may be housed in existing facilities such as hotels, schools, halls, theaters, vacant warehouses, unused factories, or available military cantonments. Otherwise, engineer support and military construction materials are required to build the facilities.

If camps must be built, they should be located near or with easy access to the following:
- Roads adequate for the arrival of construction equipment, building supplies, and DC transportation resources
- If possible and appropriate, a rail spur or noncommercial airstrip

159

- Adequate water supply
- Electricity and sewage systems (if practical—austere environments are unlikely to have these)

Also, the site selected should provide good natural surface drainage. To the greatest extent possible, camps should *not* be built in close proximity to any of the following:

- Vital communication centers
- Active, large military installations or other potential military targets
- Heavily populated regions
- International borders
- Commercial seaports, airports, or rail depots
- Low-lying, swampy areas that provide breeding grounds for disease-carrying insects
- Areas susceptible to natural or man-made disasters (e.g., flooding, air or water pollution, fire)

Construction

Camp Layout. For ease of organization, administration, and control of the camp population, the camp should be divided into sections or separate compounds. Each section can be used as an administrative subunit through which camp business is conducted. Major sections normally include:

- Camp headquarters
- Hospital/medical facility
- Dining area
- Quarters/sleeping areas

The sleeping areas must be further subdivided into separate areas for unescorted children, unattached females, families, and unattached males. When possible, construct separate camps for each category. Camp personnel must also consider cultural and religious practices and make every effort to keep families together. The accompanying figure depicts a generic camp plan.

Building the Camp. The specific type of construction resources required to build the camp vary according to the following:

- Local climate.
- Anticipated permanency of the camp. Generally, in temperate climates, construction criteria may be classified as temporary (less than six months) or semipermanent (more than six months). Obviously, the less wear and tear imposed by the climatic environment, the longer the facilities will last.

Sample Displaced Civilian Camp Layout

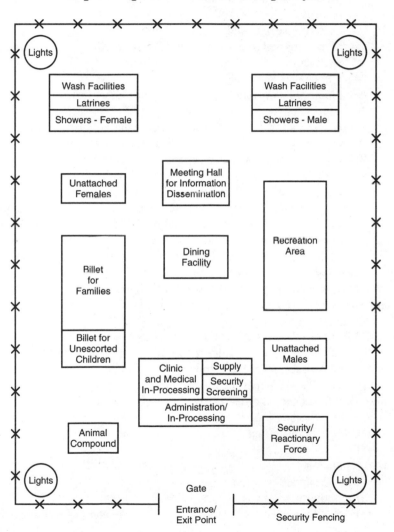

- Availability of construction materials (what is locally available and what must be shipped in).
- Extent of available construction equipment and local labor.
- Requirements to house the following categories of inhabitants:
  — Families
  — Unaccompanied children
  — Sick or injured (requiring medical facilities and possibly quarantine facilities)
  — Single male and female adults
  — Elderly or infirm adults (requiring ramps rather than stairs, special climatic protection, medical facilities)
  — Livestock that may have accompanied the population (requiring veterinary facilities, animal holding areas)

Whenever possible, DCs themselves, local agencies, or host-nation companies and labor should construct the camp. Local sources should provide materials whenever possible, pursuant to legal limitations. The supporting command's logistical and transportation assets are used to acquire and transport the required resources to build or modify existing facilities for DC operations. The supporting command also furnishes medical, food service, and other supporting assets to establish DC camps.

Dislocated civilians from antagonistic factions should never be housed in the same camp. If this is inevitable due to mission constraints, construct the camp so that the living areas for the respective factions are not contiguous.

PREPARING FOR DC CAMP OPERATIONS

Displaced civilians living in camps require rules of behavior and rules for camp operations. Rules for DC camp behavior should be prepared in consultation with CA personnel and appropriate host-nation and international authorities. SOPs should be established for the following (at a minimum):

- Entry screening
- Camp administration
- Food service
- Sanitation
- Morale support activities
- Religious activities
- Facilities maintenance, by the camp population and by facilities engineers
- Civil disturbance in the camp

Train all personnel in the performance of their duties; emphasize the ROE and the necessity of highly disciplined, humane behavior. Familiarize all personnel with the key cultural do's and don'ts that will facilitate cooperative relationships with the DC population.

OPERATING THE CAMP
Screening
Screening the DC population upon entry is necessary to prevent infiltration of camps by agitators, intelligence agents, criminals, or escaping members of belligerent factions. Although military intelligence or military police personnel generally screen DCs, friendly and reliable local civilians under the supervision of civil affairs personnel may be used to assist in this critical function. Screening is the only way to prevent infiltration by potentially disruptive elements and preclude the alienation of people who are sympathetic to friendly objectives. Blacklisted individuals or members of blacklisted groups must be segregated from the DC population immediately and transferred to separate facilities or turned over to appropriate host-nation or international authorities.

The screening process also identifies skilled technicians and professional specialists to help in camp administration. Doctors, dentists, nurses, lawyers, schoolteachers, policemen, mechanics, carpenters, and cooks are but a few of the essential people needed.

Background screening—and daily random searches—must also be conducted for all employees in the camp. Black-marketeering, money-laundering, smuggling of contraband, and other illegal activities can cause severe discipline and morale problems among the camp population. A special category of crime that should be prevented is the illegal emigration scam, involving empty promises of safe conduct to an especially desirable country in return for money, treasure, or servitude.

Camp Control
Control of the camp population is the key to successful camp operations. To meet obligations under international law, camp commanders must ensure the efficient and effective administration of camps. To control camp populations, commanders must do the following:
- Establish humane and fair rules; use PSYOPS, CA, and host-nation authorities to communicate the rules to the camp population.
- Maintain discipline. Whenever possible, use host-nation law enforcement and judicial personnel to administer camps in accordance with the culture of the DCs, *consistent with U.S. and international law.* In other words, the systems of justice and discipline may vary, but the

methods and standards must meet U.S. and international legal requirements.

- Insert or develop reliable informants. This is important in all but the most temporary camps. Remove agitators, criminals, or other dangerous personnel and transfer them from the camp to the appropriate authorities as soon as possible after identification.
- Designate a quick reaction force, thoroughly trained for the incremental use of force, to preclude or quickly quell disturbances within the camp.

Camp administrators serve as the single point of contact with outside agencies and organizations for all camp matters.

Morale of the Camp Population

Although DCs may be relieved to have escaped a dangerous situation, it is highly unlikely that any of them will want to remain in the camp longer than is absolutely necessary. Morale can be affected by a multitude of factors beyond the administering unit's control, including anxiety about the future and anguish over loss of property, possessions, family, and friends. If they have been dislocated by a human enemy, DCs may become restive and desirous of striking back.

Although it is not likely that the administering unit will be able to maintain "high morale" in the military sense of the term, DC morale can be positively affected—and the discipline problems corollary to low morale avoided—by exercising certain measures, such as:

- Maintaining different cultural groups in separate sections of the camp.
- Keeping families together but separating unaccompanied males, females, and children under the age of 18 (or abiding by the laws of the host nation regarding when a child becomes an adult).
- Furnishing necessary information regarding the status and future of DCs.
- Allowing regular, simple access to the commander for DC group representatives.
- Involving the DCs in camp administration, work, and recreation.
- Providing religious support activities, as appropriate.
- Providing recreational, sports, educational, or entertainment activities that will not agitate the DC population. For example, in some cultures, soccer matches between members of rival factions can provoke violence at the best of times. NGOs/PVOs can be of great assistance in these endeavors.

Administration

Because of the large numbers of DCs for whom control and care must be provided (experience has shown that the population for a single camp should generally not exceed 5,000, if possible), using host-nation civilians for camp administration is preferable. It promotes order in the camp by diminishing opportunities for tensions borne of cultural misunderstandings, and it streamlines law enforcement and concomitant judicial proceedings.

Involve DCs in the administration of the camp. Experience in DC operations shows that about 6 percent of the total number of DCs should be employed on a full-time basis.

It may be appropriate to coordinate assistance from international, intergovernmental, and NGOs/PVOs, especially for medical support. Certain other humanitarian and even morale support may also be available from these organizations. All such participation should be conducted under the specific provisions of memorandums of understanding (MOUs) between the camp administration and participating organizations. (Ensure thorough review by competent legal authorities.)

Medical Care and Sanitation

The need for medical care and sanitation intensifies in camp environments because of the temporary nature of the facilities and the lack of sanitation by the people. Enforcement and education can help ensure that the camp population complies with basic sanitation measures.

Supply

The camp supply officer or CA civilian supply specialist must coordinate in advance for periodic deliveries of adequate quantities of the following:

- Food (which must be inspected by qualified medical or veterinary personnel before issue)
- Water (which must be inspected by qualified medical personnel before use)
- Clothing (NGOs/PVOs can be of great help in this area. In regions supported by the United States, USAID can be helpful as well. Use U.S. military stocks as a last resort.)
- Fuel
- Portable sanitation devices
- Medical supplies
- Facilities maintenance items

Security

The camp security officer, supervised by the public safety team, is responsible for the maintenance of camp security and enforces law, order, and discipline. Sources for security officers include host-nation authorities or friendly military forces. Another potential source may be from the camp population itself. Police personnel within the population can be used to supplement any of the preceding groups or to constitute a special camp police force, if necessary. It is necessary to maintain both internal and external patrols; however, security for a DC facility should never give the impression that it is a prison.

Information Dissemination

In the administration of any type of camp, dissemination of instructions and information to the camp population is vital. Communications can be in the form of notices on bulletin boards, posters, public-address systems, loudspeakers, camp meetings and assemblies, or a camp radio station. CA information teams and PSYOPS units can be critical to planning, coordinating, and conducting an information campaign to keep the DC population informed and assist in cooperation.

Disposition

The final step in DC operations is the ultimate disposition of the DCs, although it must be considered early in the planning phase. The most desired disposition is to return them to their homes.

Allowing DCs to return to their homes as quickly as tactical considerations permit diminishes the burden on the military and the civilian economy for their support. It also reduces the danger of diseases common among people in confined areas. When DCs return to their homes, they can help restore their towns and better contribute to their own support. If DCs cannot return to their homes, they may be resettled in their country or in a country that will accept them. Guidance concerning the disposition of DCs must come from higher authorities and be coordinated with U.S. forces, national authorities, and international agencies.

Chapter 25

Conduct a Show of Force

To prevent escalation of a MOOTW situation to offensive or defensive actions, or to prevent disruption of an operation by belligerent factions, it is sometimes useful or even necessary to conduct a show of force. Ideally, such operations are conducted in concert with multinational forces, to demonstrate the united resolve of the alliance or coalition. The audience is always a potential opponent; sometimes it is multiple factions bent on initiating (or renewing) hostilities.

Shows of force are extremely delicate operations and often involve high risk; the difference between a successful show of force and a demonstration that initiates hostilities is often a function of the individual perception of a few key members of the audience. However, shows of force are sometimes the only measures that can preserve the integrity of an operation.

PLANNING A SHOW OF FORCE
Conduct reconnaissance to determine a location for the show of force that allows maximum visibility of the strengths and capabilities of the unit by the intended audience. Consider the factions' sensor array, including not only visual capabilities on the ground but also radar, electronic, and aerial or space-based sensors.

In conceiving shows of force, commanders must convince antagonistic factions of the inadvisability of hostilities, but not provoke them. Cultural and political factors play a crucial role in these determinations, so intelligence must be thorough and accurate. Generally, shows of force must convey an impression of overwhelming superiority, even if it is somewhat illusory. PSYOPS can be of exceptional utility in establishing this perception among the audience. They must *never* expose weaknesses that can be exploited by a potential enemy.

Commanders must also strike a balance between operational security and the need to deter hostilities. For example, jamming all radio nets used by belligerent factions may be impressive but it could also alert belligerent commanders to the need to devise alternative means of communicating. In such a case, jamming only selected frequencies might be wise, even though the force has the capability to jam all simultaneously. Carefully consider these trade-offs to avoid achieving consequences that are counterproductive to the mission or degrade future operations.

If feasible, notify the intended audience of the impending show of force.

MOVING TO THE LOCATION OF THE SHOW OF FORCE
Due to the unique nature and extreme sensitivity of these operations, participants must be briefed especially thoroughly. Special instructions include:
* Mission and intended outcomes
* ROE and conditions under which force may be directed against opponents
* Specific risks of the operation
* Authentication procedures for orders to commence firing
* Weapon control status and directional orientation
* Communications limitations or special uses
* Identities, types of vehicles and vehicle markings of multinational coparticipants

Clearly mark all vehicles with appropriate UN, national, or coalition insignia, and turn lights on to indicate nonhostile intent. Carefully adhering to all ROE and other legitimate restraints, assemble and move the units to the location where the show of force is to be conducted. Select movement formations and speeds that do not inherently provoke hostilities.

SHOWING FORCE
Upon arrival at the show of force site, all members of the force must maintain an especially alert, professional, yet restrained posture.

Position weapons and vehicles for maximum visibility to belligerent sensors. Array the most impressive (e.g., tanks, attack helicopters) most prominently; this arrangement will not necessarily be in a tactical formation. If allowed by ROE, orient weapons generally in the direction of the audience, but not directly at specific vehicles or positions.

Be prepared to conduct a proportional, appropriate response, up to and including attacking or defending if required upon initiation of hostilities by belligerent factions.

Chapter 26

Deliver Supplies
or Humanitarian Aid

One of the most common missions for units participating in MOOTW is the delivery of supplies or other humanitarian aid to victims of famine or natural or man-made disasters. This mission is also common when one faction is attempting to starve or otherwise deprive into submission the noncombatants of a rival faction. Typically, military units transport supplies via convoy from an assembly area—often near a port, airfield, or railhead—to locations (delivery points) where representatives of PVOs/NGOs or local authorities take possession of the supplies and subsequently distribute them to the populace.

PLANNING FOR DELIVERY

Reconnoiter the routes to the delivery points to select those that provide the best trafficability for the convoys and the least chance of interception or other attempted diversion. To the greatest extent possible, avoid population centers or areas of known belligerent activity. Confirm the following with leaders from the NGOs/PVOs or other authorities that will be distributing the supplies:

- Exact locations of delivery points
- Times at which the deliveries are expected or desired
- Types and quantities of supplies to be delivered
- Capacity for off-loading supplies at delivery points (this will influence the size, composition, and schedule of convoys to the delivery sites)

Designate an assembly area for the convoy, and establish security teams to prevent interference at likely choke points en route to the delivery points. In accordance with the ROE, security teams must also prevent pilferage or looting at the delivery points themselves, as well as at any halts along the way. Security en route and at the delivery site will be greatly aided if vehicles with "lockable" doors are used in the convoy, as opposed to the

169

open stake vehicles commonly used by military units. Securing supplies in locked military vans (MILVANs) or even CONEXes is another way to discourage or minimize potential pilferage.

Plan for communications with higher headquarters and with the leaders of the receiving/distributing organizations at the delivery points. Before departing, verify the far and near recognition signals—if any—and ensure possession of all necessary pyrotechnics, radios, codebooks, or other signaling devices to be used. Conduct rehearsals of the actions at the delivery site for all members of the convoy and security teams.

DELIVERING THE GOODS

Exchange far and near recognition signals with key leaders at the delivery point as the convoy approaches its destination. If the receiving elements are not ready, halt the convoy out of sight of the populace and establish security. Proceed when the receiving organization is ready to accept the supplies.

Secure the Area

Establish all-around security at the delivery site and conduct security operations in accordance with the ROE. Do not off-load items or break seals on containers until the receiving party is prepared to accept the supplies. If feasible and desired by the distributing agency, the security teams may remain in place until all supplies are delivered.

Transfer the Supplies

Transfer the humanitarian supplies to the appropriate receiving agent. The commander of the convoy ensures that an appropriate representative of the receiving/distributing organization acknowledges receipt of the supplies *in writing*. Receipts must be specifically written and include the types and quantities of supplies delivered. Immediately report any discrepancies or other problems to higher headquarters.

Assess Additional Requirements

Although additional requirements are usually assessed by experts from NGOs/PVOs or CA units, sometimes—especially in the case of wildcat bloodshed, unforeseen natural disasters, or other unanticipated developments in the situation—the conditions under which humanitarian assistance efforts are conducted change without notice. In these cases, other military organizations may be the only ones on site and capable of assessing the situation. The accompanying checklist, actually developed for use in Operation Restore Hope in Somalia, is an example of the sort of assessment that can be performed to adjust humanitarian operations to the new conditions.

Assessment of Required Humanitarian Assistance for a Dislocated Population

What was their previous location?
    What is the size of the original population?
    What is the size of the area and population that the village services in
       the surrounding countryside?
    What is the size of the refugee population?
    Why did they come here?
    What is the relationship of the village with the surrounding villages?
    Are they related?
    Do they support each other?
    Are they hostile toward each other?
    Is there factional antagonism within the village?

What is the food and water status of the village?
    Where do they get their food?
    What other means of subsistence are available?
    Are the villagers farmers or herders?
    What is the status of their crops or herds?
    What is the quality of the water source?

What is the medical status of the village?
    What services are available in the village?
    What is the location of the nearest medical facility?
    Is there evidence of illness and/or starvation?
    What portion of the population is affected?
    What is the death rate?
    What diseases are reported in the village?

What civilian organizations exist in the village? Who are their leaders?

What civilian/military organizations exist in the village?
    Who are their leaders?

What organization/leadership element does the general population seem
to support or trust the most?
    Which organization seems to have the most control in the village?

What NGO/PVO relief agencies operate in the village?
    Who are their representatives?
    What services do they provide?
    What portion of the population do they service?
    Do they have an outreach program for the surrounding countryside?

(continued)

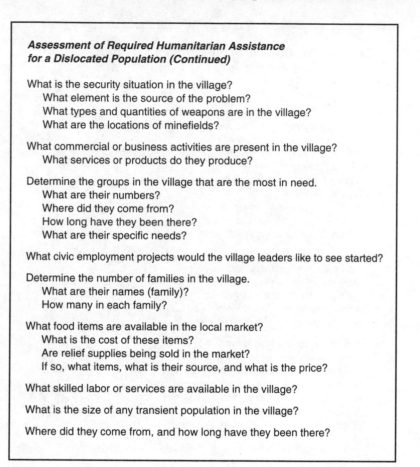

***Assessment of Required Humanitarian Assistance
for a Dislocated Population (Continued)***

What is the security situation in the village?
  What element is the source of the problem?
  What types and quantities of weapons are in the village?
  What are the locations of minefields?

What commercial or business activities are present in the village?
  What services or products do they produce?

Determine the groups in the village that are the most in need.
  What are their numbers?
  Where did they come from?
  How long have they been there?
  What are their specific needs?

What civic employment projects would the village leaders like to see started?

Determine the number of families in the village.
  What are their names (family)?
  How many in each family?

What food items are available in the local market?
  What is the cost of these items?
  Are relief supplies being sold in the market?
  If so, what items, what is their source, and what is the price?

What skilled labor or services are available in the village?

What is the size of any transient population in the village?

Where did they come from, and how long have they been there?

Chapter 27

Provide Medical Care
to Noncombatants

This mission is viewed by most Americans with significant emotion. The relief of misery and pain is a noble and admirable objective and is often intrinsic to the accomplishment of MOOTW. In this case, suitable medical assets are made available for conducting traditional medical civic assistance programs (MEDCAPs). The specific conduct of MEDCAPs is beyond the scope of this book.

Sometimes, medical relief of suffering is not a *primary* mission but remains a compelling issue for units conducting MOOTW. Under these circumstances, which may occur frequently in underdeveloped regions, units may not possess the assets to conduct MEDCAPs but must nevertheless respond to requests from noncombatants for medical assistance. Sometimes, the ROE will dictate the exact circumstances under which medical care can be provided to noncombatants; in some circumstances—especially in missions of long duration—legislation by Congress may limit or otherwise specify which medical resources may be used to treat noncombatants. In any case, as with all operations, commanders and their staffs must be thoroughly conversant with the applicable rules and the intent of higher headquarters and must act accordingly.

DEFINING THE CIRCUMSTANCES
Noncombatants may be defined as:
- Unarmed civilians
- Belligerents who are unarmed
- Belligerents who are incapacitated due to injury

Commanders must establish SOPs that address the contingency of noncombatants in urgent need of medical care. These SOPs must be congruent with all pertinent international agreements (i.e., the Geneva and Hague Conventions), U.S. statutes, military regulations, current ROE and the commander's intent. As with all plans covering sensitive issues, the SOP should be reviewed by the SJA before it goes into effect.

At a minimum, the SOP should address the following:

- Circumstances under which noncombatants may be treated.
- Limitations (if any) on the care that may be rendered or on the resources that may be expended. Resources to be considered include medicines and other medical supplies, such as whole blood; treatment procedures (X-rays, MRIs); and evacuation assets to be used (ground or air).
- Once wounded and seriously ill noncombatants are stabilized, to which PVOs, NGOs, or other civilian healthcare provider they are to be transferred (include telephone numbers, radio call signs, locations of PVOs/NGOs).
- That detainees are to be treated as though part of the friendly force until civilian care can be coordinated.
- Provisions for impartial and equal treatment of patients, irrespective of faction.
- Measures to be taken to hospitalize or otherwise billet patients that will minimize opportunities for friction between patients belonging to antagonistic factions.

TREATING AND EVACUATING PATIENTS

Sometimes, especially when units are operating from a fixed or semipermanent installation, patients may be brought to the unit by local inhabitants and treatment requested. In such cases, it is usually best to follow the SOP in effect.

More difficult is determination of the appropriate actions in the field, during the conduct of operations whose objectives do not involve the provision of medical care to noncombatants. The leaders of security patrols, reconnaissance patrols, convoy escorts, or even checkpoints may be confronted with situations in which the relief of suffering experienced by diseased or injured noncombatants suddenly becomes an important issue. In such instances, leaders should:

- Determine the urgency of the aid required.
- Evaluate the risk to the unit providing the aid (i.e., consider the impact of the absence of the soldiers allocated to transport or otherwise

attend to the casualties; weigh the possibility of communicating disease to members of the unit).
- Assist if no other options are available and if required to save life or limb.
- Transfer casualties to the care of the host nation or NGO or PVO as soon as practicable.
- Report actions to higher HQ.

Chapter 28

Protect
Noncombatants / Facilities

It is a sobering fact that during the conduct of MOOTW, those who are attempting to relieve suffering or restore peace are often the targets of violence by one or more of the belligerent factions. Saddest—and most infuriating—of all attempts to derail peace operations are attacks made against the otherwise defenseless personnel of NGOs or PVOs who are operating humanitarian aid (HA) centers such as hospitals, dislocated persons centers, or HA supply points. Although direct military action against the perpetrators of such attacks might be desirable from a purely military perspective, ROE or international exigencies might mitigate against such solutions. Rarely, however, are commanders forbidden to protect noncombatants who are assisting in the conduct of an operation. Protecting these people is often the *raison d'être* of military involvement in MOOTW.

PLANNING TO PROTECT
Commanders and staffs should visit each site in their unit AOR and develop their plans to the greatest extent practicable (based on security considerations) in consonance with leaders of the NGOs/PVOs they may be called on to protect. Commanders should formulate plans for the protection of noncombatants assisting in the operation based on the threat in the AOR.

Site Folders
One technique that facilitates planning is the creation of site folders containing critical information about each HA site potentially requiring protection. Folders for each site should include:
- Exact locations
- Routes to and from each site
- LZs/PZs in or near each site

- Physical security measures (e.g., fences, ditches) already in place
- Aerial photos/detailed diagrams of the site and immediate vicinities
- Means of communicating (e.g., radio, telephone)
- Number and nationality of NGO/PVO personnel normally at each site
- Key personnel, by name and position
- Nature of activities and types of equipment at each site
- Vulnerability assessment

Protecting Priorities
Using the information in the folders, commanders prioritize protection based on:
- Proximity of sites to known hot spots
- Purpose of sites (e.g., hospitals, supply depots, based on METT-TC)
- Ethnic group typically assisted by each site
- Forces available for protecting or evacuating the sites

Operation Plans (OPLANS)
With the priority of protection determined, commanders and their staffs use normal procedures to promulgate OPLANS for protecting the sites. Some unique factors for consideration when formulating concepts of operations are:
- Incremental use of force in proportion to the threat, in accordance with the ROE and other agreements, including nonlethal means. Nonlethal means can include:
  — CS or other irritants
  — PSYOPS
  — Sonic measures
  — Troops equipped with riot batons, shields
- Techniques or courses of action for responding to different contingencies at each site, such as:
  — Pilferage of supplies
  — Demonstrations and riots
  — Blockades
  — Armed attacks

Security Forces
The organization of security forces may differ by contingency and METT-TC. Generally, security forces consist of:

Observation Elements. Each observation element must have unobstructed vision of the most likely avenues of approach for belligerent forces. Elements should have overlapping fields of observation; remote sensors or other early warning devices should be used to cover ground not visible or visible by only one team. If possible, use video cameras to record the incident. Each observation element should possess at least two forms of communication with the command element.

Interdiction Elements. In most cases, these elements patrol the likely avenues of belligerent approach at random intervals. Their members must be armed and equipped to meet the threat, but not to encourage escalation. This is an important and sensitive decision. Sometimes, the presence of a company of soldiers presenting a phalanx of bayonet-tipped rifles is enough to discourage and disperse would-be looters; on other occasions, it can spur a crowd to a violent frenzy. Commanders must exercise judgment born of experience and the best possible intelligence to determine the appropriate composition and equipment for the interdiction element. Interdiction elements may also include PSYOPS and host-nation personnel who may be useful in defusing the situation or dispersing the belligerents. Engineers may also be useful for the hasty emplacement of obstacles or for clearing obstacles erected by belligerents.

Command Element. This element must have redundant communications with higher headquarters, subordinate elements, and the person in charge at the HA site being protected. SJA, host-nation, and CA personnel may be especially useful for on-the-spot advice and assistance in decision making.

Other Elements. Other elements could include medical treatment teams and/or elements to evacuate casualties. Under some circumstances, assets to evacuate noncombatants before the commencement of hostilities would also be useful, as would teams to remove valuable supplies.

Rehearsal and Evaluation
As with all military missions, rehearsals of the alert and reaction procedures should be conducted regularly not only to train and maintain proficiency in the tasks but also to integrate and prepare recently arrived personnel. Commanders should establish standards based on METT-TC (e.g., time interval from alert to full preparation for deployment or evacuation) and evaluate unit performance during training exercises. Consider conducting exercises on the actual HA sites to be protected if OPSEC considerations and resources allow; otherwise, conduct them off-site.

PROVIDING ON-SITE PROTECTION
Upon notification that the noncombatant personnel at an HA site are in need of protection, the commander alerts the security force. He issues a standard-

format fragmentary order, including constraints and limitations on actions, and, depending on the level of readiness of the force, a reiteration of the ROE.

Essentially, there are three basic courses of action that may be taken by a security force; the development of the situation may eventually call for using all three.

Secure the Site and Discourage Belligerent Action

In this course of action, which assumes no impending attack on the HA site but rather the conduct of a demonstration, blockade, or riot, the observation elements establish observation of the site and its environs, while the interdiction elements patrol or are posted at likely avenues of belligerent approach. The command element is located where it can best control the action, which may be co-located with the leadership of the HA site. With warning from the observation elements, the command element orders the interdiction elements to interpose themselves between the approaching belligerent factions and the HA site; in an incremental fashion, the interdiction elements then take appropriate escalating measures to ensure the continued safety of the noncombatants at the site, as well as the physical security of the site itself.

Defend the Site and Compel an End to Belligerent Action

If the situation develops to the point where physical attack on the site or on the noncombatant personnel there is imminent or in progress, the site may have to be defended. In this case, the observation element provides early warning of the approach of belligerent factions (and, if feasible, uses video equipment to record the action for use by host-nation or multinational law enforcement organizations), while the interdiction elements defend the site and the lives of the noncombatants, again using force in the incremental fashion required by the ROE. *Conduct this mission in the same way any defense is conducted, under the constraints of the ROE.* This defense may be of finite duration or may be required indefinitely. In any case, report changes in the situation as soon as they occur, and request reinforcements or augmentation as the situation requires. Designate and secure a site for the entry of additional forces (e.g., ingress point, LZ).

Evacuate the Personnel and/or Equipment from the Site

If higher headquarters determines that the two preceding courses of action are not in the best interest of the mission, it may order an evacuation. In this event, commanders and their staffs must:

- Select an assembly area for the transportation assets.
- Determine a route of egress and establish roadblocks as required.
- Determine a collection point for evacuees.
- Assemble a convoy escort, as required, or assemble evacuees in PZ posture, as appropriate.
- Devise techniques and designate elements to sweep the HA site in the event that not all evacuees are at the collection point.
- Determine the amount of personal baggage that each evacuee can bring (based on time and capacity of the transportation assets available).
- Determine any special communications equipment that may be required, especially if a sweep of an urban area is required (e.g., bullhorns, public-address sets, extra radios).
- Determine the priority of evacuation and means of personal identification.
- Determine casualty collection, treatment, and evacuation plans.
- Determine responses in the event of noncombatants' refusal to evacuate.
- Consider the need for protective clothing (e.g., helmets, flak vests) for the evacuees during the evacuation and procure sufficient quantities. Although it may not be possible to offer personal protective clothing to all noncombatant evacuees, it may be required for certain key evacuees whose survival is essential to the mission.

Chapter 29

Apprehend / Detain Noncombatants

There is a wide variety of circumstances under which forces conducting MOOTW may be required to apprehend or detain noncombatants. Usually, the detainees are people who have broken laws or violated the terms of valid agreements or rules or are suspected of doing so. They may or may not be armed or violent, and may or may not be in possession of contraband. Occasionally, units may have to apprehend and detain persons for their own protection, especially from antagonistic belligerent factions.

The best way to conduct this mission is in support of, or at least with the collaboration of, host-nation authorities. Sometimes, however, this is not possible, and forces must unilaterally apprehend and detain noncombatants.

PLANNING FOR APPREHENSION AND DETENTION
Use of minimal force consistent with mission accomplishment is axiomatic to success. Adhere to higher headquarters' written procedures and ROE for search, segregation, and security of detained noncombatants. Make specific provisions to protect the detainees from harm from belligerent factions, and clearly distinguish between the treatment afforded detainees and that of enemy prisoners of war (EPWs). Separate (and, if possible, superior) facilities of sufficient size should be arranged for detainees. In accordance with local cultural customs, prepare for segregation of sexes, families, and so forth.

Although host-nation or other local authorities may not be available to participate, make every effort to have sufficient translators on hand to explain the process and purpose of apprehension and detention. PSYOPS teams may also be extremely helpful in this task.

Procure sufficient quantities of detainee tags (DA Form 3316-R) for anticipated requirements. Also, procure quantities of restraints for use in the event of limited resistance or control problems. In accordance with cultural dictates, have appropriate types and quantities of food on hand if detainees will be under unit control for more than a few hours. Arrange for use of latrine facilities.

Rehearsals are very helpful, especially with soldiers who have not previously performed this mission or who, although trained, have most recently taken prisoners of war as part of unit operations. Leaders must reinforce that detainees are to be treated in a firm, humane, and impartial manner; they are *not* the enemy, but could conceivably become so if they are mistreated.

APPREHENDING NONCOMBATANTS

As they apprehend noncombatants, soldiers should apply the same "5 S's" they use for EPW processing: search, segregate, secure, safeguard, and speed to the rear. However, they should be aware of the distinguishing nuances of dealing with noncombatant detainees.

Use frisk search techniques to secure weapons, and consider the use of metal detectors. Use wall search (as in "up against the wall") techniques when more thorough searches are required. Whenever possible, use same-sex search personnel.

Translators and PSYOPS personnel should repeatedly explain the purpose of the operation and maintain calm among the noncombatants.

Detainees should be tagged appropriately as soon as they are apprehended.

TEMPORARILY DETAINING NONCOMBATANTS

Once noncombatants have been detained, have them prepare statements regarding important incidents they may have witnessed for submission to higher headquarters, coincident with the transfer of detainees to higher headquarters or other authorities. Use PSYOPS teams and translators not only to reassure the detainees of their status and the purpose of the detention but also to facilitate two-way communication. Detainees may have important information to pass to the commander or to higher headquarters.

Protect the detainees throughout their tenure under unit control, and be sure to segregate potentially antagonistic factions. To the greatest extent possible, allow privacy for families and, in accordance with cultural dictates, women and children. Provide water and, if detainees are under unit control for more than a few hours, appropriate food.

Continually attempt to gain the assistance of civil police and turn over detainees to the appropriate authorities as soon as possible. Report all important events and developments to higher headquarters. Reports should include, at a minimum:

- Number of noncombatants apprehended and detained, classify by gender and age (adult, child accompanied by adult, unaccompanied child)
- Contraband confiscated (if any)
- Assistance or resupply required

Chapter 30

Identify and Process Detainees

MOOTW often take place in areas in which governmental infrastructure has ceased to exist, lost its effectiveness, or even become part of the problem. In these cases, civil authorities will not be available to take custody of or process detainees, and military units may have to perform activities beyond apprehension and temporary detention.

This is a very sensitive operation. In many situations, noncombatants being detained will be frightened and distrustful—especially if belligerent factions have been detaining noncombatants for sinister purposes. Above all, effective explanation of the purpose of the detention and humane, impartial treatment will reduce friction and convince detainees of the legitimate nature of unit operations.

PLANNING TO PROCESS DETAINEES
In situations of such exceptional sensitivity, higher headquarters' guidance and intent regarding search, interrogation, segregation, and security must be clearly understood. Applicable ROE must also be known and followed. The varying cultural details and unique mission requirements of these situations require meticulous clarification of orders.

Facilities
To the greatest extent possible, detention facilities must be prepared in consonance with the cultural imperatives of the population being detained. Considerations include, but are not limited to, family, gender, religious, and caste customs and mores. Also, members of antagonistic factions must be separated, although given equal treatment. Military police are useful as advisers and/or trainers for personnel required to process and guard detainees.

Facilities must be secure, protect detainees from actions of belligerent factions, and be sanitary. Medical teams can be used to inspect and assist in sanitization of suspect facilities. Also, designate a medical team to participate in detainee reception activities.

Determine processes for the reception of seriously ill or injured detainees. Designate an evacuation procedure and/or prepare separate temporary medical facilities for detainees in need of treatment or quarantine.

Supplies
Procure sufficient food and water for the anticipated maximum quantity of detainees. To the greatest extent possible, ensure that it is nutritionally and culturally suitable. Local vendors and NGOs/PVOs may be especially helpful in making these arrangements. CA teams are particularly well suited for dealing with local vendors.

In the event that detainees are delivered without tags, procure sufficient quantities of DA Form 3316-R so that each detainee can be tagged. Devise temporary identity tags to simplify the issuance of supplies or rations. Adequate restraints must also be on hand.

IDENTIFYING AND CLASSIFYING DETAINEES
Whenever possible, receive detainees in the presence of MPs or other law enforcement authorities. Screen appropriate documents establishing the detainees' identities and factions to which they belong (if applicable), and record them. Interpreters and/or CA teams can greatly assist in this process and, together with PSYOPS teams, can help calm and reassure the detainees about the situation.

Medically screen detainees for obvious injuries or diseases. After screening, issue ID tags. Evacuate or assign to on-site medical facilities all detainees requiring medical attention.

DETAINING PERSONNEL
After detainees have been identified, issued ID tags, and medically screened, explain the rules of the holding area, including on- and off-limits facilities; location of latrines; feeding schedule; standards of conduct; and, if feasible, anticipated length of stay and future activities.

Report the situation to higher headquarters. At a minimum, reports should generally include:
- Number of detainees, by faction, gender, and age (adult, child accompanied by parent, child unaccompanied by parent)
- Number of injured or sick detainees, by type
- Resupply, augmentation, and/or reinforcements required or anticipated

Chapter 31

Monitor Prisoner Exchange

Often, one of the most encouraging signs of progress in the process of stabilizing a situation is when factions agree to exchange prisoners. Sometimes, this is a relatively straightforward procedure involving two antagonistic sides that exchange prisoners under the observation of a peacekeeping force. Sometimes, however, prisoner exchanges can be extremely complex affairs, especially if there are more than two factions involved.

Factions often attempt to use these exchanges for propaganda purposes and may attempt to cheat or renege on some or all aspects of the agreement. Stability force units taking part in prisoner exchanges must therefore remain scrupulously neutral in their actions and must be meticulous in their accounting of exchanged personnel.

PLANNING TO MONITOR PRISONER EXCHANGES
Plans and preparations for prisoner exchange require leaders to:
- Obtain information about prisoners to be exchanged, including number and medical condition (ambulatory/nonambulatory).
- Coordinate appropriate transportation and medical assets for moving exchanged prisoners.
- Coordinate with receiving parties to ensure that they have similarly appropriate transportation and medical assets on hand at the agreed linkup points.
- Assess belligerent factions' reaction to media presence.
- Reconnoiter the exchange site.
- Determine the size and composition of the force needed to secure the exchange site.
- Depending on weather conditions, determine the requirement for temporary shelter during accountability procedures.
- Determine what barriers, signs, and other markings (e.g., engineer tape, road cones) may be necessary.

- Provide supplies and other resources, such as:
  — Barriers, multilingual signs, and other marking materials to form a cordon, or passage point
  — Tents, stoves, and the like for temporary shelter during accountability procedures
  — Communications between the security element and the monitor element
  — Medical support
  — PAO to handle media representatives
  — CA teams to coordinate with host-nation authorities, UN agencies, and NGOs/PVOs that may be involved
  — Receipts for prisoners

Prisoner Exchange Point

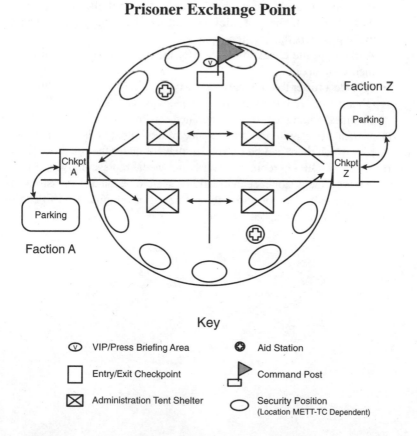

Key

- Ⓥ VIP/Press Briefing Area
- ☐ Entry/Exit Checkpoint
- ☒ Administration Tent Shelter
- ✪ Aid Station
- ⚑ Command Post
- ◯ Security Position (Location METT-TC Dependent)

MONITORING/CONTROLLING THE EXCHANGE

U.S. military forces often mediate and control exchange of prisoners between factions, such as when the force is involved in peacekeeping operations. In peace enforcement operations, U.S. forces could be directly exchanging prisoners with belligerent factions. In either case, prisoner exchange operations include the following actions:

- Secure the exchange site with armed troops, in accordance with the ROE and other pertinent agreements.
- Establish the site (see the sample).
- Meet prisoners at the checkpoint. Separate nonambulatory personnel.
- Obtain a roster from faction representatives or NGO/PVO intermediaries.
- Provide a receipt for the prisoners, by name.
- Escort prisoners through the exchange area in groups of manageable size; ten can usually be safely and adequately controlled by an escort party of two. If there are delays, and weather conditions warrant, move prisoners into shelters.
- At the opposite checkpoint, transfer the prisoners to the control of their own faction.
- Provide a roster to the receiving party.
- Obtain a signed receipt for the prisoners by name.

Sometimes, willingness to be repatriated can be an issue. A way to handle this delicate issue with minimal chance of recrimination is to establish a line across which there can be no return; place it under the observation of intermediary NGO/PVO representatives (and media representatives, if present). This way, the prisoners can clearly be seen to be making decisions of their own free will, and not under the influence or intimidation of peacekeeping forces or the antagonist faction.

Chapter 32

Interdict Smuggling Operations

Factions often attempt to smuggle contraband across borders to finance continued hostilities. Sometimes, if buffer zones have been established between belligerent factions, smuggling is conducted to pass arms or other contraband to foster or support an insurgency.

Interdiction of the international flow of illicit drugs is often one of the pillars of counterdrug operations. It is usually performed in concert with civil law enforcement efforts at the source of supply of the illegal substance, as well as in concert with diplomatic efforts to stem production and interdict traffic within the producing nation.

U.S. Armed Forces' direct participation in interdiction activities *within U.S. territory* is limited by law and is generally unacceptable except in time of war—and even then, it is restricted to certain specific operations. Essentially, this support is limited to detection and monitoring, which at the tactical level, means reconnaissance and surveillance. Military forces may not collect intelligence on U.S. citizens, nor may they be placed in a situation in which they will have to use their weapons, except in self-defense.

PLANNING INTERDICTION OPERATIONS

The unit must be in possession of specific orders from higher headquarters to conduct search and seizure of contraband. Seek the assistance of host nation authorities to determine the type of items being smuggled, and assess transportation and delivery means. Specifically, leaders of interdiction operations must:

- Gain detailed information about the type of products being smuggled.
- Determine what concealment techniques or disguises are likely to be used by the smugglers to conceal the contraband or to deceive personnel conducting interdiction operations.
- Determine the transportation assets typically used or available for use by smugglers.

- Familiarize all personnel on the specifics of prohibited items and contraband. Due to the sensitivity of this mission, unless unit personnel are highly experienced in search and seizure activities, conduct especially demanding training in this mission.
- Determine likely entry points, drop-off points, delivery sites, or locations of transshipment of contraband. Reconnoiter and determine secure routes to all of these.
- Prepare patrol plans that emphasize coverage of the most likely sites (above) but that also (less frequently) cover other possible sites.

Supplies and Resources

Typical resources needed for interdiction operations include:
- Restraints for detainees
- Evidence containers for contraband
- Tags for marking contraband and detainees
- Transportation for contraband (if expected in large quantities)
- Surveillance devices, such as night observation devices and still and video cameras (preferably with night nonflash capabilities)
- Detection devices, as appropriate:
  — Metal detectors (for guns and other hardware)
  — Military working dogs (for explosives, narcotics)
  — Test kits (mainly for narcotics)
- Assistance from:
  — Host-nation/local authorities (use them to make arrests whenever possible)
  — Military police
  — Military intelligence, such as interrogators, identification specialists, and sensors (e.g., ground surveillance radars, REMBASS)
  — Civil affairs teams (coordination with host-nation/local authorities)
  — Army aviation units or UAVs for reconnaissance

Organization

Search Teams. Search teams are needed at checkpoints or as reaction elements for patrols. Personnel should be trained in appropriate search techniques. Whenever possible, arrange for females to search female noncombatants. If no military personnel are available, use host-nation personnel. Sometimes, female NGO/PVO personnel are willing to assist in this sensitive task.

Each search team should be supported by representatives of host-nation authorities and should have maximum appropriate detection resources (e.g., detectors, dogs). All members must understand their jurisdiction and the source of their authority.

Patrols. Mounted patrols are likely to be needed to cover vehicular routes. Organize dismounted patrols to cover likely footpaths and helicopter-borne reaction patrols.

All personnel must understand the ROE; use of incrementally escalating force is critical. Each patrol should be accompanied by a translator and representative of host-nation authorities. If the terrain or weather precludes this, they must have rapid access to each of them. All members must understand their jurisdiction and the source of their authority.

Observation Posts and Checkpoints. See chapters 13 and 14.

INTERDICTING SMUGGLING

Establish OPs to constantly monitor the most likely entry points, drop off points, delivery sites, or transshipment locations. Establish checkpoints on most likely routes by which contraband will be transported. Intensify searches at existing checkpoints. Conduct mounted and dismounted patrols to cover less likely areas, and use reaction patrols to respond to sightings made by OPs or aerial assets, or through sensor or human intelligence. Integrate aerial reconnaissance assets (Army aviation and UAVs).

When contraband is found, follow search and seizure procedures outlined in higher headquarters' guidance/ROE. Render appropriate reports to higher headquarters and exchange information about operations with adjacent units.

Turn over contraband to higher headquarters or host-nation authorities as quickly as practical following seizure.

SPECIAL LEGAL CONSTRAINTS

When conducting interdiction operations on U.S. borders, consult with legal experts regarding precisely what information about U.S. citizens may be collected, retained, and disseminated. Presidential executive orders, statutes, and Army regulations on this sensitive subject—and their legal interpretations—sometimes change, so leaders must be aware of implications for the conduct of interdiction operations.

Chapter 33

Disarm Belligerents

Although some MOOTW—such as peacekeeping—may occur in relatively static situations, many of these operations are executed in dynamic environments such as peace building or peace enforcement. As situations evolve pursuant to diplomatic developments, disarmament of one or more belligerent factions may be ordered. This disarmament is rarely voluntary or a process to which the contentious factions happily assent. Therefore, disarming belligerents must be done carefully and with vigilance for efforts to circumvent or even reverse the process. To the greatest extent possible, conduct this mission in a nonconfrontational, nonhostile, or nongloating manner. Adhere strictly to all pertinent treaties, agreements, or directives from higher headquarters

ESTABLISHING LIAISON WITH BELLIGERENT FACTIONS

Generally a task performed at the battalion level or higher, the establishment of liaison with the belligerent factions to be disarmed is a key to setting the conditions for the successful performance of this mission. Factions should withdraw to or remain at distances from one another that are beyond their indirect fire systems' ranges. Establish routine channels of communication for the exchange of information necessary to conduct disarmament; regularly scheduled meetings to discuss the status of the disarmament process can be very helpful, and reliable 24-hour communications are essential. Commanders may also need to coordinate prisoner exchange or free passage of noncombatants as part of the disarmament effort.

OCCUPYING AND ESTABLISHING MILITARY MATERIEL COLLECTION POINTS

Reconnoiter the Site for Suitability

Whenever possible, the site must be large enough for inspection areas, discrete storage areas, and cantonment or administrative areas. Access by vehicles and dismounted personnel must be controllable within the means of the unit, as augmented or reinforced. If equipment is to be destroyed or altered on site, appropriate facilities must be available. If equipment is to be stored and subsequently transferred out of the area, adequately sized areas or buildings must be accessible. CA personnel are valuable for the determination of cultural or political issues connected with the establishment of such a site. For example, be sensitive to the historical heritage of the area—establishing a military materiel collection point in the vicinity of the birthplace of a national war hero or on the site of a famous victory in a previous war can easily be seen as inflammatory behavior.

Establish Security
Establish 24-hour security at the site at which weapons and other equipment are to be collected. Ensure that the members of the security force are fully knowledgeable of the ROE, especially regarding the force that can be used to secure the collected equipment. Active security measures generally include checkpoints, OPs, and even roving patrols. Passive measures include barricaded areas (fenced or barbed-wire enclosed), sturdy buildings well back from wood lines, and, if feasible, bright illumination for hours of limited visibility.

Inspect Equipment for Safety and Completeness
Ideally, a team from an ordnance, intelligence, or other specialized unit is on hand to perform this task. With some specialized training, armorers, communications repair personnel, and mechanics can be used to inspect turned-in weapons and other equipment, especially that of American origin. Designate an area located a safe distance from friendly cantonment areas or other facilities for this inspection. Establish emergency procedures, including isolation of the area, first aid, MEDEVAC, ordnance disposal, firefighting, and evacuation processes in the event of booby-trapped or other unsafe conditions of turned-in materiel. Report all violations of the terms of the turn-in procedure to higher headquarters so that the appropriate authorities can take action to ensure compliance by participating factions.

Maintain Accountability of Equipment
Establish a method for maintaining accountability of all materiel collected, stored, transferred, or destroyed. The accurate identification of equipment is often important to the success of the peace process. Although military intelligence personnel are usually best able to accurately identify enemy equipment, sometimes the age or diversity of equipment makes it difficult for

them to precisely identify every weapon or piece of equipment turned in. One technique that has been used with great success is for commanders to canvass the unit for weapons buffs, hobbyists, historians, or other experts in equipment identification. Often, such efforts yield surprising results; a battalion commander in Somalia in 1993 found that the battalion physician's assistant—a collector of military long arms—was an extremely valuable adjunct to the intelligence personnel's knowledge and capabilities.

Record the items turned in by serial number whenever possible; provide a receipt to the party turning in the equipment. If items are not suitably marked already, mark them for future identification and accountability. A wood-burning tool or metal etcher (the same one used to mark high-dollar-value items stored in the barracks) can be useful for this task. Gummed labels or tape provide an alternative if the equipment is not to be permanently altered. After the equipment is identified, marked, and recorded, it is moved to a storage area. Maintain a register that includes the identifying marks, type, and location of each piece of equipment; ensure that there is a backup copy of the register, if possible.

DISPOSING OF EQUIPMENT

Often, units are required to store turned-in weapons and equipment only until they are picked up by higher headquarters. Ensure that all storage areas are accessible by the type of transportation equipment that will be used for shipment of the turned-in materiel, or at least designate routes and means by which the equipment can be moved to the pickup point.

In some cases, units receiving turned-in materiel are required to destroy some or all of it or to "demilitarize" it in certain ways. In this case, destroy or demilitarize the equipment in accordance with designated procedures, and forward destruction reports as required. Ensure that "souvenir" policies are clearly understood and adhered to by all members of the command; to the greatest extent possible, limit temptations to all ranks. Souvenir hunting is an old and, until recently (in the U.S. Armed Forces, at least), widely accepted military custom. Today, however, depending on the situation and the regulations or policies in effect, it can result in severe disciplinary or even international legal sanctions.

Chapter 34

Interact with
Media Representatives

There is no avoiding it—this is the Information Age, characterized by the pervasive presence of media representatives. Only rarely are reporters and camera crews *not* allowed access to military personnel during the conduct of MOOTW. For some time now, it has been U.S. Department of Defense policy to grant considerable press access to enhance domestic and world public understanding of American military missions. In many ways, interacting with representatives of the news media is an important part of high-profile missions, and many MOOTW missions fit that description.

PLANNING FOR MEDIA INTERACTION

As part of the operation order, or as a fragmentary order, apprise soldiers of the possibility of media presence. All soldiers should understand the following:

1. Soldiers do not have to talk with the media.
2. Soldiers may decline to answer any question. They can end the interview at any time. If they exercise this option, they should do so tactfully, without causing animosity, anger, or frustration.
3. If a soldier chooses to talk with a media representative, he or she may do so without fear of adverse repercussions or punishment.

Soldiers must understand that what they say can instantly be broadcast to fellow soldiers, allies, the American and world audience, and potential adversaries. A confident, prepared professional sends a more positive, effective message to all those audiences and supports the overall objective of deterrence and readiness.

Leaders must determine whether media representatives are accredited; if they are, they should be escorted by PAO representatives from higher headquarters. If media representatives arrive in the unit area under circumstances other than these, leaders must ask them to wait while they contact the chain of command. Do not detain them, but report them to their supervisors and/or higher headquarters before providing support or allowing access to the area. Assist reporters in getting proper authorization for access to the area, if allowable.

Provide media representatives access to all aspects of the operation, within the limitations of operational security. Explain the reasons for not granting access to those areas or activities that are inappropriate.

CONDUCTING INTERVIEWS
Use the following lists of do's and don'ts when dealing with the media:
Do
- Know the name of the reporter and what medium and organization he or she represents.
- Behave professionally and courteously. If necessary, soldiers should ask reporters to repeat, clarify, or rephrase questions.
- Provide answers that are short and to the point. Soldiers should avoid rambling explanations full of jargon and acronyms.
- Tell reporters *why* a question cannot be answered. If the reason is valid, most media representatives will accept it. Soldiers should not avoid questions that make them uncomfortable or embarrassed by conjuring specious reasons to support that avoidance. Most reporters appreciate and respect openness and honesty.
- Talk only about familiar topics pertinent to one's level of expertise and responsibility. It is wise for soldiers to answer "I do not know" if they are not absolutely sure.

Do Not
- Lie or prevaricate.
- Speculate or repeat rumors.
- Violate operations security. Actual and potential adversaries have access to the information published by news media representatives. The best way to protect information that may jeopardize the soldiers, unit, or mission or may be used as propaganda against U.S. and allied forces is to practice security at the source. Leaders must ensure that their soldiers know what topics pertain to operations security. In MOOTW, situations may change rapidly, and issues that once were cleared for dissemination may now require protection under operations security. In contrast, leaders may want to emphasize some topics normally considered operations security (e.g., equipment types, numbers, capabilities) as a deterrent during MOOTW.

- Allow the media to jeopardize or interfere with the mission or the safety of soldiers.
- Stage events for the media. The media should be passive onlookers to normal activities. The presence of media representatives should not result in special events solely to get favorable coverage or to cover up an unfavorable situation. Before meeting with media representatives, soldiers should be made aware of public affairs guidance; be informed of the unit perspective, themes, and messages; and be briefed to ensure that their information is accurate and up-to-date.
- Tell soldiers what they can and cannot say.
- Lose control of emotions or be sarcastic. Soldiers must stay in control of the situation and their emotions.
- Threaten, detain, apprehend, or physically interfere with a reporter or confiscate film. If information is inadvertently provided to or obtained by the media, soldiers must remain professional, seek the news media representative's assistance and cooperation, or obtain assistance through the chain of command. If soldiers explain to a reporter why something is classified and that the release of such information could endanger soldiers and the mission, most reporters will understand and comply with requests to prevent dissemination.
- Answer any inappropriate question.

SUPPORTING MEDIA REPRESENTATIVES

Generally, U.S. Army policy is to treat media representatives and attached noncombatants with the protocol due an officer with the rank of major. If media representatives have been escorted to the unit area by division or higher headquarters PAOs and are left with the unit for 24 to 72 hours, units must provide appropriate quarters and messing.

Chapter 35

Establish an Operating Base

When entering a new area of operations, units must establish and continually improve their operating bases. Force protection measures must include not only standard military fortifications but also specially designed antiterrorist measures. Additionally, units may be required to include temporary lodging facilities for the protection of noncombatants.

PREPARING FOR ESTABLISHMENT
Reconnoiter the Site
Select a site that has the following qualities:
- Dispersion of facilities. This reduces base vulnerability to indirect fire attacks. Dispersion must not preclude mutual support, however.
- Accessibility to routes of travel, including roads, railroads, airfields, and waterways.
- Close proximity to the most important portions of the unit's area of responsibility.
- Accessibility to lines of communication. Consider and *test* FM, high-frequency, and mobile subscriber equipment (MSE) communications from potential base locations throughout the area of responsibility to adjacent units and to higher headquarters. Also, the site must facilitate communications with appropriate satellites.
- Defensibility (e.g., good observation and fields of fire, control of key terrain).
- Appropriate visibility to host-nation personnel and members of belligerent factions. This decision is METT-TC dependent. For example, if the mission requires establishment of presence in a relatively peaceful area, the site should be obvious. If the operational environment is one in which attacks or terrorist activities are likely, then the site should be relatively obscure to visibility.
- Appropriate proximity to NGO/PVO sites.

- Close proximity to—or inclusion of space for—LZs/PZs or airfields.
- Absence of unexploded ordnance (UXO), obstacles, mines, and so forth. After selection of the site, use engineers to conduct UXO operations and EOD personnel to thoroughly sweep the area and dispose of all UXO.
- Absence of low-lying areas that could be breeding grounds for disease-carrying insects.

Prepare a Plan

Prepare a schematic diagram of the base, including (at a minimum):
- Sectors for each subunit, crew-served weapons, and night vision devices
- Location of envisioned facilities
- OPs/guard towers
- Vehicle emplacement and orientation
- Fighting positions and other fortifications
- Command post and alternative command post
- Routes of ingress and egress and barrier plans

Validate the plan with engineers. Ensure that soil, drainage, and the like are conducive to healthy occupation of the site over the projected period of use of the base. Establish medical evacuation SOPs.

ESTABLISHING THE BASE

Occupy the Site

- Establish and maintain security in accordance with ROE.
- Emplace and build defensive positions for crew-served weapons first, then all others.
- Emplace hasty roadblocks and checkpoints to limit access to the site.
- Continue engineer mobility operations and EOD activities as required.

Construct the Base

- Build personnel and vehicle shelters for personnel and equipment on site plus 10 percent.
- Build a protected command post.
- Build an aid station.
- Emplace barriers around the perimeter in accordance with the threat and ROE. Barrier materials may vary from signs and tape markers to barbed wire or other fences, concertina, earthen berms, and even prefabricated concrete walls. Consider installing anti-observations

barriers, such as fabric woven through fences or wire, to prevent observation of activities inside the base (METT-TC dependent).
- Construct field sanitation and personal hygiene facilities.
- Install lighting for the perimeter in accordance with ROE and other pertinent regulations and agreements.

Improve Facilities
As time and resources permit, build the following improvements:
- Electrical power—first for the command post and perimeter lights, then for personnel shelters
- Gravel or macadam roads and motor parks
- PT, instructional/classroom, and recreational areas (e.g., volleyball courts) for soldiers who are not on duty

CONDUCTING BASE SECURITY ACTIVITIES
Base security activities include at least the following:
- Patrol the perimeter (inside and out) as required. Determine joint responsibilities for security with host-nation authorities (if appropriate). In many cases, the unit is responsible for security inside the perimeter of the base, and host-nation authorities are responsible for security on the outside.
- Establish reliefs for OPs/guard towers, crew-served weapons positions, and night vision devices.
- Ensure that all personnel understand SOPs and special orders for the following:
  — Requests for medical assistance, food, and the like by local civilians
  — Media visits
  — Off-base travel requirements (e.g., wear of body armor, helmets; minimum size of party; pass procedures; possession of SOFA cards)
- Check passes and ID at the gate to the base; coordinate with CA and MI personnel about allowing noncombatants into the base. Use host-nation authorities to assist with the screening of local civilians if they are to be allowed onto the base.
- Establish a reaction force and rehearse for appropriate missions (e.g., quelling civil disturbances, reacting to terrorist attack).
- Vary the timing of repetitive activities on the base; avoid establishing a routine.

- Establish and rehearse drills for general reaction to car bombs, demonstrations, tear gas attacks, and so forth.
- Use PSYOPS units to discourage undesirable civilian activities in the vicinity of the base (e.g., loitering, heckling, begging).

PREPARING FOR BASE DEFENSE ACTIVITIES

Base defense activities include the following:

- Establish and periodically update the fire support plan, including at a minimum, the use of smoke to obscure activities inside the base, illumination, and final protective fires.
- Establish and periodically update the air defense plan.
- Improve defensive positions and obstacles.
- Build alternative and supplementary positions.
- Periodically vary the arrangements of obstacles to deter efforts at sabotage or breaching.
- Rehearse occupation of defensive positions/shelters at all times of the day, using announced and unannounced drills, at varying intervals.
- Establish signals (e.g., pyrotechnic, sound) for the occupation of positions and potential threats.
- Develop and rehearse drills for reaction to small arms fire (including snipers), indirect fire, and air attack.
- Rehearse MEDEVAC procedures, including actual evacuation to the designated supporting medical facility, using announced and unannounced drills.

Chapter 36

Escort and Defend a Convoy

Convoys are an intrinsic part of all military operations, but their conduct under the conditions common in MOOTW presents special challenges. Convoys can move or deliver humanitarian relief supplies, supplies needed by the unit, refugees, VIPs, media groups, casualties, or any combination of these. They are often highly visible operations, and the challenges presented are many.

Under administrative (peacetime) conditions, convoys can be dangerous and difficult to complete successfully—mechanical problems, route coordination, driver training, maintenance of communications, and many other factors can break up a convoy under the most peaceful of circumstances. The conduct of convoys in the austere theaters in which most MOOTW take place is much more difficult. Their conduct in an area where antagonistic factions may have much to gain by halting or disrupting convoy operations is a major undertaking. Make no mistake, in *most* MOOTW, conducting convoys is an important and sensitive operation requiring extensive planning, coordination, rehearsals, discipline, and teamwork.

ORGANIZING CONVOY ESCORTS

Basically, convoy escorts are organized into three elements:

Advance Guard. The advance guard reconnoiters the route, reduces obstacles, and clears opposition as necessary. It is equipped with a global positioning system, if available.

Main Body. The main body comprises the cargo and passenger vehicles, as well as the command and control elements for directing actions of the convoy, including fire support if required. An infantry unit is usually included for local defense and security at halts. The main body may be divided into multiple march units (also called serials, or "chalks") for easier command and control; these usually consist of five vehicles, but the number may vary with METT-TC.

Rear Guard. The rear guard secures the convoy from the rear and supports onward movement with recovery, limited fire support, medical, and selected special operations forces (SOF) capabilities.

PLANNING AND PREPARING FOR A CONVOY

Because they often consist of so many disparate elements—many of which may not even be military, or whose members may not speak a common language—convoys must be meticulously planned and prepared. Once the convoy crosses its start point, especially in austere environments, it is very difficult to adjust for shortcomings in preparation or planning.

Prepare Vehicles

Mechanical Considerations. Convoys inevitably consist of a variety of equipment, some of which may be in questionable condition—especially if the convoy includes nonmilitary vehicles from the host nation. These vehicles must be identified before commencement of convoy operations, and, if possible, their cargo should be transferred to other vehicles. At a minimum, be prepared to tow them when they break down. Schedule maintenance halts during long motor marches to help prevent vehicle breakdowns, and establish and maintain security at all times.

Survivability Measures. Enhance the survivability of the convoy's vehicles to the maximum extent consonant with the mission. Survivability preparations include:

- Sandbag vehicles, especially the vehicle cabs and floors.
- When practical, remove windshields and windows to reduce fragmentation effects.

Basic Convoy Composition

Rear Guard	Main Body	Advance Guard
2 x Bradley IFVs or hardshell HMMWVs w/ Mk. 10s or MGs*	Infantry platoon in three 2 1/2 ton trucks	2 x Bradley IFVs or hardshell HMMWVs w/ Mk. 19s or MGs*
Recovery vehicle	Fire support officer/forward observer	Forward observer (if available)
Ambulance	Cargo trucks, buses, automobiles, etc.	Engineer squad
CA and PSYOPS Teams	Convoy commander's vehicle	CA rep/interpreter
Mortar section		

* Types of weapons mounted are METT-TC dependent

Direction of Travel →

- Position expedient wire cutters on at least the lead vehicle of each serial.
- Install chicken wire or chainlink fencing across the front bumper frame to deflect rocks, bottles, firebombs, and hand grenades.
- Remove the canvas from vehicles carrying soldiers so that they can see and shoot in all directions.
- Position cargo along the outside walls of vehicles to allow soldiers to stand in the center of the cargo area, using the cargo for protection.
- Position ammunition for ready access.

Other Preparations. Inspect cargo vehicles' load plans to ensure that the proper supplies are being carried and no illegal or contraband supplies are loaded. Spot-check the contents of cargo. It is also useful, if possible, to position cargo where it can be quickly off-loaded in the event that the vehicle is damaged.

Leaders must also spot-check the maintenance of the vehicles, and it is wise to check that drivers possess strip maps and knowledge of the planned route.

Plan Fire Support

The fire support element of the headquarters initiating the convoy should develop a fire plan to support the convoy. Normally, this is a simple plan consisting of priority targets on which the supporting artillery or mortars are laid and shifted as the convoy progresses along its route. This keeps the artillery focused on the general area of the convoy and greatly improves its responsiveness.

Whenever possible, a fire support officer should assist in the planning of a convoy; it is also extremely beneficial to have that officer accompany the convoy commander. A forward observer (or at least someone trained and equipped to call for and adjust fires) must be a member of the advance guard. Convoys through high-risk areas always profit from a forward observer in an aircraft flying in support of the convoy, as long as the air defense threat is low.

Priority (preplanned) targets are the most responsive way to get indirect-fire support, because the weapons of the supporting artillery unit are then prepared to put a round on the target immediately when called. If the unit has a priority target, the commander establishes targets off to the side of the route of march (not on the road or trail) and shifts the priority target from one target to the next as the unit passes each target.

Certain air assets can also be extremely helpful. Attack helicopter escort is ideal, as it can simultaneously reconnoiter and provide armed escort. The utility of joint or multinational close air support may be somewhat limited by reaction time, but AC-130 gunships, with long loiter capabilities and precision sensors and fire support systems, are also close to ideal.

Rehearse Actions

As with any military operation, rehearsals are critical to success. In convoy operations, because elements from so many different military—and civilian—organizations are involved, rehearsals are essential. Rehearse the following to standard before commencing convoy operations (See the sample operation order later in this chapter for types of drills within each of the following categories.):

- Actions on enemy contact
- Actions at danger areas
- Actions at obstacles
- Actions on vehicle emergency and accident recovery procedures
- Actions on short halts
- Actions on long halts

DEFENDING A CONVOY

Convoy commanders must be aware of the latest intelligence concerning their routes. If intelligence is not current or reliable, or if the threat is high, Army aviation or joint or multinational aerial assets can be used for near-real-time reconnaissance. Remotely piloted vehicles are extremely useful for this purpose.

Advance Guard

Far Ambushes. Generally, convoys attempt to drive through far ambushes, or those directed from a distance at which the fire is not sufficiently concentrated or intense to halt the vehicles.

Near Ambushes. Upon initiation of a near ambush, the advance guard provides immediate suppressive fire and, if possible, fights through the ambushing force. If the ambushing force is too large, the advance guard fixes the enemy while the convoy commander directs maneuver elements from the main body and/or rear guard against the enemy; he also directs indirect fires against them. If resistance still cannot be eliminated, the convoy commander calls for the reaction force, which is usually an air assault force on standby. Designate and mark LZs.

Obstacles. The engineer element must be sufficiently robust to quickly breach and clear obstacles. Overwatched by the maneuver element of the advance guard, the engineers must breach the obstacle or, if too complex, quickly find a way for the convoy to safely bypass the obstacle.

Main Body

Since this element includes the bulk of the cargo- and passenger-carrying vehicles—whose safe delivery to the destination is usually the *raison d'être* for the convoy—the main body needs all-around protection.

Lead the element with a military vehicle. Intersperse the combat elements throughout the main body. No more than a squad should be placed in a single vehicle. (In Somalia, units of the 10th Mountain Division recommended that at least a platoon of combat power move in the main body.)

Maintain radio or visual contact with the advance guard and rear guard security elements. If the main body is a large element (more than seven vehicles), divide it into serials commanded and controlled by leaders reporting directly back to the convoy commander. Immediately report all obstacles or enemy contacts to higher headquarters. If an ambush or obstacles cannot be reduced by elements organic to the convoy, request assistance from higher headquarters.

Rear Guard

The rear guard defends the rear of the convoy against ambush in much the same way as the advance guard. It provides a reaction force to assist the advance guard or main body in counterattacking against enemy ambushes. When appropriate, the rear guard contains CA and PSYOPS elements to assist in negotiation, dispersal of crowds blocking the route, and so forth.

CONVOY OPERATION ORDER

Because of the importance and frequency of convoy operations in MOOTW, we have included a sample convoy operation order:

Sample Convoy Operation Order

1. SITUATION:
   a. Enemy Forces.
     (1) Weather and Light Data.
       (a) Temperature *(may affect speed, coolant/antifreeze requirements, etc.).*
       (b) Wind speed and direction *(especially important if roads are dry and dusty).*
       (c) Forecast.
       (d) Light data *(affects speed, interval, etc.).*
       (e) Effect on convoy operations.
     (2) Terrain and Vegetation.
       (a) Description.
       (b) Effect on enemy *(likely chokepoints, ambushes, etc.).*
       (c) Effect on convoy *(low-lying areas may be marshy; bridges may be out, towns or urban centers will affect speed).*

      (3) Road Conditions.
         (a) Description.
         (b) Construction materials.
         (c) Substantial loads and speeds/considerations.
         (d) Road width.
         (e) Road signs.
         (f) Bridge classification/width.
         (g) Overpass restrictions *(height)*.
         (h) Fords *(locations, depths, velocity of current, etc.)*.
      (4) Identification of Belligerent Factions' Forces.
         (a) Uniforms.
         (b) Weapons, vehicles, aircraft type, and markings.
      (5) Locations of Belligerent Factions' Forces.
         (a) Suspected.
         (b) Known.
         (c) Minefields.
         (d) Obstacles.
      (6) Disposition of Belligerent Factions' Forces.
         (a) Strength.
         (b) Morale.
         (c) Reinforcement capability.
         (d) Expected courses of action.
  b. Civilians/Noncombatants: ROE.
      (1) Populated areas.
      (2) Probable reactions.
  c. NGOs/PVOs, and Neutral Nation Observers, as applicable.
      (1) Uniforms/clothing/identification insignia.
      (2) Locations.
  d. Friendly Forces.
      (1) Mission of next higher headquarters.
      (2) Intent of next higher commander.
      (3) Locations of adjacent and supporting units.
      (4) Planned actions of adjacent and supporting units.
      (5) Units providing fire support.
  e. Attachments/Detachments.
      (1) Effective times.
      (2) Unit identification.
      (3) Type of control *(OPCON, attached, direct support, etc.)*.

2. MISSION:
Written in the directive form, using the second-person voice. Example: "Company A, 1-274th Infantry conducts a convoy commencing 010400 JAN along Route Black to transport cargo and noncombatant passengers from SP vic. BISCHWILLER (MV 164023) to RP vic. WIMMENAU (LV 836195) NLT 010900 JAN."

3. EXECUTION:
Commander's intent *(succinct definition of what must be done to succeed with respect to the enemy, the terrain, and the desired end state)*.
  a. Concept of the Operation *(summarizes what is to be done to achieve success)*.

    (1) Maneuver *(purpose and overall description of the operation)*.
    (2) Fire support.
       (a) Target list.
         — Target numbers.
         — Locations and terrain features.
         — Description, munitions, size.
         — Type (linear, and so forth).
         — Purpose.
       (b) Priority of fires *(usually to Advance Guard, then element in contact)*.
       (c) Control of fires.
       (d) Frequencies.
  b. Subunit Missions.
    (1) Advance guard.
       (a) Reconnoiter Route Black from SP to RP. Report changes in road conditions and serious incidents ASAP upon discovery.
       (b) Conduct mobility operations by clearing all obstacles on Route Black.
       (c) Clear all resistance by belligerent factions IAW ROE. Use CA rep/interpreter to negotiate passage if possible. Use incrementally increasing force as necessary. Take all actions to protect convoy members' lives and limbs, but request permission to engage belligerents with 25mm (or Mk. 19s). Hasty authentication word from convoy commander is "Pinwheel."
    (2) Main body.
       (a) Transport cargo and noncombatant passengers from SP to RP along Route Black.
       (b) Commercial cargo and passenger vehicle order of march as follows:
        — Quantity, type, and order of march of vehicles in each march unit.
        — Crew and vehicle assignments.
    (3) Rear guard.
       (a) Secure the convoy from the rear. Report all serious incidents ASAP upon observation.
       (b) Recover convoy vehicles on order.
       (c) Provide mortar support to the convoy on call, with permission of convoy commander. Hasty authentication of permission of direction or permission to fire by convoy commander is "Archer."
       (d) Provide medical treatment and evacuation of convoy casualties.
       (e) Provide CA operations and PSYOPS in support of onward movement on order.
  c. Coordinating Instructions.
    (1) Submit load plans including the following information NLT 311900 DEC:
       (a) Type of vehicle.
       (b) Names of crew.
       (c) Gross vehicle weight.
       (d) Detailed description of cargo/manifest of passengers.
       (e) Weapons aboard.
       (f) Sequence of loading and off-loading.

(2) Order of movement: advance guard, main body, rear guard.

(3) March intervals and speed.

    (a) Day.

    (b) Periods of limited visibility.

    (c) Special roadway conditions (ice, snow, rain, dust, etc.).

(4) Sequence of loading and off-loading.

(5) Routes (see overlay).

    (a) Primary.

    (b) Alternate.

    (c) Start and release points (SP and RP).

    (d) Known danger areas.

    (e) Major intersections.

    (f) Checkpoints.

    (g) Phase lines.

    (h) Route clearance plan.

    (i) Traffic control points (TCPs).

    (j) Staging or marshaling area.

    (k) Destination point and de-trucking point.

(6) Actions on enemy contact.

    (a) Near ambush.

      — Maneuver into ambush with armored/protected vehicles if possible.

      — If assault not possible, lay down base of fire and call for support.

      — Support maneuver of reinforcements.

      — Adjust indirect fires onto enemy.

    (b) Far ambush.

      — Attempt to drive through. If not possible, then as for near ambush.

    (c) Mines.

      — Treat and evacuate casualties.

      — Actions per mechanical breakdown.

      — Engineers reconnoiter ahead for more, and remove as necessary.

      — Report to higher HQ.

    (d) Sniper contact.

      — Attempt to drive through. If not possible, then as for near ambush.

    (e) Aerial attack.

      — Halt vehicles in herringbone pattern off road (alternating to right and left, at oblique angles to the road—minimizes effects of strafing damage).

      — Personnel dismount and take cover.

      — Engage with air defense weapons, including MGs and small arms.

      — Report and request counter air support.

    (f) Indirect fire.

      — Attempt to drive through.

      — If not possible, halt vehicles in herringbone pattern off road (alternating to right and left, at oblique angles to the road—minimizes effects of parallel sheafs).

— Personnel dismount and take cover.
— Report and request counterbattery fires.
(g) Roadblock and illegitimate demands for search.
— Report to higher headquarters.
— Use NGO/PVO, CA, host-nation, and/or UNHCR representative and interpreter to negotiate passage without agreeing to search demands.
— If search of cargo vehicles is unavoidable (least offensive measure, avoids escalation of hostility, may facilitate passage further along route), keep the loss of time to a minimum.
— Convoy personnel say as little as possible during inspections.
— Never bribe or allow confiscation of equipment in return for permission to pass. Await arrival of reaction element.
(7) Actions at danger areas.
METT-TC dependent. May require nothing more than special vigilance, or may require halting the main body and rear guard while advance guard reconnoiters.
(a) Known intersections.
(b) Fording sites and bridges.
(c) Large open areas/lengthy straightaways.
(d) Defiles, sharp inclines, and overpasses.
(e) Roadblocks or illegitimate traffic control points.
(8) Actions at obstacles.
(a) Minefields.
— Halt convoy and establish security.
— Report to higher headquarters.
— Reconnoiter for bypass—use if found.
— If there is no bypass, engineers breach the minefield.
— If the minefield is too extensive for the escorting engineers to breach, request assistance.
(b) Obstructive debris. Same as for minefields.
(c) Unmanned roadblocks. Same as for minefields.
(9) Actions upon vehicle emergency and accident recovery procedures.
— Convoy commander directs all elements to halt and establish security.
— Attempt emergency repairs on site while vehicles retain march interval.
— If emergency repairs are not possible, tow vehicle to destination.
— If towing is impossible, transfer cargo to other vehicles.
— Remove critical vehicle parts.
— Move vehicle off road to avoid traffic obstruction.
(a) Actions upon short halts *(who dismounts, how far they push out to establish local security perimeter, etc.).*
(b) Actions upon long halts.
(c) Actions upon break in contact.
— Convoy commander notifies higher HQ.
— Halt convoy, establish security, and send an armored (or protected) vehicle to determine the problem.
— If a breakdown, then action per mechanical failure (above).

— If a result of enemy action *(mine, etc.)*, then action per enemy contact (above).

   (10) Driver rotation and relief during extended drives.

   (11) Driving during periods of limited visibility.

      (a) Rules for using night observation devices.

      (b) Speed adjustments.

      (c) Rules for catch-up following breaks in contact.

   (12) MOPP level.

   (13) Preventive maintenance checks and services completion time.

   (14) Time and location of marshaling.

   (15) Technical inspection.

   (16) Initial inspection.

   (17) Communications exercises.

   (18) Briefbacks.

   (19) Rehearsals.

   (20) Final inspection time.

   (21) Load time.

   (22) SP time.

   (23) All vehicles will have a designated commander.

   (24) All vehicles will have at least one map and at least one person with the operations graphics committed to memory.

4. SERVICE AND SUPPORT:
  a. Rations and Water.
    (1) Rations and water for each convoy member.
    (2) Emergency rations.
  b. Equipment/Supplies.
    (1) Basis of issue items/pioneer tools.
    (2) Rucksack plan (for military personnel).
    (3) Resupply plan.
    (4) Refuel plan.
  c. Maintenance Plan.
    (1) Vehicle services.
    (2) Recovery plan.
    (3) Bumper number and location of mechanics in each serial.
    (4) Bumper number and location of tow bars.
  d. Casualty Procedures.
    (1) Location of medical vehicles and aidmen.
    (2) Method of evacuating casualties.
  e. Evacuation of Captured Personnel and Equipment.
    (1) Evacuation and handling of PWs and noncombatant detainees.
    (2) Evacuation, processing, and reporting captured equipment, documents, and intelligence requirements.

5. COMMAND AND SIGNAL:
  a. Command.
    (1) Chain of command.
    (2) Location of key leaders and radiotelephone operators.
  b. Signal.

   (1) Ideally, each vehicle will have a radio; in practice, this is rarely possible; key leaders get priority of radios. List all vehicles with radios and radio type.
   (2) Channels, frequencies, and call signs for internal communications and external, adjacent, supporting units.
   (3) Authentication table, SOI, current time period in effect.
   (4) Code words (such as "Pinwheel" for advance guard permission to engage with 25mm or Mk. 19s, or "Archer" for permission for rear guard to engage with mortar fire).
   (5) Brevity codes, operational schedules.
   (6) Location of cryptographic devices, if any.
   (7) Number combinations, challenges, and password by time period.
   (8) Arm-and-hand signals.
   (9) Pyrotechnics, flares, and other signals.
  (10) Personnel status, logistics status, and status reports required.

LINKING UP WITH A CONVOY

In addition to escorting and defending convoys, in the course of MOOTW, units often have to link up with convoys as they cross from one area of operation or zone of responsibility into another. In the multinational and interagency environments in which other military operations often occur, this is an important and frequently conducted mission. Typically, convoys are escorted to a linkup point on the edge of two areas of responsibility, linkup occurs, and the new escort assumes responsibility for the convoy.

Recon and Secure the Linkup Point

Using a small element from the escort element, recon the linkup point. The site must facilitate staging and inspection of the convoy. It must also be free of obstacles and easily traversed. If not, notify higher headquarters and be prepared to accept attachment or control of engineer assets to clear the linkup point. If the site is suitable, leave a small detachment with communications capability for security, and return to bring forward the convoy escort element.

Prepare the New Escort Force

Task organize the escort force prior to arrival at the linkup point. Elements typically include:

- Perimeter security element to secure the area around the linkup point
- Ground guides/vehicle inspection element
- Support element to prepare vehicles for convoy
- Command/liaison element

The commander must monitor the progress of the approaching convoy with higher headquarters or, if possible, on the radio, following the announcements of pass times at checkpoints. In this way, the commander can tailor the linkup force as required by the anticipated conditions at the linkup site. Depending on the situation, the commander may include the following in his force at the linkup site:

- Military working dogs (to check for bombs and/or contraband)
- EOD team
- CA and/or legal representative
- Representatives of the local authorities, to resolve matters of territorial sovereignty or other sensitive issues
- PAO or media representatives
- Representatives of NGOs/PVOs or other civilian agencies supporting the transporting element, or associated with the convoy or its cargo
- Medical elements to treat or evacuate casualties
- Maintenance personnel to repair rolling stock and facilitate onward movement through the escorting unit's area of responsibility

Before departing for the linkup site, verify the far and near recognition signals, if any, and ensure possession of all necessary pyrotechnics, radios, codebooks, or other signaling devices. Conduct rehearsals of the actions at the linkup site for all members of the escort party and attachments.

Conduct Linkup

The unit arrives at the linkup site generally no later than 60 minutes prior to the linkup. Exchange far and near recognition signals with the convoy as it approaches the linkup point.

Secure the Area. The perimeter security element establishes all-around security at the site and conducts security operations in accordance with the ROE. This element remains in place until the convoy is ready for onward movement or until the escort commander releases it from its mission.

Inspect the Convoy. The ground guide/vehicle inspection element directs vehicles to appropriate positions in the site and immediately commences inspection. Inspections normally include the following:

- General mechanical condition (tires, oil, coolant, canvas, doors, fuel levels)
- Bills of lading, locks, security seals
- Safety devices, such as lights, wipers, directional signals

If the convoy has been in combat prior to the linkup, treat or evacuate casualties, inspect for unexploded ordnance or bombs, and record damage to cargo noted at the time of linkup. Render necessary reports to higher headquarters. Repair damage that may prevent onward movement of the convoy, or transfer cargo from damaged vehicles to ones more likely to complete the mission.

Sometimes, factions use convoys to attempt to smuggle contraband (weapons, ammunition, drugs, money) from one zone of responsibility to another. Be prepared to inspect for and confiscate contraband items; report the discovery and confiscation to higher headquarters and the convoy commander.

PREPARING FOR ONWARD MOVEMENT

The escort force commander confers with the convoy commander and confirms details of security measures, actions on contact, vehicle recovery policy and procedures, and so forth. At a minimum, all elements of the convoy must be briefed on:

- Formations and intervals
- Rate of march
- Actions upon hostile contact, such as ambush or receipt of indirect fire
- Checkpoint procedures
- ROE
- Actions upon breaks in contact, separation of convoy elements, or breakdown
- Planned halts
- Demands for inspections by belligerent factions
- Casualty treatment and evacuation procedures
- Communications/signals
- Operations under conditions of limited visibility

Safety briefings are also required and may include:

- Areas of poor trafficability along the route
- Dangerous uphill or downhill sections
- Broken pavement
- Restrictive sections such as tunnels, narrow bridges, low-clearance viaducts
- Icy, muddy, dusty, or snowy roadway surfaces
- Areas obscured by fog or smoke from fires
- Dangerous curves or drop-offs from the shoulders

Other items that may be necessary to cover are the locations and/or distances of the lines of separation; locations of buffer zones; and locations of recent ambushes or other actions taken to interfere with convoys, such as roadblocks, obstacles, or demonstrations.

If necessitated by the threat, vehicle inspectors may identify vehicles in need of additional preparation or protection. The support element may sandbag floors or sides of vehicles, emplace ballistic protection "blankets," apply anti-grenade chicken wire to windows or other apertures, and add other measures to protect the vehicles during convoy operations.

Convoy vehicles are often marked for recognition by local authorities and/or belligerent factions. To prevent abuse of these markings, they are sometimes changed from day to day, or even within different areas of operations. Symbols or alphanumeric designations may be chalked, spray-painted, or fastened on vehicles to signify and preserve the legitimacy of the convoy. The support element marks vehicles as necessary and appropriate for movement through the unit's area of responsibility.

Time permitting, all convoy elements should rehearse critical actions, such as actions upon hostile contact.

When all preparations have been completed, the ground guide/search element reassembles the convoy. The command/liaison element emplaces the escort. The lead security patrol departs no earlier than 15 minutes ahead of the convoy.

Chapter 37

Evacuate Noncombatants

Military forces play a key supporting role in planning and conducting non-combatant evacuation operations (NEO). Nevertheless, the U.S. government often views the military as the last resort in a series of evacuation options. It is important for leaders to understand this role when preparing an evacuation plan. Planning evacuation operations in a vacuum, without regard for the ambassador's requirements for or perspective on the operation, can lead to serious problems. This is a potentially serious flaw in the coordination between the Department of State (DOS) and the military when preparing and conducting evacuation operations.

PREPARING FOR DEPLOYMENT
Advance Party
As early as possible in the planning, the JTF commander forms the advance party and requests permission to send it to the site of the operation. The advance party may consist of two elements:

1. The forward command element (FCE) coordinates with in-country State Department personnel and host country authorities (when authorized by the DOS) and establishes a communications link among the JTF, the geographic combatant commander, and the DOS. The FCE normally submits SITREPs to the JTF. When the main body enters the country, the FCE rejoins the evacuation force and continues operations with the JTF.

2. The evacuation site party conducts reconnaissance to determine and establish assembly areas and evacuation sites.

These two elements are covered in more detail later in this chapter.

In a permissive or uncertain environment, the FCE should be inserted before any evacuation site parties. In a hostile environment, the ambassador's decision will probably be to insert the entire NEO force to commence the operation immediately.

Deployment of the advance party is METT-TC dependent. Use the least conspicuous method to transport the advance party to the host country; civilian clothes on civilian aircraft is one good way, but this is possible only if the necessary passport and visa arrangements can be made and the environment is permissive. An uncertain or hostile environment may require forced entry. Use of military aircraft allows the advance party to carry additional equipment that may be needed in setting up the evacuation site and establishing communication and liaison.

The following tasks should be accomplished during this phase:

- Request permission from the U.S. Embassy for the advance party to enter the country. Leaders must inquire regarding the number of FCE members allowed and the preferred insertion method.
- Deploy as soon as possible to allow maximum time for coordination and to determine external support requirements.
- Develop and brief a communication plan for the advance party.
- Acquire and review appropriate maps.
- Review the embassy's evacuation checklists.
- Assemble and inspect required equipment.
- Develop and brief an escape and evasion plan for the advance party.
- Obtain visitor visas for all members of the advance party.
- Due to possible sensitivity of the political situation in the host country, determine whether the advance party should deploy in civilian clothes.
- Consider weapon and ammunition requirements based on the threat assessment.
- Examine the need for specialized equipment; for example, ordnance to assist State Department officials in the destruction of classified equipment and documents, or sufficient satellite communications (SATCOM) systems to establish communications with the JTF or combatant command headquarters.
- Determine medical requirements.
- Identify translator and linguistic requirements.
- Request overflight and landing rights for appropriate countries.
- Review all available intelligence on the proposed NEO; obtain assistance to fill gaps created by missing data.
- Assess news media interest in the situation and activities of the JTF and its involvement in the evacuation.

Forward Command Element

The JTF commander determines the size and composition of the FCE in conjunction with the ambassador or his or her designated representative. The FCE may include the following personnel:

Officer in Charge (OIC)

The OIC provides direct liaison with the senior State Department official at the embassy to ensure that orders of the JTF commander and the desires of the State Department are accomplished.

Intelligence Officer

- Provides a conduit for intelligence directly from the embassy and evacuation sites.
- Coordinates with the DAO, CIA chief of station, and RSO to provide the evacuation force with updated intelligence estimates. The DAO can facilitate access to the daily embassy SITREPs and other intelligence.
- Obtains information and intelligence to satisfy JTF intelligence requirements from the country team and other embassy sources.
- Provides a signal intelligence function with equipment that is interoperable with the rest of the communications detachment.
- Considers the following when evaluating the intelligence picture and developing essential elements of information and other intelligence requirements.
  — Climatological, tidal, astronomical, and lunar phase data
  — Intelligence on assets, characteristics, and capabilities of ports, airfields, beaches, helicopter landing zones (HLZs), and drop zones (DZs) and key facilities of the host-nation government for communications, utilities, and health services
  — Identification of hostile and potentially hostile forces, including local government forces, rebel groups, dissident forces, student groups, and unorganized mob action, with the focus on location and the ability of potential threat forces to become organized
  — Identification of any third parties (e.g., external countries) that may attempt to hinder evacuation operations
  — Identification of friendly third parties that could assist the NEO
  — Potential for hostile infiltration of evacuees
  — Satellite imagery of required areas (if available)
  — Liaison with intelligence representatives of other U.S., third-country, and host-nation agencies as appropriate
  — Need for linguists to assist with debriefings or conduct liaison with foreign nationals

Operations Officer
- Briefs State Department representatives on the capabilities of the advance party and the JTF.
- Answers operational questions concerning the evacuation plan.
- Briefs the OIC concerning any information the embassy presents that may affect the evacuation plan.
- Ensures that support is provided to prepare the passenger manifest for noncombatant evacuees.
- Assesses the requirement for deployment of combat forces.
- Coordinates the efforts of the fire support, air operations, PSYOPS, and CA officers.

Logistics Officer
- Coordinates host-nation transportation assets needed by the advance party and JTF.
- Arranges for supplies required by the JTF to minimize what is brought with them (such as water, medical supplies, and rations).
- Coordinates heavy equipment and materials handling equipment support required by the JTF.
- Provides on-site logistics assistance to facilitate the evacuation.

Communications Detachment
- Sets up and operates necessary communications equipment.
- Determines areas of compatibility between military and DOD and/or State Department on-site communications equipment.
- Resolves frequency conflicts or other problems.
- Determines whether host-nation communications equipment is similar to, or compatible with, U.S. equipment.
- Ensures that required single-channel communications equipment is planned for and deployed (high frequency, very high frequency, ultra high frequency, and SATCOM).
- Develops an understanding of the operation of the host country's phone system. Existing domestic telephone lines can be used to back up the military communications systems. Although telephone lines are not secure, manual encryption devices can be used to pass classified traffic and should be planned for. Telephone lines may be the most reliable form of communication, especially to remote evacuation sites. Communications personnel should verify the serviceability of these lines, record numbers, and ascertain dialing procedures for possible use during execution of the NEO.
- Establishes positive communications between the diplomatic mission, the geographic combatant commander, and the JTF commander.

Communications must be established between the embassy and JTF commander so that diplomatic and politically sensitive situations can be controlled.

Medical Team
- Advises the FCE OIC of medical considerations affecting the NEO.
- Provides immediate medical assistance as required.
- Determines characteristics of the evacuation area that are related to the cause and spread of disease, such as terrain, soil, climate, animals, plants, sanitary standards of the native population, and endemic and epidemic diseases present.
- Determines the need for special preventive medicine units.

Air Operations Officer
- Coordinates both fixed- and rotary-wing aircraft.
- Determines air traffic control requirements.
- Provides advice concerning the number and type of air assets required, the technical aspects of HLZs and DZs (including the type of security required), fixed-wing landing strips, and air evacuation routes.
- Selects landing zones (LZs).
- Provides interface for air-to-ground operations.
- Surveys air facilities to support follow-on forces for conduct of defensive operations.

Fire Support Officer
- Identifies and confirms prospective targets to support the NEO (uncertain and/or hostile environments).
- Coordinates targets with appropriate embassy personnel.
- Provides initial terminal guidance support and supporting arms control as required.

Public Affairs Officer (PAO)
- Advises and assists the OIC FCE on matters concerning the news media.
- Serves as a liaison between the FCE and embassy staffs for public affairs (PA).
- Works with the embassy to publicize evacuation efforts in an effort to generate confidence in and a positive perception of the operation.

This is always accomplished in close coordination with the embassy's staff and within the guidelines of approved DOD PA policy.

• Provides clear, concise, and timely information through the combatant command PA staff to senior DOD PA agencies. Provides information to the PAOs at temporary safe havens concerning media opportunities before the arrival of evacuees.

• Provides security review of media products to ensure that operational security is not compromised.

• Establishes an effective command information program.

Psychological Operations (PSYOPS) Officer
• Advises the FCE OIC on PSYOPS-related matters.
• Serves as liaison between the FCE OIC and the supporting PSYOPS organization.
• Coordinates and monitors execution of PSYOPS to support the NEO.
• Coordinates with the JTF PAO, embassy PAO, and USIS director to ensure that themes and messages are congruent.
• Validates the PSYOPS plan.
• Obtains the ambassador's approval for PSYOPS products and execution of the PSYOPS plan.

Civil Affairs (CA) Officer
• Advises the FCE OIC on how to minimize population interference with evacuation operations.
• Maintains close liaison with embassy officials to ensure effective coordination and delineation of CA responsibilities and activities.
• Assists the JTF in accomplishing its mission by obtaining civil or indigenous support for the NEO.
• Assists embassy personnel in receiving, screening, and debriefing evacuees.

Joint Force Legal Adviser
• Advises the FCE OIC on legal issues that may arise on scene in preparation for and during execution of the NEO.
• Reviews and assists in preparing instruction packages on ROE, use of force, use of riot control agents, applicable SOFAs, host-nation law enforcement practices, weapons confiscation, searches and seizures, and civilian detention.
• Conducts liaison with embassy and local officials as required.

Unit Ministry Team
- Advises the FCE OIC on any personal evacuee issues that may have an impact on the evacuation process.
- Provides any required pastoral care.
- Coordinates with other teams such as the medical team.
- Functions as the FCE OIC's representative to local and evacuee religious officials.

Forward Control Element Tasks
The FCE accomplishes the following:
- Initiates liaison with the diplomatic mission.
- Briefs State Department representatives on the capabilities and missions of the advance party and the JTF.
- Establishes a forward command post that can be expanded to accept the JTF staff.
- Provides a continuing presence for planning and ensures a complementary role with State Department personnel.
- Determines whether the operational environment is permissive, uncertain, or hostile
- Makes recommendations to the JTF commander regarding the size and composition of forces required. If specified in the initiating directive, determines whether the JTF is appropriate for the mission.
- Makes recommendations to the JTF commander regarding the time, place, and method of arrival of the evacuation force.
- Advises the JTF commander about the political conditions and attitude of the local population in the JTF AOR.
- Establishes communications between the forward command element and the JTF.
- Allows the senior State Department representative access to the communications link to the JTF.
- Maintains continuous communications.

Evacuation Site Party
The evacuation site party identifies and, when possible, establishes assembly areas, evacuation sites, and the Evacuation Control Center (ECC) site. When the evacuation force enters the country and the evacuation commences, the evacuation site party becomes the operations center and/or section of the ECC.

Composition. The evacuation site party includes the following:
Headquarters commandant or OIC
Operations officer
Intelligence officer
Communications and/or electronics officer
Personnel officer
Logistics officer
Security officer
Civil affairs officer
PSYOPS officer
Public affairs officer
Legal adviser
Air operations officer

Evacuation Site Party Tasks. The evacuation site party accomplishes the following:

- Plans, organizes, and establishes the FCC in preparation for the main body.
- Provides direct liaison with the chief of the Embassy Consular Office.
- Maintains liaison with civilian or local host-government agencies involved in the evacuation.
- Conducts ground reconnaissance of proposed assembly areas, evacuation sites, beaches, LZs/PZs/DZs, airports, and ports; obtain photographs, where possible. To ensure that aircraft configurations are taken into account, the air operations officer must be fully aware of the requirements of potential pickup and delivery sites.
- Recommends and/or confirms assembly areas, evacuation sites, and LZs/PZs/DZs. If assembly area operations must be moved, coordinates approval with the CIA chief of mission.
- Prepares initial evacuation site defensive plan and evacuation security requirements.
- Plans and coordinates emergency aeromedical operations for evacuees with serious medical problems.
- Plans and coordinates operations of assembly areas and evacuation areas with State Department representatives.
- Conducts initial preparation of assembly areas and evacuation sites, including the following:
  — Clears minor obstacles.
  — Plans and lays out assembly areas and evacuation sites.
  — Plans and provides for initial terminal guidance at beaches and HLZs and/or DZs.

- Collects essential planning information, including the following:
  — Assessment of hostage threat
  — Quantity and categories of evacuees
  — Medical status of evacuees
  — Temporary safe havens determined by the State Department
  — Political constraints
  — Number of host-country personnel and third-country nationals (TCNs) to be evacuated.
- Assists State Department personnel with news media.
- Establishes and maintains communications with the FCE and embassy.
- Coordinates additional security requirements that the host-nation police may be able to provide.
- During permissive NEO, coordinates for overflight rights. In uncertain or hostile environments, considers the need for operations security and airspace coordination prior to coordinating overflight rights.
- Initiates PSYOPS.

EVACUATING NONCOMBATANTS

As the advance party rejoins the main body, the main body generally consists of an HQ, marshaling element, security element, logistics element, and special operations forces. Briefly, the Evacuation Force HQ commands and controls the operation. The marshaling element locates and safely transports the evacuees to assembly areas, and then to the ECC. The logistics element supports the operation. The security element provides basic and reactive protection for the overall operation. Special operations forces support the operation with CA, PSYOPS, and possibly direct action missions (SOF missions are beyond the scope of this book).

Evacuation Force HQ

The JTF HQ coordinates and directs the evacuation. Its headquarters may or may not enter the JTF AOR, based on METT-TC. In addition to the usual staff components, the following elements are part of the HQ:

Forward Command Element. The FCE joins the evacuation force and continues operations with the JTF HQ. The FCE continues communications between the embassy and the JTF commander.

Liaison Team. Liaison activities with the embassy and other agencies are continued as required.

Administrative Team. The administrative team joins the evacuation site party to form the ECC.

Marshaling Element

The marshaling element accomplishes the following:

- Moves to and secures predesignated assembly areas.
- Locates, transports, and escorts evacuees to the assembly areas.
- Transports and escorts evacuees to the ECC.

The marshaling element consists of multiple marshaling teams. Each marshaling team controls one assembly area and evacuates the citizens in that area. Each marshaling team should consist of search squads and security squads.

Search Squads. Search squads locate evacuees and escort them to the assembly area. To do this, they must:

- Obtain a list of potential evacuees from the consular officer.
- Obtain copies of the instructions given to each potential evacuee.
- Use copies of the "Waiver of Evacuation Opportunity" for evacuees who refuse to leave.
- Brief each evacuee on the baggage limitations set by the embassy, the positive identification requirements at the ECC, and restricted items that may not be transported.
- Record the name, sex, age, potential medical problems, and citizenship of each evacuee.
- Escort evacuees from the vehicle parking area to the ECC. (Evacuees may drive their own vehicles directly to the ECC, and search personnel should note the individual's name and intent.)
- Identify evacuees not on the list provided by the embassy.

Each search squad should have an interpreter and, if possible, a guide. Interpreters may be required to assist the search squads in moving from the assembly areas and to locate evacuees who are not at home or whose addresses are incorrect.

Search squads may not be needed if the embassy's evacuation plan has been successfully implemented and all evacuees have been notified. If it has been determined that all evacuees have been informed, then search squads should not leave the assembly area except in emergency cases.

Security Squads. Security squads provide security to the team during movement and in the assembly area.

Other Assets. Other marshaling element assets can include:

- PSYOPS loudspeaker teams to facilitate communications with the local populace and noncombatant evacuees. Additionally, depending on the country, PSYOPS personnel may be able to provide interpreters.
- CA personnel or teams to assist in dealing with the local populace and the lower-level host-nation authorities that may be encountered

during evacuation. They, too, may be able to act as interpreters for the marshaling team.

- Transportation assets (air, ground, or watercraft) sufficient to move all elements of the marshaling force, including each search squad, the accompanying security squads, and all anticipated evacuees and their luggage (as specified in the evacuation order). Plan on a 15 percent overage for personnel and luggage.

Actions in the Assembly Area. Assembly area operations include (1) establishment of perimeter security, even in a permissive environment; and (2) marshaling sufficient transportation to move evacuees to the ECC. The marshaling element should consider using local drivers, if in a permissive environment, because of their experience and familiarity with the local road network. Ground movement control is the same as for any convoy (see chapter 36). Vehicles belonging to the evacuees may be used to transport personnel to the ECC.

Security Element

Security forces are used as necessary at the evacuation sites; ECC perimeter; PZs/LZs, aircraft, staging, and/or parking areas; and landing sites for naval landing craft. Security forces can also provide a reaction force if a marshaling team or other unit encounters difficulty or requires assistance. To determine the size of the security force, consider the following:

- Enemy threat to evacuation operations
- Anticipated response of host-nation police, military forces, and other friendly forces in and around the evacuation objective area
- Crowd control requirements at each site
- Number of evacuees
- Number of marshaling and search teams required to search for evacuees
- Number of evacuation sites
- Size of the ECC
- Transportation available to cover the assigned areas
- Personal security of the ambassador
- Type of resources used to evacuate personnel

Logistics Element

The logistics support provided should be limited to the minimum essential support required for the evacuation. Consideration should be given to the following factors in determining requirements for logistic support of the JTF:

- Characteristics and resources of the evacuation area, such as:
  — Existing and potential facilities for support to the JTF, such as facilities for the storage and distribution of supplies, transportation means, airfields, fuel points, medical facilities, medical supplies, and other facilities
  — Food, water, fuel, and consumables
  — Climate, weather, and terrain
- Number of evacuees and their needs
- Potential threats to the evacuation
- Strength and composition of the JTF, including total troop strength; composition of the JTF in terms of ground, air, and naval combat forces, combat support, and combat service support units; and logistic support capabilities of each component and separate unit
- Time constraints and duration of operation
- Logistic support required by the embassy and evacuees
- Availability and suitability of host-nation support as an alternative to deploying U.S. military logistic support
- Prearranged host-nation and/or inter-service support agreements as appropriate
- Transportation system to provide rapid evacuation of combat and noncombat casualties

PROCESSING EVACUEES

Evacuee processing may take place in country at an air terminal or near an airstrip, onboard ship, or at a temporary safe haven site. Regardless of location, a comprehensive plan for the reception and care of evacuees should be implemented. The JTF's primary duties include maintaining order in the evacuation site and supporting the ambassador's efforts to care for noncombatant evacuees.

Evacuation Control Center (ECC)

The ECC supports the State Department, which conducts processing, screening, and selected logistic functions associated with emergency evacuation of noncombatants. The JTF should, however, be prepared to perform functions that are State Department responsibilities, if required. Size and composition of the ECC are determined by the number of evacuees, evacuation environment, and location of the evacuation area. Of primary importance is the nature of the emergency causing the evacuation; it may be a natural, political, or military one.

Evacuation Control Center for NEO

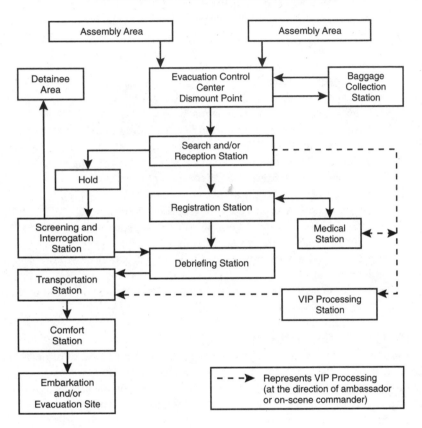

The ECC should be located in a building, tent, or other appropriate place to provide shelter and safety to the evacuees. The ECC should be staffed with security, interpreters, and local immigration, embassy, support liaison, and medical personnel.

Procedures During Processing. The effective and efficient processing of noncombatant evacuees involves a number of key considerations:

- Use easily recognizable markings on U.S. personnel, vehicles, and equipment.
- Disarm evacuees prior to evacuation processing.

- Establish a policy concerning JTF responsibility to secure evacuee valuables during processing.
- Provide interpreters for bilingual information at control sites.
- Affix tags to clothing after initial screening to simplify visual identification.
- Establish provisions for searching women, children, and those who are disabled and/or injured. Use personnel of the same sex to search evacuees.
- Establish procedures for VIPs, government officials, and TCNs.
- Organize evacuees to ensure that there is a single point of contact between the evacuee group and the JTF commander.

Minimum Processing Requirements. Minimum processing requirements are used when there is concern about the protection and safety of evacuees and the JTF. Basic rules include the following:

- Security of JTF personnel and equipment will not be compromised to expedite processing.
- Processing of persons with life-threatening medical problems will be expedited.
- All evacuees will be screened for verification of identity and documentation as well as prioritization.
- Prior to implementation, the ambassador and the JTF commander will agree on procedures for minimum evacuee processing.

Actions at the ECC. The purpose of the ECC is to prepare the evacuees for eventual overseas movement to a temporary safe haven or the United States. The three guiding principles for ECC operations are:

1. *Accuracy.* Everyone who should be accounted for is accounted for.
2. *Security.* Evacuees and the JTF are safeguarded from all threats.
3. *Speed.* Processing is accomplished quickly and efficiently.

As the marshaling teams deliver the evacuees to the ECC, the processing center assumes control of the evacuees. The OIC or NCOIC of the marshaling teams should ensure that the ECC has positive control of all evacuees before departing; consider using a roll call and/or getting a signed, by-name receipt for the evacuees. All evacuees should be screened to certify identification and to ensure that documentation is accurate and all information provided is current. Representatives from the embassy's consular affairs office should be in the ECC to assist in determining the eligibility of questionable evacuees. If evacuees arrive without escort, processing personnel should verify their identity and eligibility for evacuation before allowing the evacuees to enter the ECC.

The various ECC sections perform the necessary screening, registration, medical, and transportation functions to ensure an orderly evacuation.

Headquarters Section. The HQ section is responsible for the following:
* Planning, organizing, and supervising the operation of the ECC
* Maintaining liaison with local representatives of the State Department and other agencies involved in the evacuation
* Advising the JTF commander on the progress of the evacuation
* Maintaining communications with all elements of the evacuation force, including ships, control aircraft, remote sites, evacuation vehicles, State Department personnel, host-nation security forces and the ECC

Reception and/or Search Station. Reception personnel collect all available information from the marshaling teams who escort the evacuees. The evacuees should be moved into a holding area where reception and search personnel can receive, search, segregate, and brief incoming evacuees in conjunction with State Department representatives. The initial briefing should be given by senior officials, who provide sufficient information to ease fears about the evacuation process. It should include the following:
* Summary of the reasons for the evacuation
* Stations through which the evacuees will process
* Need for an inspection of personnel and baggage
* What support to expect at the temporary safe haven
* What to expect upon arrival in the United States
* What the repatriation center will provide
* Amnesty opportunity for any restricted items

The evacuees are then organized into groups to maintain family integrity where possible. Reception personnel should:
* Maintain a roster noting the name of each evacuee, with his or her nationality, date of birth, evacuation classification, profession, destination, and name, address, and/or phone number of a point of contact (POC) in the United States for notification.
* Provide an escort for groups of personnel going through the processing center. VIPs and emergency medical cases should be provided individual guides if available.
* Inspect for restricted items. Each evacuee and all baggage should be inspected at the conclusion of the briefing. Areas used for individual inspections should be screened. Hand-held metal detectors can expedite the inspections. All restricted items should be confiscated.

Many foreign countries sell drugs over the counter that U.S. law requires a prescription to obtain. Medical personnel on the inspection team can aid in identifying these drugs.

All weapons, excluding those of U.S. government personnel, are impounded, and receipts are issued to the owners. Embassy or customs officials should be consulted about the disposition of these weapons. Unless the weapons are illegal in the United States, they will be returned to the owners at the repatriation center.

The persons, property, papers, and families of foreign ambassadors authorized to go to the United States are exempt from search under any circumstances without specific direction from the State Department. The persons, property, papers, and families of foreign diplomats (other than ambassadors) authorized passage to the United States are exempt from search. However, personal baggage may be searched if there is reasonable cause to believe that the baggage contains restricted items. All searches should be conducted in the presence of the diplomats or their authorized agents. Diplomatic pouches are *not* searched.

Based on reasonable cause, the JFC may refuse to evacuate any baggage suspected of containing weapons or explosives.

Evacuees suspected of being enemy agents or criminals should be separated and escorted to the screening and interrogation station. The screening should be voluntary but is considered a prerequisite to evacuation. At the conclusion of the interrogation, the evacuees should be allowed to continue the processing, be set free, or be placed in a detainee area.

Registration Station. The registration section should ensure that evacuees complete all administrative paperwork prior to leaving the country. Foreign nationals must either be on the list of potential evacuees provided by the embassy or secure approval from the U.S. Embassy before they can continue processing. The ambassador or designated State Department representative is the final authority on the acceptability of evacuee identification. If there are doubts about a person's identity, the matter should be turned over to the State Department and the person should not be evacuated. Registration station personnel supervise foreign nationals until they are cleared for evacuation or escorted outside the ECC. Military police should be available to react to any hostile incidents.

Each evacuee should do the following:
- Prove identity by using passports, dependent ID cards, seaman's papers, or anything that unquestionably establishes U.S. citizenship.
- Provide information to the registration clerks concerning background and personal history. The State Department's *Evacuee Processing Handbook* provides for a standard one-page Evacuee Documentation Card (OF-28) that has three carbon copies. All critical information is recorded on the form, including personal data, health and citizenship status, privacy warning, and promissory note. The original of the

form remains at the ECC; the copies can be used as boarding passes for evacuation transportation and for in-processing at the temporary safe haven.

- Receive a copy of DD Form 2585, *Repatriation Processing Center Processing Sheet* which should be completed before arrival at the repatriation center.

Debriefing Station. This station is optional, depending on the situation and the time available to conduct the evacuation. It should be staffed by counterintelligence personnel. Each evacuee should be debriefed to obtain information that may affect the evacuation force, its mission, the evacuees, or other U.S. government activities in the country. Areas of interest might include the following:

- Locations of other potential evacuees
- Changes in the political situation
- Movements and activities of indigenous groups, entities, and other parties that might oppose the evacuation, with special regard to these questions:
  — Is the party capable of carrying out a threat?
  — Can the party be influenced?
  — Can the potential threat be stopped or countered?

Medical Station. The medical station provides emergency medical treatment and immunizations required by the safe-haven country. Injured or ill evacuees may proceed through the medical station for first aid and to identify medical conditions that may have an effect on the evacuation process. Serious medical cases receive top priority for evacuation. However, the medical officer ensures that any seriously ill, injured, or wounded persons complete processing. Medical personnel should:

- Screen to determine whether an evacuee requires emergency medical treatment or evacuation.
- Perform emergency treatment as required.
- Isolate persons with contagious diseases.

Transportation Station. Transportation personnel prepare each group of evacuees for embarkation aboard aircraft, ships, or surface vehicles. The personnel at this station accomplish the following:

- Coordinate surface or air transportation including movement of personnel to the evacuation area, transportation of evacuees to designated aircraft and/or landing craft, and internal evacuation site requirements.
- Provide loading control personnel to supervise loading of personnel aboard vehicles, aircraft, and/or landing craft.

- Maintain a roster of all embarked personnel showing destination and identifying information.
- Organize evacuees into transportation groups ("chalks"), issue boarding passes for aircraft, and verify baggage tags.
- Ensure that information on the passenger manifest agrees with information provided on the evacuee register.
- Ensure sufficient transportation assets to transport evacuees and their baggage to the point of embarkation.

Comfort Station. The comfort station is a temporary waiting area for evacuees until they board evacuation aircraft. Comfort station personnel should make the evacuees' stay as untroubled as possible and provide some degree of privacy. To the extent allowed by the situation, the following should be available:

- Sufficient shelter, cots, blankets, food, water, and infant supplies
- Sufficient sanitation facilities
- Medical personnel and unit ministry teams to counsel evacuees, especially families with young children
- Male and female personal items

Classification of Evacuees

For organizational purposes, all evacuees receive a priority and classification designator. These categorizations are critical to the smooth execution and success of the operation and are used when identifying, moving, and locating evacuees. The JTF staff keeps abreast of changes in the total numbers of potential evacuees based on periodic updates from the embassy's staff. These updates indicate the total number of evacuees and the number by category.

The following system of major and minor categories governs the priority of evacuations. A complete priority designator includes a Roman numeral and capital letter indicating major and minor priorities assigned to each individual. Aliens for whom the United States has accepted responsibility are afforded the same major and minor category consideration as U.S.-sponsored evacuees.

Major Categories

Category I. U.S. citizens in the following order:

1. Those with current identification, such as passports, birth certificates, DOD identification cards, seaman's papers, aircrew cards, and anyone designated as first priority by the ambassador, regardless of national affiliation. The ambassador is the final authority.

2. Those with expired U.S. passports less than 10 years old.

3. Those with expired U.S. passports over 10 years old.

Category II. Aliens who are immediate family members of American citizens.

Category III. Foreign Service national and TCN employees of the U.S. government.

Category IV. Eligible non-Americans who are seriously ill or injured or whose lives are in imminent peril (but who do not qualify for a higher priority).

Category V. Others who are eligible, as directed by the ambassador or joint force commander.

Minor Categories
A. Pregnant women
B. Unaccompanied minors under 18
C. Aged and infirm
D. Adults with children
E. Adults (18 or older)

Thus, an 82-year-old citizen of the host country who was employed by the U.S. Foreign Service would receive an evacuation priority of III.C.

GUIDELINES FOR INTERACTION WITH EVACUEES

Evacuees are *not* enemy prisoners of war; they must be treated with dignity and respect. Most are your countrymen and will be glad to see you. The minimum force required should be used.

Evacuation can be an unsettling experience, especially for children and families who have become separated. As a rule, presenting a patient, courteous, and professional attitude will do much to calm the situation and the evacuees.

Depending on the situation, personal baggage may be limited; however, people should not be separated from their baggage.

The JTF commander should establish a policy concerning pets. Some people refuse to evacuate or delay their departure if they cannot bring their pets. Therefore, whenever possible, allow pets to accompany evacuees, except when human lives will be jeopardized or security compromised. If pets arrive for evacuation, a pet control facility must be established. The logistics officer should bring pet travel containers, if possible.

Personnel should not accept gifts, tips, or bribes. All personnel must be aware of this prohibition.

All questions about an evacuee should be referred to the State Department representative.

Persons of higher priority may elect evacuation in a lower priority to avoid separating families. If it is necessary to MEDEVAC a member of a family, the entire family will be evacuated medically.

Well-established liaison with local airport security and an ambulance service is highly useful.

Medical personnel should consider wearing distinctive clothing or markings to aid in identification. When possible, patients should be given written instructions for medical care, especially care for children.

REQUESTS FOR ASYLUM OR TEMPORARY REFUGE

International law and custom have long recognized the humanitarian practice of providing temporary refuge to anyone, regardless of nationality, who may be in imminent physical danger. It is the policy of the United States to grant temporary refuge in a foreign country to nationals of that country or to TCNs solely for humanitarian reasons when extreme or exceptional circumstances, such as pursuit by a mob, put the life or safety of a person in imminent danger. The officer in command of an aircraft, ship, station, or activity decides which measures can prudently be taken to provide temporary refuge.

State Department representatives handle asylum requests through the appropriate channels. No information shall be released to the media concerning requests for asylum until cleared by the State Department. Any requests by foreign governments for the return of an individual must be reported to the State Department representative. Until a determination is made by the State Department, safeguard those who have requested asylum or temporary refuge. Do not release personnel against their will to a third-party force. The safety of JTF personnel and the security of the unit must be taken into consideration.

MEDICAL CONSIDERATIONS DURING NEO

During evacuation operations, it may be difficult or impossible to insert and establish the medical support function for the JTF because of time and operational constraints. Comprehensive and detailed casualty and medical support planning should be implemented to cover immediate medical and surgical treatment points. Special units organized for this purpose may save lives and permit a more expeditious evacuation. Depending on the size and scope of the evacuation operation, there may be the potential for large numbers of both military and civilian casualties.

The Theater Patient Movement Requirements Center (TPMRC) is a joint agency established to regulate and monitor the flow of patients to medical treatment facilities. The TPMRC matches patients with the most appropriate medical treatment facility based on patient needs and bed availability in the area of operations.

Primary casualty receiving and treatment ships (PCRTSs) may provide medical treatment resources offshore. The classes of ships with this capability include:

- General purpose amphibious assault ship
- General purpose amphibious assault ship (with internal dock)
- Amphibious assault ship
- Aircraft carriers

Aeromedical evacuation (AE) is the movement of patients under medical supervision to and between medical treatment facilities by air transportation. The Air Force is responsible for operating a common-user, fixed-wing AE system. HQ, Air Mobility Command (AMC) is responsible for serving as the single AE proponent for the Air Force, managing and operating the intertheater and CONUS AE systems. Intratheater AE is a responsibility of the geographic combatant commander. USTRANSCOM tasks HQ AMC to provide AE forces to strategic airfields in theater to evacuate casualties between theaters or from a theater of operations to CONUS reception airfields. Distribution of patients within CONUS from these strategic airfields is an HQ AMC responsibility. Intratheater common-user AE is provided using a combination of theater-assigned AE units and/or deployment of theater-specific AE elements.

Experience has shown that the common medical complaints of personnel being evacuated are nausea, dehydration, and diarrhea. Most frequently, sick evacuees are children.

Particularly effective medical staffs during NEO include general medical officers, family practitioners, pediatricians, internists, and psychiatrists and/or psychologists. Similarly, well-established liaison with local airport security and an ambulance service is essential.

A separate area close to the disembarkation point should be designated to perform medical assessments, dispense medication, and conduct patient staging. Medical staff should consider wearing distinctive clothing or markings to aid in identification.

Medical staffs may anticipate requests for antibiotics, diarrhea medicines, pain relievers, Silvadene, eye and ear drops, cough and cold formulas, and high blood pressure medications. When possible, patients should be given written instructions on how to continue care for themselves or for children under their supervision.

Special plans and attention to the situation are required to move and evacuate personnel hospitalized in host-nation medical facilities. AE missions may require movement of urgent or priority patients in aircraft that are not completely filled. Due to patients' severe conditions, such aircraft are normally not delayed while nonmedical evacuees are moved to the airfield to fill the aircraft.

LEGAL CONSIDERATIONS DURING NEO

The JTF commander and subordinate commanders of the evacuation and intermediate support base should have a legal adviser attached to their staffs to advise on military and international legal matters. They must ensure that JTF personnel abide by the standards of international law, as well as the provisions of the operation's ROE. The JTF commander should establish procedures and policies for immediately reporting and investigating violations. The JTF commander must report all suspected violations in accordance with applicable DOD and service regulations and should notify the embassy of a suspected violation within 24 hours of its occurrence.

JTF Legal Adviser

The JTF legal adviser provides guidance on legal issues involving NEO, in coordination with higher headquarters, State Department agencies, NGOs/PVOs, IOs, foreign governments, and the host-nation government. The emphasis is on assisting with the interpretation of and compliance with applicable U.S. laws and regulations; relevant international agreements, including any pertinent SOFAs; and multilateral and bilateral transit agreements impacting NEO.

Legal Imperatives and Input

When planning and conducting NEO, commanders must be cognizant of legal imperatives derived from the U.S. Constitution, domestic law, international agreements, and customary international law. In view of this governing framework of laws and regulations, as well as the complexity of legal issues relating to NEO, commanders must obtain legal guidance at all phases of NEO planning and execution, particularly during the early planning stage.

Commanders should ensure that legal advisers at all levels are full participants in all aspects of NEO planning, operational guidance and decisions, and national policy directives. Additionally, operation plans (OPLANs), warning orders, commander's estimates, ROE, operation orders (OPORDs), executive orders, and other operational documents should be systematically reviewed by the JTF legal adviser to ensure compliance with international and domestic law.

Specific Guidance and Terminology

Foreign Diplomat. A foreign diplomat of an embassy staff authorized to go to the United States for evacuation is entitled to special treatment in accordance with international law. Ideally, the individual, as well as his or her personal effects and papers, should not be searched, detained, or seized. Family members are entitled to the same immunity unless they are citizens of the United States. The diplomatic pouch of a diplomatic courier from a state recognized by the United States is also immune from any search, inspection, detention, or seizure by U.S. personnel.

Political Asylum or Temporary Refuge. JTF commanders may not grant political asylum to any foreign national. They may grant temporary refuge under emergency conditions when there is imminent danger to the safety, health, or life of any person. All requests for asylum should be referred to the embassy or senior State Department representative.

Status-of-Forces Agreement. Any SOFA between the host nation and the United States should be reviewed to determine how it applies, if at all, to the current situation involving the NEO. If time permits, it should be modified as necessary prior to the JTF arrival. If no agreement exists and if time permits, the embassy may negotiate a temporary agreement with the host nation covering criminal jurisdiction, procurement, customs, and other legal matters. Given the emergency nature of the NEO, however, it is likely that no special SOFA provisions will be negotiated.

Status of Detainee. The embassy should determine the status of a detainee in advance of the JTF deployment. In the absence of this determination, it is U.S. policy to treat a hostile detainee humanely and in accordance with international humanitarian law. Anyone actively detained by U.S. forces in an attempt to deter or in response to hostile action will be accorded the rights of an EPW, even though he or she may not be an EPW within the context of the Geneva Convention. The embassy, with the host nation, will negotiate the disposition of the detainee.

Claims. The JTF legal adviser or designated claims officer shall develop a plan for the processing and adjudication of claims against the United States. The plan will be coordinated with the appropriate embassy staff member.

International Legal Considerations

Law of Armed Conflict. Traditional legal issues associated with the law of armed conflict do not normally arise in the context of NEO, as NEO typically occur during times of escalating confrontation short of armed conflict. However, the protections afforded civilians, sick, and wounded under the law of armed conflict are almost universally accepted humanitarian norms and are respected in many cases despite the absence of international armed conflict. NEO planning and execution should adhere as closely as possible to international humanitarian law principles as a matter of consistent practice.

Commanders must report, investigate, and initiate appropriate disciplinary disposition of allegations of law of armed conflict violations, as follows:

- With respect to alleged violations of the law of armed conflict committed by or against members of, or persons accompanying or serving with, their commands, promptly investigate, collect and evaluate evidence, and report in accordance with applicable DOD and military department guidance.
- With respect to alleged violations of the law of armed conflict committed by or against allied military or civilian personnel, conduct an appropriate preliminary investigation to determine the involvement of JTF personnel and report as required through U.S. operational channels. Once a determination is made that the JTF was not involved, further U.S. investigation will be undertaken only at the direction of the combatant commander.
- In *all* instances of reported violations of the law of armed conflict, make immediate message notification to the appropriate combatant commander. Service component commanders should provide such notification as soon as the tactical situation permits, rather than awaiting complete investigation. Additional details may be supplied by supplemental reports.

National Sovereignty. Commanders must ensure that the NEO does not violate the sovereignty of foreign nations other than the host nation. NEO planners and operators must be cognizant of the potential impact of operations on relations with other nations and of all relevant international agreements, including pertinent SOFAs and multilateral and bilateral transit agreements.

Host-Nation Support

Commanders must be aware of applicable basing rights and the status of U.S. forces within the country when planning and executing NEO.

Particular attention must be paid to ensuring the advance procurement of landing, embarkation, and transit rights required to support a given operation. Additionally, the changing political and military situation must be taken into account before relying on previously negotiated host-nation agreements. Liaison with State Department officials responsible for the particular NEO site must be accomplished in a timely manner.

TYPICAL DILEMMAS
Although each NEO is unique, situations typically arise that require special considerations. JTF personnel should be briefed and prepared to deal with the following:
- Questions concerning when the use of deadly force or a given weapon system is authorized
- Interpretation of the ROE
- Hostile detainees who present themselves to or are captured by the JTF
- Civil disturbance, from passive resistance or civil disobedience to violence
- Terrorism (see chapter 38)
- Bomb threats (see chapter 15)
- Snipers
- Nonambulatory evacuees
- Language problems
- Religious constraints
- Potential evacuee's name not on list provided by the embassy but appearing to be a bona fide evacuee
- Deaths of evacuees and evacuation of remains
- Listed evacuees or unlisted potential evacuees with unknown identifications
- Evacuees carrying contraband, and disposition of the contraband
- Overwhelming numbers of civilians coming to assembly areas or evacuation sites to request evacuation
- Listed evacuees refusing evacuation
- Evacuees attempting to pay bribes to gain favor
- Inaccurate evacuation lists
- Large numbers of international journalists converging on the area

The following NEO planning checklist provides questions that may be used to provide a common framework for evacuation planning and operations. These questions may serve as foci for the detailed planning and operational dialogue between diplomats and military forces that must precede any successful evacuation operation.

NEO PLANNING CHECKLIST

1. Will this be a permissive, uncertain, or hostile NEO? If the evacuation is permissive, are unarmed hostilities expected? If the evacuation is uncertain or hostile, will pursuit forces be necessary? What is the likelihood of terrorist activities?
2. What multinational forces will be operating in the area?
   a. Are multinational forces integrated into the JTF plan?
   b. How are plans being deconflicted if evacuations are separate?
3. What is the current situation in the country? In the embassy? Near the U.S. citizens?
4. Who is the senior U.S. official in charge of the evacuation operation?
5. Who will give the JTF permission to complete the evacuation and to leave the evacuation site?
6. What is the chain of command for U.S. military forces?
7. What is the relationship between the JTF commander and the ambassador?
8. Will all U.S. mission and/or embassy officials be leaving? If not, who will remain? What action should be taken in the event an embassy official refuses evacuation?
9. Who will screen the evacuees?
   a. Are there embassy personnel assigned to screen?
   b. Are there any evacuees (e.g., wardens) who will be able to help with processing and screening?
   c. What are the JTF requirements for screening?
10. Who makes the final determination of evacuee accounting prior to final evacuation departure?
11. Is the embassy's EAP available? Is it up-to-date?
12. Who is the primary point of contact within the embassy to work with the JTF on details of the operation?
13. What steps are being taken by the embassy to get the evacuees ready for evacuation?
14. Are there any members of the JTF, or anyone reasonably available, who have been in the host nation recently?
15. Is there any intelligence needed immediately from the evacuees?
16. Have the primary and alternative assembly areas, evacuation sites, and routes been verified and surveyed?
17. Have the screening and processing areas been verified?
18. What is the total number of U.S. personnel to be evacuated?
19. What action should be taken concerning individuals not on the list of evacuees (e.g., TCNs)? What is the total number of TCNs to be evacuated?
    a. Number per priority category.
    b. Identification.
20. What will be the composition of the evacuees? Will there be a cross section of those listed in the EAP?
21. What discipline problems are expected from the evacuees? Who are the potential troublemakers?
22. What action should be taken if there is an outbreak of violence among evacuees?
23. What action should be taken if someone asks for political asylum?

24. Will it be necessary to search the baggage and personal property of all evacuees for weapons or explosives?
25. Who will be available to physically search female evacuees?
26. What proof of U.S. citizenship is acceptable?
27. Are there any changes in the standard priorities for evacuation?
28. Will the U.S. Embassy be able to assign evacuation priorities before it schedules evacuation?
29. What are the arrangements for evacuee housing, security, and transfer? Will protective clothing be required? Will food be required?
    a. Type.
    b. Quantity.
    c. Location.
30. Are any animals (pets) prohibited from traveling on the designated transportation? Have restrictions concerning animals been identified at the safe-haven location?
31. Will JTF search teams be sent after missing evacuees?
32. Is there any sensitive equipment or material that will need to be evacuated or destroyed? Will personnel with requisite clearances be required to assist in evacuating or destroying sensitive equipment or material?
33. Are there procedures to handle claims against U.S. civilians?
34. If required, who will provide an emergency resupply of ammunition for the advance party?
35. What cultural nuances and customs should be known by the JTF evacuation force to avoid confrontation?
36. Who are the key host-country personnel, and what are their attitudes toward the evacuation?
37. Will medical support be available from the embassy or host country? Have MEDEVAC procedures been coordinated with the host country? Where are the host-country health services?
    a. Location.
    b. Availability.
    c. Capability.
38. What is the policy concerning seriously wounded evacuees? Should they be given precedence over all other evacuees? What is the physical condition of all evacuees? Are AE assets required? If so, is there a need to pre-stage those assets nearby, and what are the MEDEVAC procedures?
39. Where are the host-country police forces?
    a. Location.
    b. Availability.
    c. Capability.
    d. Loyalty to the host government.
    e. Hostility to the United States.
    f. Factional infighting present.
40. Where are the host-country fire services?
    a. Location.
    b. Availability.
    c. Capability.
41. Where are the host-country military forces?
    a. Location.

    b. Availability.

    c. Capability.

    d. Loyalty to the host government.

    e. Hostility to the United States.

    f. Factional infighting present.

42. Will the host government be providing any security for the assembly areas of evacuation sites?

    a. Location.

    b. Unit.

    c. Size of security force.

43. What is the potential threat?

    a. Strength.

    b. Composition.

    c. Disposition.

    d. Probable tactics.

    e. Weapons available.

44. Will interpreter support be available from the embassy or the host country?

45. What communications support will be available from the embassy, and how will the communication architecture be set up to support the operations (i.e., networks, frequencies, secure equipment availability, need for relays)?

46. Can portable communications equipment be sent to the embassy to facilitate improved and secure communication?

47. Will transportation support be available from the embassy or the host country?

    a. Type.

    b. Location.

    c. Capacity.

    d. Condition.

    e. Operators required.

48. Who will prepare the PA plan? How often will it be updated? Who is the lead PA director? Will media representatives be evacuated?

49. Are there areas from which the media are restricted access? Is there a media support plan?

50. What are the ROE for the JTF?

51. What is the guidance on the use of PSYOPS?

52. What coordination has been made with the host-nation media to support the NEO and/or the NEO PSYOPS plan?

53. Will the host-nation media provide support for the NEO and/or the NEO PSYOPS plan?

54. What is the role of Civil Affairs in NEO?

55. Does the JTF have permission to drop sensors and insert special operations forces?

56. Who provides country studies for the JTF with information such as LZs, concentration of U.S. citizens, port facilities, landing beaches? How will this information be transmitted to the JTF?

57. Have all requirements for strategic transportation system been directed to the USTRANSCOM command center and/or crisis action team?

58. What is the best means of transportation to evacuate personnel?

    a. Can commercial airlift provide more timely evacuation than deploying U.S. military assets?

    b. Have air requirements for units and equipment been identified in the Joint Operation Planning Execution System?

    c. Are U.S. naval assets readily available to stage off the coast?

59. What are the appropriate command and control arrangements if the NEO is conducted as a combined operation?

60. Who will provide climatological, meteorological, and oceanographic information?

61. What support is available from other U.S. sources?

62. What support is required by other U.S. agencies?

63. What support is available from other participating nations?

64. What support is required by other participating nations?

65. Are trained EOD personnel available through the host nation?

66. Are map products of the JOA and the embassy compound available? What are the sources?

67. Who controls and ensures familiarity with NEOPACKs and other geographic information?

68. Which evacuees have special medical needs, such as pregnancy, infectious disease, exceptional family member, or pediatric healthcare problems?

69. What are the ROE?

70. Is an ISB available? Where? How extensive are its facilities and support capabilities?

71. Will the ambassador allow an FCE to deploy?

Chapter 38

Employ Personal
Antiterrorism Measures

Any member of the Department of Defense can become a target for terrorists, especially when deployed in the conduct of MOOTW. Antiterrorist measures include precautions to avoid being victimized and behaviors in the event of terrorist attack. Leaders should ensure that all subordinates engaged in foreign MOOTW are familiar with these measures and, to the greatest extent possible, should ensure that they employ them.

PRECAUTIONS
The following measures are taken by individuals to avoid victimization from terrorist acts; due to the similar nature of criminal acts, they are not unlike those taken to avoid criminal depredation.

At All Times
At all times, all personnel should:
- Be alert for surveillance attempts, the presence of suspicious persons, or the conduct of unusual activities. Report them to the proper authorities. *Trust your instincts.*
- Vary personal and even duty routines whenever possible.
- Routinely check in with fellow soldiers and friends to let them know where you are or when to expect you.
- Know how to use the local phone system, and always carry enough local currency to make calls. Know the emergency numbers for local police, fire, ambulance, and medical support (if any).
- Know the locations of civilian police, military police, government agencies, the U.S. Embassy, and other safe locations where you can find refuge or assistance.
- Avoid public disputes or confrontations with local civilians.

- Promptly report any harassment or other trouble to the proper authorities.
- Learn certain key phrases in the native language such as:
  — "I need a policeman."
  — "Take me to a doctor."
  — "Where is the hospital?"
  — "Where is the police station?"
- Set up a simple signal system to alert associates via telephone or conversation that you are in danger. Do not share this information with anyone who is not involved in your signal system.
- Carry identification showing your blood type and any special medical conditions. Keep a minimum one-week supply of essential medication on your person at all times.
- Keep a low profile. Shun publicity. Do not flash large sums of money.
- Do not unnecessarily divulge your billet location, phone number, or family information.
- Be aware of unexplained or unusual absences of local civilians as an early warning of possible terrorist actions.
- Keep your personal affairs in good order.
- Keep wills current, have powers of attorney drawn up, take measures to ensure your family's financial security, and develop a plan for family actions in the event you are taken hostage.
- Do not carry sensitive or potentially embarrassing items.

When Traveling by Ground Transportation

Whenever traveling, regardless of the length of the trip, take these precautions:

- Use a plain car that is common in the area.
- Vary your daily travel behavior, including times, routes, and modes of transportation, whenever possible.
- Safeguard car keys at all times.
- Check for suspicious activity or objects around your car before getting into or out of it. Do not touch your vehicle until you have thoroughly checked it (look inside it, walk around it, and look under it).
- Secure your vehicle when it is not in use. Make absolutely sure that you have immobilized the steering wheel (with a chain or club) and have removed all desirable property from view. If possible, equip your vehicle with a locking gas door or gas cap.
- Drive with windows closed and doors locked.

- Travel with a group of people or a convoy—there is safety in numbers.
- Travel on busy routes; avoid isolated and dangerous areas.
- Park your car off the street in a secure area.
- Do not routinely use the same taxi or bus stop. Note: Buses are preferable to taxis; trains are better still.
- Know the locations of save havens (e.g., police and fire stations) along your route.
- Be alert for suspicious-looking vehicles and surveillance, and be aware of possible danger when driving or riding in a car.
- If you think you are being followed, move as quickly as possible to a safe place, such as a police or fire station; do not attempt to complete your journey.
- If your car breaks down, raise the hood, then get back inside the car and remain there with the doors locked and the windows up. If anyone offers to assist, ask the person to call the police.
- Do not pick up hitchhikers.
- Drive on well-lit streets whenever possible.
- Prearrange a signal with your driver (if you have one) to indicate that it is safe to get into the vehicle. Share this information only with persons having a need to know.
- Keep your vehicle's gas tank at least half full.

When Traveling by Air
When you must travel by air, do the following:
- Use military air transportation whenever possible.
- Avoid travel through high-risk areas; book reservations on foreign flag airlines and/or indirect routes to avoid such areas.
- Do not use rank or military addresses on tickets, travel documents, hotel reservations, or luggage.
- Select a window seat on aircraft, because they offer more protection and are less accessible to hijackers than are aisle seats.
- Select a seat in the midsection of the aircraft, because it is not one of usual areas of terrorist activity.
- Do not discuss your U.S. government affiliation with any other passengers.
- Consider using a tourist passport when traveling in high-risk areas; if you use a tourist passport, store your official passport, ID card, travel orders, and other official documents in your carry-on bags.

- Use plain civilian luggage; avoid using B-4 bags, duffel bags, and other military-looking bags. Remove all indications of your rank and any military patches, logos, and decals from your luggage and briefcase.
- Do not carry official papers in your briefcase.
- Travel in conservative civilian clothing. Do not wear the following:
  — Military-oriented organizational shirts or caps
  — Military rings
  — Military-issue shoes or glasses
  — Obviously American clothing such as cowboy boots and hats
  — American-logo T-shirts
  — Cover visible U.S.-affiliated tattoos with a long-sleeved shirt
  — If possible, check your baggage with the airport's curb service
  — Adjust your arrival at the airport to minimize waiting time; be alert for any suspicious activity in the waiting area, and proceed immediately to the departure gate.

In Hotels

When staying in a hotel:
- Keep your room key on your person at all times.
- Be observant for suspicious persons loitering in the area.
- Do not give your room number to strangers.
- Keep your room and personal effects neat and orderly so that you will recognize tampering or out-of-place objects.
- Know the location of emergency exits and fire extinguishers.
- Do not admit strangers to your room.
- Know how to locate hotel security personnel.

HOSTAGE DEFENSE MEASURES

The mission of any American hostage is to survive with honor. In the event you become a hostage, do the following:
- Maintain your composure.
- Take mental note of the direction, time in transit, noise, and other environmental factors that may help you identify your location.
- Note the numbers, names, physical characteristics, accents, personal habits, and apparent hierarchical structure of your captors.
- Anticipate isolation and terrorist efforts to confuse and frighten you.
- Mentally prepare yourself for the situation as much as possible. Stay mentally active.

- Do not be fooled by a friendly approach by abductors—it may be used to get information from you.
- Avoid political or ideological discussions with your captors; comply with their routine instructions, but maintain your dignity.
- If at all possible, find some way to exercise daily.
- Read anything you can find to keep your mind active.
- Eat whatever food is offered to you to maintain your strength.
- Establish a slow, methodical routine for every task.
- When interrogated, take a simple, tenable position and stick to it. Be polite and maintain your temper. Give short answers about nonessential matters, but do not discuss substantial issues or reveal operational or classified information.
- If forced to present terrorist demands to authorities in writing or on tape, do only what you are told to do. Avoid making a plea on your own behalf.
- Affirm your faith in basic democratic principles, but do not discuss particular political policies, parties, or personalities.

RESCUES

In the event of a rescue attempt:
- Drop to the floor.
- Do not move until instructed to do so by the rescuing force.
- If you notice the attempt before your captors do, do not allow your body language to tip them off. Be quiet and do not attract your captors' attention.

Rescue forces may initially treat you as one of the terrorists until you are positively identified as a "friendly." Cooperate, even if you are initially handcuffed or bound.

Once released or rescued, do not make comments to the news media until you have been debriefed by the proper U.S. authorities and have been cleared to do so by the appropriate military commander.

Chapter 39

Conduct Negotiations

Few missions better highlight the special challenges facing NCOs and officers conducting MOOTW than this one. Although civil affairs (CA) officers and NCOs are specially trained to conduct this task, leaders of units participating in these operations are sometimes called on to negotiate disputes between antagonistic factions. These negotiations can often prevent the outbreak of further hostilities and thus contribute significantly to the achievement of stability.

The aim must always be to resolve problems at the lowest level as quickly as possible to prevent small incidents from escalating into serious disputes. Leaders conducting MOOTW often find themselves acting as intermediaries between militia-based forces. In this type of situation, real power is often held at the lower levels by the belligerents; a platoon leader may resolve a minor matter on the spot, at the local level. If it becomes apparent that an issue cannot be resolved at a low level, it should be referred up to the level where a quick decision can be made.

ESTABLISHING LIAISON TO NEGOTIATE WITH FACTION REPRESENTATIVES

Leaders conducting this sort of mission must gain a detailed knowledge of the nature of the conflict, its sources, and the issues surrounding the situation in which they are operating. Specifically, during negotiations, they must ascertain the viewpoints and negotiating positions of both sides. CA personnel are usually extremely conversant with the situation and should be consulted whenever possible to educate unit leaders—and soldiers—about the relevant facts. Intelligence personnel are also useful in this role.

Determine the assets of each side, and what they would require in exchange for an asset. Establish who will represent each side and what, if any, restrictions have been placed on their ability to reach a decision or compromise. Both sides should agree to be represented by an official of *equal* rank and authority. Find out what agreements have been made at higher-level meetings that have a bearing on the subject. If appropriate, obtain copies of any texts issued at those meetings. Rehearse the negotiation process.

Prepare the Negotiation Site

Ensure that both sides are prepared for the meeting. Select an appropriate place for the meeting that is acceptable to both sides, such as the U.S. forces barracks. Consider the security and travel arrangements of the delegates. Units may be asked to provide transportation for the delegates. Coordinate or provide the following:

- Interpreters. Delegates are likely to use their own interpreters. If using local civilian interpreters, the negotiator must consider that they may not be considered neutral by the belligerents. Substitute interpreters should be available if accuracy of translation is in question.
- A recorder for the preparation of minutes or written agreements.
- Communications. Delegates may wish to consult with their superiors.
- Maps.
- Media coverage, if applicable (arrange through the PAO).
- If hosting the meeting, arrangements for each delegate to be met and escorted to the negotiations.
- Waiting area for bodyguards, drivers and other ancillary personnel.
- Refreshments.

CONDUCTING NEGOTIATIONS
Initiate Negotiations

Negotiations generally start with the following actions. The leader introduces himself and his assistants and makes a few opening remarks. If appropriate, delegates introduce themselves. (Be sure that names are correctly spelled by the recorder.) Invite the belligerents to state their cases or opinions, and allow them to do so without interruption. Initial statements are likely to be contrived, full of innuendo, and occasionally irrelevant to the aim of the meeting, but they must be heard. Record the main points of the arguments and highlight the main points of agreement or disagreement.

Adjourn the meeting for a few minutes. The adjournment gives each side a chance to consider its position in light of what has been said during opening remarks.

Negotiate

Having heard both sides, the chairman has a good idea of the room for maneuver. Prior to reconvening the meeting, the chairman may also wish to consult with advisers to plot a strategy to achieve compromise.

During negotiations, it is important that the chairman take firm control and attempt to direct both sides toward a compromise. He can do this by summarizing the points of agreement and disagreement, then prioritizing the issues. He should confirm that both sides would still like to find a compromise solution and invite one or both sides to propose a compromise. A period of heated discussion is likely to follow. If the meeting is being conducted in a foreign language common to both belligerents, the chairman should allow them to talk directly to each other. An interpreter should keep the chairman informed of the main points of the discussion.

Intervention to reestablish order requires careful timing. A well-trained interpreter can provide advice. Adjourning the meeting is another way to reestablish order. During the break, the chairman should consult privately with both sides to try to establish the compromise. The chairman should now have an idea of what is acceptable to both sides.

After reconvening the meeting, the chairman might propose a compromise based on what is acceptable to the unit and the belligerents, and then seek comments from both sides. It is important for the chairman to remain impartial, if not neutral; true neutrality is often impossible due to vested interests in resolving the problems. If both sides are still too far apart, consider imposing a time limit on the discussion to focus attention. Also, consider emphasizing the definite and potential consequences of failing to arrive at a compromise solution.

Conclude Negotiations

As in any negotiation, it is appropriate to highlight agreements and outstanding areas of disagreement. If necessary and appropriate, arrange a tentative time and date for the next meeting.

Before the next meeting, visit the belligerents to confirm compliance, clarify any misunderstandings, and prepare the ground for subsequent meetings. Procedures for monitoring compliance, reporting violations, and making complaints must be included. Report results to higher headquarters.

In conclusion, the negotiator must be insistent but not belligerent; he should find out what the real issue is, as it may not be apparent. Do not threaten; it may backfire. And never, under any circumstances, provide unauthorized information to the other side.

Under no circumstances should military units participating in or supporting negotiations surrender equipment, documents, or rights afforded under pertinent agreements or ROE. They should remain neutral in all dealings with belligerent factions and not make promises or agreements that are not authorized or feasible.

PART IV

An Encyclopedia of Prominent NGOs and Federal Agencies Involved in MOOTW

Before, during, and even after deployment to MOOTW, military leaders and planners have to coordinate with a broad variety of NGOs/PVOs, IOs, U.S. federal agencies, and other organizations to achieve effective interagency cooperation. This often presents significant challenges due to organizational cultural differences; nevertheless, it is in the interest of all parties to learn as much as they can about one another, and be involved in the development of goals, priorities, and plans.

The following chapters are provided to facilitate parallel planning and multiechelon coordination and to promote a more comprehensive understanding of the agencies most prominently involved in MOOTW over the last seven years. The information contained in this part was accurate as of the time of publication. To obtain more current information, refer to the points of contact listed for each organization, or access the organization's web site. NGOs or PVOs that have web sites but are not listed here can be found using an Internet search engine or one of several "clearinghouse" web sites for NGOs. These are described in chapter 43.

Chapter 40

Nongovernmental and Private Voluntary Organizations

A nongovernmental organization (NGO) is a transnational organization of private citizens that maintains a consultative status with the Economic and Social Council of the United Nations. NGOs may be professional associations, foundations, multinational businesses, or simply groups with a common interest in humanitarian assistance activities (development and relief). NGO is a term normally used by non-U.S. organizations.

A private voluntary organization (PVO) is a nonprofit humanitarian assistance organization involved in development and relief activities. PVOs are normally U.S.-based. PVO and NGO are often used synonymously.

ACTION INTERNATIONALE CONTRE LA FAIM (INTERNATIONAL ACTION AGAINST HUNGER) (AICF)

Overview. AICF/USA was founded in 1985 as American Friends of AICF. It promotes local development efforts to help improve living standards and provides emergency assistance in Africa, Asia, and Central Europe. It focuses its efforts on health, drinking water, and agriculture-based income-generation projects. Its central criterion for assistance is need, without regard to race, religion, age, sex, or ethnic group.

Capabilities. AICF is available to provide agriculture and food production programs to improve agriculture-based income generation; to carry out disaster and emergency relief with health services, water supply, environmental sanitation, and shelter; to provide primary healthcare, health education, maternal and child healthcare, training, and supervision of primary healthcare services and primary healthcare facilities; and to provide potable water and sanitation.

Interagency Relationships. AICF/USA cooperates with local agencies and communities and the international aid community, including its sister organization, AICF/France. The organization is funded by private individuals, the Soros Humanitarian Fund for Bosnia-Herzegovina, the Christopher Reynolds Foundation, USAID, Britain's Overseas Development Administration, Oxfam/UK, UNICEF, and UNHCR.

Organization. AICF/USA is headquartered in Washington, D.C. It has four field offices based on specific target countries or programs; Cambodia, northeast Somalia, Bosnia-Herzegovina, and Rwanda.

Point of Contact. Action Internationale Contre la Faim/USA, 1511 K Street, N.W., Suite 1025, Washington, DC 20005

ADVENTIST DEVELOPMENT AND RELIEF AGENCY INTERNATIONAL (ADRA)

Overview. The Adventist Development and Relief Agency was established in 1983 as the humanitarian arm of the Seventh-Day Adventist (SDA) Church. ADRA works in more than 100 countries around the world in Asia, Africa, Eastern Europe, the South Pacific, and Central and South America.

Authority and Responsibilities. ADRA is an independent agency established by the SDA Church for the specific purposes of individual and community development and disaster relief.

Capabilities. ADRA is equipped to provide mother and child healthcare, AIDS and primary healthcare, growth monitoring, oral rehydration therapy, breast-feeding education, and immunization; to educate parents in nutrition, hygiene, child spacing, and child care; to provide supplementary food aid for pregnant women, preschool children, and nursing mothers; to develop infrastructure, schools, day-care centers, roads, hospitals, and bridges; to assist small-enterprise development and human resources development and training; to construct irrigation with deep-water wells, water reservoirs, irrigation systems, sewage and storm drainage projects, and potable water projects; to provide agricultural training for soil improvement and reforestation; and to maintain food, clothing, and shelter warehouses in Germany, Australia, Japan, Canada, the former Yugoslavia, the Philippines, and the United States (California and Maryland).

Interagency Relationships. ADRA cooperates with the USAID to receive food for distribution to developing countries and receives USAID reimbursement for ocean freight for shipment of food, clothing, bedding, medicines, and hospital and vocational equipment. The agency advises NGOs, PVOs, and advocacy groups. It operates with the Church World Service, United Nations (UNDP, UNHCR, World Food Programme [WFP], World Health Organization [WHO], and UNICEF), American Council for Voluntary International Action (InterAction), Australian Development

Assistance Bureau, Canadian International Development Agency, Cooperative for Assistance and Relief Everywhere, Danish International Development Agency, and the European Union. ADRA is funded by donor countries and government and international humanitarian agencies, as well as by public support from individuals and corporations.

Organization. ADRA is headquartered in Silver Spring, Maryland. Fieldwork is coordinated through 12 regional offices in Abidjan, Berne, Brasilia, Harare, Johannesburg, London, Miami, Moscow, Nicosia, Hosur (India), Singapore, and Sydney.

Point of Contact. Adventist Development and Relief Agency International, 12501 Old Columbia Pike, Silver Spring, MD 20904

Tel: (301) 680-6380; Fax: (301) 680-6370; Telex: 440186, SDAY-UI

E-mail: *74617.1652@compuserve.com*

Web site: *http://www.interaction.org/mb/adra.html*

AFRICARE

Overview. Africare is dedicated to improving the quality of life in rural Africa in five principal areas: agriculture, water resource development, environmental management, health, and emergency humanitarian aid. With a fiscal-year 1996 budget in excess of $35 million, more than 150 Africare programs reached 28 nations in northern, western, eastern, central, and southern Africa.

Africare works in all the major regions of the continent to assist in human and economic development by developing water resources, increasing food production, delivering basic health services, protecting the environment, and providing emergency assistance to refugees.

Capabilities. Africare works to construct rural access roads, buildings, irrigation, dams, wells, and health centers; to support production cooperatives, vegetable gardening, forestry, livestock, and poultry raising; to support fodder production and storage and reforestation and soil conservation; to supply blankets, high-protein foods, cooking utensils, and agricultural equipment to refugees; to supply oxen, animal traction equipment, and farm equipment and supplies for long-term development; to provide medicine and public health with family planning services; to provide pharmaceutical supplies and medical equipment and supplies, village-based primary healthcare services, medical distribution systems, comprehensive healthcare plans, dispensaries, maternal and child health centers, and village health team training; to meet short-term needs for potable water, medicine, healthcare, seeds, and tools; and to assist small business with credit, technical, advisory, and managerial assistance.

Interagency Relationships. Africare consults with African planners, field experts, village leaders, and workers and attends briefings between African ambassadors and U.S. leaders through the African Diplomatic Outreach Program, co-sponsored by Africare and the Georgetown University Institute for the Study of Diplomacy. Africare projects address the needs and involve the collaboration of the Africans they assist. Funding is derived from the governments of Canada, Great Britain, Switzerland, Guinea, Malawi, Niger, Nigeria, Zambia, Zimbabwe, and the United States (through USAID) from multinational organizations, such as the African Development Bank, the European Union's European Development Fund; from UN agencies, such as UNDP, WHO, UNICEF, and UNHCR; and from charitable foundations, corporations, the religious community, other private organizations, international agencies, foreign institutions, and private citizens. Africare is a member of International Service Agencies, a part of the Combined Federal Campaign, and is the recipient of many corporate as well as state and local government campaigns.

Organization. Africare is headquartered in Washington, D.C. It has field offices in 24 African countries: Angola, Benin, Burkina Faso, Central African Republic, Chad, Cote d'Ivoire, Eritrea, Ethiopia, Guinea, Guinea-Bissau, Liberia, Malawi, Mali, Mozambique, Namibia, Niger, Nigeria, Rwanda, Senegal, Sierra Leone, South Africa, Tanzania, Zambia, and Zimbabwe. Africare also has nine U.S. chapters: Chicago, Illinois; Columbia, Maryland; Columbus, Ohio; Detroit, Michigan; Los Angeles, California; McLean, Virginia; Milwaukee, Wisconsin; Seattle, Washington; and Tampa, Florida.

Point of Contact. Africare, Africare House, 440 R Street, N.W., Washington, DC 20001

    Tel: (202) 462-3614; Fax: (202) 387-1034

    Web site: *http://www.africare.org/*

AID WITHOUT BORDERS

Overview. Aid Without Borders was created by a group of Israelis with an unwavering commitment to promoting the fundamental need and basic right of individuals to receive meaningful and lasting assistance, and a profound desire to provide aid to individuals in situations of suffering and distress throughout the world because of circumstances beyond their control. The organization's activities vary widely both in type and in location, and they are all developed with careful attention to the stated needs of the local community the project will serve. All projects are designed to have the greatest impact in the long term, and they are developed in close coordination with local community authorities.

Capabilities. Aid Without Borders provides disaster relief and education and is concerned about issues related to the environment, health, poverty, and hunger.

Point of Contact. Aid Without Borders, P.O. Box 7255, Jerusalem, 91071, Israel

Tel: 972-2-5638375; Fax: 972-2-5638375

E-mail: *rwandety@eyetravel.org*

Web site: *http://www.eyetravel.org*

AMERICAN JEWISH WORLD SERVICE (AJWS)

Overview. American Jewish World Service is a nonprofit organization dedicated to providing nonsectarian humanitarian assistance, technical support and emergency relief to people in need in Africa, Asia, Latin America, the Middle East, Russia, and Ukraine. AJWS is guided by the principle that every human being has the basic right to food, shelter, health, and education. It works in partnership with local grassroots NGOs to support and implement small-scale self-sustaining international development projects. Through its Jewish Volunteer Corps, it also sends skilled Jewish men and women to volunteer in health, education, agriculture, and economic development projects throughout the developing world.

Capabilities. AJWS provides community service and volunteering; disaster relief; and economic development.

Point of Contact. American Jewish World Service, 989 Avenue of the Americas, 10th Floor, New York, NY, 10025

Tel: (800) 889-7146; Fax: (212) 736-3463

E-mail: *jul@jws.org*

Web site: *http://www.ajws.org*

AMERICAN RED CROSS (ARC)

Overview. The American Red Cross is a humanitarian organization led by volunteers. It provides relief to victims of disasters and helps people prevent, prepare for, and respond to emergencies. The ARC does this through services that are consistent with its congressional charter and the fundamental principles of the International Red Cross and Red Crescent Movement, of which it is a part.

Authority and Responsibilities. ARC is chartered by Congress (Act of Congress of 5 January 1905, as amended, 36 USC Sections 1–9) to undertake relief activities to mitigate the suffering caused by disasters. It is the only NGO chartered by Congress to provide relief to victims of major disasters.

Capabilities. The ARC is ready to position advanced communications equipment such as satellite uplinks, high-frequency radios, and cellular phones in disaster-prone areas; to train citizens to teach courses in everything from first aid, cardiopulmonary resuscitation, and water safety to proper nutrition and healthcare; to train disaster team members to help those in need with emergency shelters and food; to provide nurses for crucial education, disaster, and blood-related services; to provide biomedical services: blood for transfusion and tissue for transplantation, human bone, heart valves, veins, skin, tendons, and cartilage for transplantation, blood drives and tests for infectious diseases, biotherapeutics made from donated plasma for trauma and hemophilia, and a registry of rare blood donors and rare blood; to trace people, exchange Red Cross messages, and reunite family members separated by disaster, civil disturbance, or war; to support international relief efforts with personnel, financial aid, and gifts of goods and services; to provide refugee and immigrant language banks and health and safety courses in foreign languages; to assist members of the armed forces, their families, and veterans with emergency communications, to relay urgent messages to service personnel far from home, notify them of births, deaths, serious illnesses, and other family emergencies, verify information contained in requests for emergency leave, provide interest-free loans and grants for expenses related to emergency travel or personal crisis, and provide counseling, referrals, and other social services; to provide money to disaster and hazardous materials victims for essentials, repairs, transportation, household items, medicines, and shelter; to determine the level of damage to homes in a disaster; to provide hot meals to disaster-stricken communities and emergency workers; to move vehicles and supplies across the country; to interview individuals and families to assess their needs; to provide the media with information on the disaster and the ARC response; to provide computer, communications, or accounting support; to resolve inquiries from concerned family members outside the disaster area; and to provide mass care with emergency food, shelter, medicine, first aid, and long-term recovery assistance when victims exhaust other resources.

Interagency Relationships. The ARC works with the U.S. government and other organizations, including the American Psychological Association, American Counseling Association, and mental health professionals for counseling; the U.S. Centers for Disease Control and Prevention for HIV/AIDS education programs; FEMA's Family Protection Program to educate the American public about safety precautions and coping with disasters; the National Oceanic and Atmospheric Administration to educate the public about heat waves, winter storms, thunderstorms, and hurricanes; the Coast Guard through an agreement on "Cooperation during Disasters"; and the U.S. Geological Survey to educate the public about earthquakes.

Organization. The International Red Cross Movement encompasses the International Committee of the Red Cross, which acts to protect victims of armed conflict; and the International Federation of Red Cross and Red Crescent Societies which helps coordinate international relief efforts for disaster victims, displaced persons, and refugees. As an active member of the ICRC, the ARC supports the movement's mission to protect human life and relieve suffering worldwide.

The national headquarters of the ARC is located in Washington, D.C. There are almost 2,600 Red Cross chapters throughout all 50 states, U.S. possessions, and dependencies. Nearly every community in the United States has a Red Cross unit. Each unit has its own array of services and programs based on the needs of the community it serves. All Red Cross services are provided free of charge. The largest relief efforts are directed from the Disaster Operations Center in Alexandria, Virginia, which is ready to respond 24 hours a day. It typically launches a new relief operation about two times a week. In addition, the ARC has a national Quick Response Team that can deploy on four hours' notice.

Point of Contact. American Red Cross, 431 18th Street, N.W., Washington, DC 20006

Tel: (202) 737-8300

Web site: *http://www.crossnet.org/*

AMERICAN RESCUE TEAM INTERNATIONAL EPRC (ARTI)

Overview. Founded in 1985, the American Rescue Team International EPRC (ARTI) is a nonprofit, nonpolitical, NGO and an internationally recognized humanitarian rescue organization operating within the framework of the Geneva Convention and Protocols. Its purpose is to save lives, reduce suffering, and assist in the devastating aftermath caused by catastrophic events. The key point of lifesaving is its ability to respond to the unexpected. ARTI has worked most of the major disasters worldwide since 1985, earthquake, explosion, tornado, landslide, hurricane, mudslide, mine collapse, rockslide, water rescue, toxic cloud, firestorm, mountain rescue, and cave rescue. As of May 1996, ARTI had formed broad-based cooperative alliances with rescuers and rescue teams in 16 countries that unite the best resources and people to solve critical lifesaving and disaster problems.

Capabilities. ARTI provides disaster relief and addresses housing and homelessness and poverty and hunger.

Point of Contact. American Rescue Team International EPRC (ARTI), P.O. Box 489, Alameda, CA 94501

Tel: (510) 523-5493; Fax: (510) 523-5493
E-mail: *AmerRescue@aol.com*
Web site: *http://www.amerrescue.org*

CAREFORCE INTERNATIONAL
Overview. Careforce International focuses its energy and resources to meet the needs of children suffering from hunger, poverty, disease, illiteracy, abuse, and despair. Serving globally through national leadership and maintaining high standards of excellence, integrity, and accountability, Careforce demonstrates God's love by bringing hope through word and action.

Capabilities. Careforce serves children and youth, provides disaster relief, and alleviates poverty and hunger.

Point of Contact. Careforce International, 945 Syscon Road, Burlington, Ontario, L9A 3W6, Canada
Tel: (905) 639-8525; Fax: (905) 639-8482
E-mail: *info@careforceinternational.org*
Web site: *http://www.careforceinternational.org*

CATHOLIC RELIEF SERVICES (CRS)
Overview. Catholic Relief Services was founded in 1943 by the Catholic bishops of the United States to assist the poor and disadvantaged outside the United States. Its first project was to provide aid to refugees in Europe during World War II. The agency's principal mission is to alleviate human suffering, encourage human development, and foster charity and justice for poor and disadvantaged people around the world. Today, CRS is active in countries in Africa, Eastern Europe, the Middle East, Asia, Latin America, and the Caribbean.

Authority and Responsibilities. CRS serves as the overseas humanitarian and development agency of the U.S. Catholic Conference. The policies and programs of the agency reflect and express the teachings of the Catholic Church—assisting people on the basis of need, not creed, race, or nationality.

CRS draws its financial, material, and moral support from the Catholic community in the United States, but it also reaches out for support to individuals of many faiths and to governments and community organizations, foundations, corporations, and student groups.

Through education and advocacy, CRS is active in raising the awareness of governments, civil servants, intergovernmental organizations, and the public concerning issues of relief, reconciliation, rehabilitation, human development, and human rights outside the United States.

Capabilities. CRS is available to respond to victims of natural and man-made disasters, famine, epidemics, civil wars and unrest, and economic emergencies; to provide assistance to the poor to alleviate their immediate needs; to support self-help development programs of job-skills training, community development, poverty lending, education, and agricultural improvement; to assist refugees and displaced people with emergency relief, repatriation, and rehabilitation, as well as local reintegration and resettlement; to promote and support efforts aimed at conflict mitigation, reconciliation, justice, and peace; and to distribute lifesaving food and non-food emergency and medical supplies, as in its recent efforts in Haiti, the former Yugoslavia, Rwanda, Somalia, Burundi, and India.

Interagency Relationships. CRS is part of the U.S. Catholic Conference and is affiliated with the Interfaith Hunger Appeal, National Council of Catholic Women, and Italy's Caritas Internationalis, a network of national Caritas agencies worldwide. CRS is also a member of InterAction and has collective relationships with a number of other NGOs, PVOs, and UN agencies.

Organization. CRS is headquartered in Baltimore, Maryland. It has offices in 48 countries around the world through assistance directed to local project holders. The staff includes approximately 275 American personnel, half of whom work overseas. However, the majority of staff are nationals of countries in which the CRS works.

Point of Contact. Catholic Relief Services, 209 West Fayette Street, Baltimore, MD 21201-3443

Tel: (410) 625-2220

Web site: *http://www.catholicrelief.org*

CHILDREACH

Overview. Childreach is an international humanitarian, child-focused development organization without religious, political, or governmental affiliation. Child sponsorship is the basic foundation of the organization. Childreach's vision is of a world in which all children realize their full potential in societies that respect people's rights and dignity. Childreach strives to achieve lasting improvements in the quality of life of deprived children in developing countries through a process that unites people across cultures and adds meaning and value to their lives by enabling deprived children, their families, and their communities to meet their basic needs and to increase their ability to participate in and benefit from their societies; fostering relationships to increase understanding and unity among peoples of different cultures and countries; and promoting the rights and interests of the world's children.

Capabilities. Childreach focuses on children and youth, economic development, and poverty and hunger.

Point of Contact. Childreach, 155 Plan Way, Warwick, RI 02886
Tel: (800) 556-7918; Fax: (401) 738-5608
E-mail: *sookikis@plan.geis.com*
Web site: *http://www.childreach.org*

CHILDREN'S CUP INTERNATIONAL RELIEF

Overview. Children's Cup International Relief is a Christian response to international disaster and relief for needy people with an emphasis on children in hard places.

Capabilities. Children's Cup addresses children and youth, disaster relief, poverty and hunger, religion, and veterans of wars.

Point of Contact. Children's Cup International Relief, 121 North Iowa Avenue, Eagle Grove, IA 50533
Tel: (515) 448-5110; Fax: (515) 448-3720
E-mail: *ohlerking@childrenscup.org*
Web site: *http://www.childrenscup.org*

CHRISTIAN CHILDREN'S FUND

Overview. Under the Judeo-Christian ethic of helping one's neighbor without regard to race, creed, nationality, or gender, Christian Children's Fund and its international associated organizations are dedicated to serving the needs of children worldwide—primarily through person-to-person programs, in the context of family and community, and using a developmental approach through national and local partners.

Capabilities. Christian Children's Fund deals with children and youth, education, health, and poverty and hunger.

Point of Contact. Christian Children's Fund, 2821 Emerywood Parkway, Richmond, VA, 23261
Tel: (804) 756-2700; Fax: (804) 756-2738
E-mail: *warrenf@ccfusa.org*
Web site: *http://www.christianchildrensfund.org*

CONCERN WORLDWIDE LIMITED

Overview. CONCERN Worldwide Limited was created in response to the 1968 Biafran famine to provide humanitarian relief and development assistance to disaster-afflicted people and to those whose vulnerability is due to inadequate income, education, and access to power—the "poorest of the poor."

CONCERN feeds the hungry, works for the development and improvement of conditions of extreme poverty, and provides emergency and rehabilitation programs to rebuild shattered communities in the least developed countries, as defined by the United Nations. Within these countries, it targets the urban poor, refugees, and disadvantaged women and children.

Capabilities. CONCERN is equipped to assess relief needs, identify required resources, and ensure fair distribution of supplies; to train members of the community, who in turn pass their newly acquired knowledge and skills in agriculture, crafts, hygiene, and public health to their neighbors; to provide sanitation and water supply services; to assist women to become more economically independent through job skills, health, credit, and training facilities; to help farmers learn new skills and techniques in agriculture, horticulture, forestry, fertilizers, and pesticides; to provide credit schemes and seed and repair and replace damaged agricultural tools; to construct roads, bridges, clinics, schools, public buildings, and low-cost housing; to monitor nutrition in its countries of operation, scientifically assess the nutritional status of populations at risk for starvation, and distribute emergency rations; to help mothers recognize infection and take appropriate action; to operate prenatal clinics and vaccination programs; and to provide healthcare worker training.

Interagency Relationships. CONCERN cooperates with other humanitarian agencies and local governments. Funding is received from the governments of Ireland, Great Britain, France, and Tanzania; the European Union (EU) and the EU's Humanitarian Office; the UNDP, UNHCR, UNICEF, and WPF; and USAID.

Organization. Areas of operation are African and Asian countries, including Angola, Bangladesh, Cambodia, Ethiopia, Kenya, Laos, Mozambique, Rwanda, Somalia, Sudan, Tanzania, and Uganda. CONCERN is also involved in Haiti in its first long-term project in the Caribbean. In each country, a field director oversees the work of volunteers and local staff.

CONCERN is headquartered in Dublin, Ireland. An affiliate, CONCERN Worldwide USA, is based in New York. Its Belfast-based subsidiary, CONCERN Worldwide (UK) Limited, operates in Northern Ireland and Great Britain. *Note:* CONCERN Worldwide Limited should not be confused with Center of Concern in Washington, D.C.; CONCERN/America in Santa Ana, California, or World Concern in Seattle, Washington.

Points of Contact. CONCERN Worldwide Limited, Camden Street, Dublin 2, Ireland

Web site: *http://www.concern.ie/*
CONCERN Worldwide USA, 104 East 40th Street, Room 903, New York, NY 10016
Tel: (800) 59-CONCERN or (212) 557-8000; Fax: (212) 557-8004
E-mail: *swalshkoc@aol.com*
Web site: *http://www.irishnet.com/concern/*

COOPERATIVE FOR ASSISTANCE AND RELIEF EVERYWHERE (CARE)

Overview. CARE was founded to aid victims of World War II in Europe and, soon after, Asia. CARE USA, CARE Canada, and CARE Deutschland joined together to create CARE International in 1982. CARE International is a confederation of 11 national CARE partners that addresses poverty and responds to emergencies worldwide. CARE currently has 128 health and population projects in 40 countries, 140 income projects in 40 countries, 55 emergency relief and rehabilitation projects in 25 countries, and 15 education projects in 10 countries. Some 400,000 individuals, 300 U.S. corporations, and dozens of private foundations, and government and international organizations support CARE.

CARE's purpose is to help the developing world's poor in their efforts to achieve social and economic well-being. It supports processes that create competence and lead to self-sustainment over time. CARE's task is to reach new standards of excellence in offering disaster relief, technical assistance, training, food, and other material resources and management in combinations appropriate to local needs and priorities. It also advocates public policies and programs that support these ends.

Capabilities. CARE is available to assist agricultural and environmental efforts to plant trees, manage forests, irrigate land, start vegetable gardens, conserve soil, promote natural pesticides, and build fish ponds and to lend on-site technical advice on improving production; to supply clean and plentiful water, nutritious food, immunizations, improved sanitation, AIDS prevention counseling, and healthcare for pregnant women and new mothers; to offer family planning and other reproductive healthcare services; to support small businesses with loans, training in basic accounting and bookkeeping, and savings for future investments; to deliver emergency aid, clothing, clean water, medicine, tools, and food; and to handle requests for commodities from CARE country offices, negotiate grants for U.S. government funds, deliver food to CARE countries worldwide, track food supplies overseas, and ensure that supplies reach their destination safely and are used in ways that best promote self-sufficiency.

Interagency Relationships. CARE programs are partnerships, carried out under agreements among NGOs, PVOs, national government agencies, local communities, the UNHCR, WFP, UNICEF, the Peace Corps, USAID, and foreign governments (especially the government of the Netherlands).

CARE requires a written basic agreement with the host government of every country where it establishes a presence to secure a broad legal base for its projects. The basic agreement is always augmented by specific project activity agreements that outline the terms of each project.

Organization. CARE International is headquartered in Brussels, Belgium. CARE USA is the U.S. partner in CARE International. In the regular course of its operations, CARE USA makes certain grants to CARE International and its member organizations, and likewise receives certain funding from members of CARE International. CARE USA's headquarters is in Atlanta, Georgia. CARE USA also has 15 regional offices located in New York, New York; Concord, Massachusetts; Philadelphia, Pennsylvania; Washington, D.C.; Chicago, Illinois; Minneapolis, Minnesota; Atlanta, Georgia; Miami, Florida; Dallas, Texas; Houston, Texas; Denver, Colorado; Kansas City, Missouri; Los Angeles, California; San Francisco, California; and Seattle, Washington.

CARE USA operates in over 50 developing nations in Asia, Africa, and Latin America. Each country with a CARE mission is represented by a CARE country director, acting country director, or representative. To coordinate operations, one CARE partner within CARE International is designated the "lead member" in each country represented by CARE. CARE USA is the lead member of CARE International in over 30 nations.

Points of Contact. CARE International, Boulevard du Regent 58/ 10, B-1000 Brussels Belgium

CARE USA, 151 Ellis Street, N.E., Atlanta, GA 30303

Tel: (800) 521-CARE

E-mail: *info@care.org*

Web site: *http://www.care.org*

CARE USA Regional and Liaison Office, 2025 I Street, N.W., Suite 1024, Washington, DC 20006

FOOD FOR THE HUNGRY INTERNATIONAL (FHI)

Overview. Food for the Hungry International is an organization of Christian motivation working to end physical and spiritual hunger in more than 25 countries in Africa, Asia, and Latin America through disaster relief and integrated self-help development programs. Because children often suffer the most from poverty, FHI focuses on their special needs. Program areas include agriculture, health, clean water resources, microenterprise development, education, child sponsorship, and spiritual nurturing.

Capabilities. FHI focuses on religion, poverty and hunger, and disaster relief.

Point of Contact. Food for the Hungry International, 7729 East Greenway Road, Scottsdale, AZ 85260

    Tel: (800) 2-HUNGER (248-6437); Fax: (602) 998-4806

    E-mail: *hunger@fh.org*

    Web site: *http://www.fh.org*

GLOBAL DEVELOPMENT CENTER

Overview. The Global Development Center is a nonreligious, nonprofit, nonpolitical organization dedicated to providing development and relief assistance wherever it is required by working with local organizations to directly help those who need assistance.

Capabilities. The Global Development Center specializes in community service and volunteering, disaster relief, and economic development.

Point of Contact. Global Development Center, 1250 24th Street, N.W. Suite 300, Washington, D.C. 20037

    Tel: (202) 467-8366; Fax: (202) 467-2793

    E-mail: *center@globaldevelopment.org*

    Web site: *http://www.globaldevelopment.org/*

GLOBAL SOLUTIONS

Overview. Global Solutions is a nonprofit service that offers consultation to other nonprofits on domestic and international emergency planning, crisis management, disaster and civil emergency, kidnapping and recovery, and safety issues for staff and volunteers. All consultations are free of charge, confidential, and closely held. Global Solutions emphasizes written plans and policies as a way of better handling unexpected emergencies. Global Solutions will also advise senior management and, if desired, participate in crisis management.

Capabilities. Global Solutions consults on disaster relief and peace and conflict resolution.

Point of Contact. Global Solutions, 3607 Van Ness Street, N.W., Washington, DC 20008

    Tel: (202) 277-4742

    E-mail: *paladin@consulting.org*

GLOBAL VOLUNTEERS

Overview. Global Volunteers, a private nonprofit international development organization, was founded in 1984 with the goal of establishing a foundation for peace through mutual international understanding. Its programs center around one-, two-, or three-week work experiences in Asia, Africa, the Americas, the Caribbean, or Europe. At the request of local leaders and indigenous host organizations, Global Volunteers sends teams of volunteers to live and work with local people on human and economic development projects identified by the community as important to its long-term development. In this way, the volunteers' energy, creativity, and labor are put to use, and they gain a genuine, firsthand understanding of how other people live day to day.

Capabilities. Global Volunteers addresses children and youth, community building and renewal, community service and volunteering, economic development, the environment, health, housing and homelessness, multiservice community agency, peace and conflict resolution, race and ethnicity, and rural issues.

Point of Contact. Global Volunteers, 375 East Little Canada Road, St. Paul, MN 55117

Tel: (800) 487-1074; Fax: (612) 482-0915

E-mail: *E-mail@globalvolunteers.org*

Web site: *http://www.globalvolunteers.org*

GRASSROOTS INTERNATIONAL

Overview. Grassroots International is an independent development information agency that channels humanitarian aid to democratic social change movements in the Third World. The partnerships it builds at the grassroots level provide it with a unique basis to inform the U.S. public about Third World conflicts and crises and the U.S. role in them. Grassroots International is supported entirely by private donations. It provides cash grants and material aid to more than 30 community-based organizations in Africa, the Middle East, Asia, Latin America, and the Caribbean. It offers poor and disenfranchised people the resources to make use of their own creativity and power. Grassroots International believes that people know their own communities, understand their own needs, and, with a little support, can solve their own problems.

Capabilities. Grassroots International addresses civil liberties and human rights, community building and renewal, disaster relief, education, farming and agriculture, health, mental health, job training and workplace issues, peace and conflict resolution, poverty and hunger, voting and democracy, and women's issues.

Point of Contact. Grassroots International, 179 Boylston Street, 4th Floor, Boston, MA 02130

Tel: (617) 524-1400; Fax: (617) 524-5525

E-mail: *grassroots@igc.apc.org*

INTERNATIONAL ACTION CENTER

Overview. The International Action Center coordinates activism and information opposing domestic and international injustices, including U.S./UN sanctions, U.S./NATO expansion, the Cuba blockade, Pentagon global military incursions, racism, homophobia, workfare and other anti-labor legislation, anti-immigrant laws, the death penalty, and environmental pollution from depleted uranium. The center publishes books, produces videos, organizes forums, and supports activists and activities relevant to its mission.

Capabilities. The International Action Center focuses on civil liberties and human rights, environment, and poverty and hunger.

Point of Contact. International Action Center, 39 West 14th Street, #206, New York, NY 10011

Tel: (212) 633-6646; Fax: (212) 633-2889

E-mail: *iacenter@iacenter.org*

Web site: *http://www.iacenter.org*

INTERNATIONAL AID, INC.

Overview. International Aid provides food, health, and hope in the name of Christ to those in need in the United States and throughout the developing world. In 1997, it provided assistance to over 160 countries, collaborating with thousands of partners to keep costs down and leverage donors' dollars. It has 40 employees and 750 direct volunteers. It moves $40 million in gifts-in-kind with $4 million total overhead.

Capabilities. International Aid deals with children and youth, disaster relief, and health.

Point of Contact. International Aid, Inc., 17011 Hickory, Spring Lake, MI 49456

Tel: (616) 846-7490; Fax: (616) 846-3842

E-mail: *intlaid@xc.org*

Web site: *http://www.internationalaid.org/*

INTERNATIONAL FOOD CONGRESS

Overview. The International Food Congress is composed of farmers, peasants, and workers committed to the end of hunger and environmental degradation. Members see their actions as directed toward feeding people rather than creating profit, and they see their role on earth as spiritual caretakers of the earth and its people. The direct, local action of individuals and groups is emphasized in creating and developing a spiritual connection to the earth and to the food supply. The organization receives no governmental support or approval and seeks none from any government, corporation, or foundation. Membership is free.

Capabilities. The International Food Congress is concerned with poverty and hunger, farming and agriculture, and the environment.

Point of Contact. International Food Congress, P.O. Box 15, Hallsville, MO 65255

Tel: (573) 696-1058

E-mail: *hunger@tmn.com*

INTERNATIONAL MEDICAL CORPS (IMC)

Overview. The International Medical Corps was founded in 1984 to address the critical need for medical care in war-torn Afghanistan. Its charter is to help people become self-sufficient. Volunteer physicians and medical personnel provide emergency medical relief, healthcare services, and training to people in devastated regions worldwide where health resources are scarce and few organizations dare to serve. The IMC provides humanitarian assistance and helps rebuild healthcare systems devastated by war and disaster. It conducts programs of public awareness of human suffering and acts of atrocity throughout the world through testimony, published reports, and visual images.

Capabilities. The IMC is available to dispense teams of qualified doctors, nurses, physician assistants, medics, logisticians, and support staff to help rebuild healthcare systems and restore self-sufficiency; to train people to diagnose and treat common diseases, disorders, and injuries encountered within their country; to train vaccinators, traditional birth attendants, village health workers, and trauma and emergency medicine specialists; to conduct efforts in child mental health, "cold chain" vaccine management, immunization, health assessments, maternal and child healthcare, midwifery and obstetrics/gynecology, nutrition and sanitation management, and tuberculosis control; and to treat war-related injuries.

Interagency Relationships. Partnerships with local health workers, community leaders, and village elders provide a self-sustaining healthcare system that can flourish independent of international relief efforts. IMC is funded by individuals, foundations, corporations, UNHCR, USAID/OFDA, WHO, UNICEF, the European Union's Humanitarian Office, the Overseas Development Administration (UK), Soros Humanitarian Fund, and Swedish International Development Authority.

Organization. IMC is headquartered in Los Angeles, California. It has five regional offices that are located in Brussels, Belgium; London, England; Nairobi, Kenya; Split, Croatia; and Windhoek, Namibia.

Point of Contact. International Medical Corps, 12233 West Olympic Boulevard, Suite 280, Los Angeles, CA 90064

Tel: (310) 826-7800; Fax: (310) 442-6620

E-mail: *imc@imc-la.com*

Web site: *http://www.imc-la.com*

INTERNATIONAL ORGANIZATION FOR MIGRATION (IOM)

Overview. The International Organization for Migration was created to deal with the problem of displaced persons and refugees in Europe after World War II. As problems of voluntary and forced movement of people increased, its work expanded worldwide. The IOM provides technical assistance and advisory services to promote the orderly transfer of refugees, displaced persons, and other individuals compelled to leave their homelands, as well as nationals who desire to migrate to countries where they may achieve independence through their employment. It also works to advance the economic, social, and cultural conditions of the receiving countries.

Capabilities. The IOM is equipped to recruit, select, and process migrants; to provide language training, orientation activities, medical examinations, and document processing for placement, reception, and integration into the host country; to respond to emergencies through its Emergency Response Unit for assessing complex emergency migration situations; and to maintain an emergency response roster of internal and external personnel for emergency operations or for urgent dispatch to the field.

Interagency Relationships. The IOM cooperates on migration assistance at the request of or with the agreement of interested nations and in coordination with regional and international organizations, NGOs, PVOs, and the UN Department of Humanitarian Affairs. Major partners include the Economic and Social Commission for Asia and the Pacific, Economic Commission for Latin America and the Caribbean, International Labour Organization, WHO, International Bank for Reconstruction and Development, International Maritime Organization, Council of European Communities,

OAS, Inter-American Development Bank, Italian–Latin American Institute, and ICRC.

UN agencies with which the IOM has strong bonds include the UN Economic Commission for Africa; UN Disaster Relief Coordinator; UN Conference on Trade and Development; UNDP; UN Center for Human Rights; UN Population Fund; UN Research Institute for Social Development; Food and Agriculture Organization of the UN; UN Educational, Scientific, and Cultural Organization; UN Industrial Development Organization; and UNHCR.

Organization. IOM headquarters is in Switzerland, and it has over 70 field offices in 52 member and 40 nonmember and/or observer countries. U.S. field offices are located in Washington, D.C.; New York, New York; San Francisco, California; Rosemont, Illinois; and Miami Springs, Florida.

Points of Contact. International Organization for Migration, 17 route des Morrilons, C.P. 71, CH 1211 Geneva 19 Switzerland
    Tel: (41 22) 717-9111; Fax: (41 22) 798-6150
    E-mail: *hq@iom.int*
    Press relations: (41 22) 717-9418
    Web site: *http://www.iom.ch*

INTERNATIONAL RESCUE COMMITTEE (IRC)

Overview. The International Rescue Committee was founded in 1933 to assist opponents of Hitler. Its first mission was to rescue people in Europe from Nazi oppression and find them new homes in free countries. Today, the IRC's mission is to help victims of racial, religious, and ethnic persecution and oppression, as well as people uprooted by war and violence. Since its inception, the committee's work has evolved to include the assistance of displaced people within their own borders and refugees during repatriation.

Capabilities. The IRC is available to provide refugee relief services in sanitation, medical services, food, training, education, and income-generating and self-reliance projects; to train refugees to be community workers as the first line of defense against diseases, epidemics, and malnutrition (training individuals to be health educators, birth attendants, midwives, immunization teams, paramedics, physicians assistants, and nursing aides); to provide educational support for preschool, primary, and secondary education and specialized courses in teacher training, public administration, math, science, health education, engineering, and language development; to encourage self-sufficiency through self-reliance training, income generation, and leadership development; to preserve the cultural and community values of those uprooted and respect for the authority of community leaders; and to resettle refugees into American society, provide basic needs—food, shelter, and clothing—and help refugees become self-sufficient by teaching them English and new job skills and finding employment opportunities.

Interagency Relationships. The IRC cooperates with the Bureau for Refugee Programs of the U.S. Department of State, Office of Refugee Resettlement of the U.S. Department of Health and Human Services, USAID and OFDA, Immigration and Naturalization Service of the U.S. Department of Justice, USIA, UNHCR, UNDP, Food and Agriculture Organization of the UN, UNICEF, UN Fund for Women, WFP, International Organization for Migration, and European Union. IRC programs are coordinated with many private groups, especially the American Council for Voluntary Action (InterAction) and its Subcommittee for Refugee and Migration Affairs. The IRC communicates with the National Security Council and officials of the U.S. Departments of State and Defense, the media, human rights groups, and related organizations.

Organization. The IRC is headquartered in New York City. It has 15 domestic offices in Atlanta, Georgia; Boston, Massachusetts; Dallas, Texas; Los Angeles, California; Miami, Florida; New York, New York; San Diego, California; San Francisco, California; San Jose, California; Fresno, California; Sacramento, California; Santa Ana, New Mexico; Seattle, Washington; Washington, D.C.; and West New York, New Jersey. The committee has eight offices abroad in Madrid, Spain; Rome, Italy; Paris, France; Geneva, Switzerland; Vienna, Austria; Zagreb and Split, Croatia; and Moscow, Russia.

Point of Contact. International Rescue Committee, 122 East 42nd Street, New York, NY 10168

Tel: (212) 551-3000; Fax: (212) 551-3184

E-mail: *barbs@intrescom.org*

Web site: *http://www.irc@intrescom.org*

LUTHERAN WORLD RELIEF (LWR)

Overview. Lutheran World Relief was founded in 1945 to help Europeans displaced by World War II. Today, LWR works in the field of overseas development and relief on behalf of the Evangelical Lutheran Church in America and the Lutheran Church–Missouri Synod. LWR provides food, medicine, clothing, and shelter to alleviate human suffering resulting from natural disaster, war, social conflict, or poverty. It acts in partnership with local organizations to support the poor and oppressed of less-developed countries as they try to meet basic human needs and participate with dignity and equity in their communities.

Capabilities. LWR is ready to pledge cash on behalf of local organizations and the Lutheran World Federation to provide medicine, food, clothing, and shelter; to send clothing and relief supplies from its U.S. warehouses; to train in management, project planning, and evaluation; to provide water and soil management, build wells, introduce dry-season gardening, and plant trees; and to strengthen the leadership role of women, offering literacy and vocational education and village healthcare training.

Interagency Relationships. LWR cooperates with humanitarian agencies, governmental and nongovernmental organizations, religious and secular agencies, international and regional organizations, and local implementing partners in the following countries: Angola, Bangladesh, Botswana, Cambodia, Croatia, Dominican Republic, El Salvador, Eritrea, Ethiopia, Haiti, India, Israel, Kenya, Liberia, Malawi, Mauritania, Mozambique, Nepal, Peru, Swaziland, Tanzania, Uganda, Venezuela, Zambia, and Zimbabwe. LWR is funded through the International Service Agencies, a work-place fund-raising federation. LWR participates in a number of workplace employee campaigns, including the Combined Federal Campaign; state, county, and municipal campaigns; and in the private sector. It receives significant donations from individuals, foundations, and USAID.

Organization. LWR is headquartered in New York City. Regional offices are in Quito, Ecuador; Nairobi, Kenya; and Niamey, Niger.

Point of Contact. Lutheran World Relief, 390 Park Avenue South, New York, NY 10016

Tel: (212) 532-6350; Fax: (212) 213-6081

E-mail: *lwr@lwr.org*

Web site: *http://www.lwr.org*

MEDECINS SANS FRONTIERES (MSF) (DOCTORS WITHOUT BORDERS)

Overview. Medecins Sans Frontieres, translated as Doctors Without Borders, was established in 1971 by doctors to offer emergency medical assistance wherever man-made or natural disasters occur, independently of all states, institutions, and political, economic, and religious influences, and irrespective of race, religion, creed, or political affiliation. Annually, more than 2,000 volunteers representing 45 nationalities work in some 80 countries in front-line hospitals, refugee camps, disaster sites, towns, and villages. MSF operates with strict neutrality and impartiality, unhindered freedom in the exercise of its functions, and respect for its professional code of ethics.

Capabilities. MSF is prepared to initiate field missions to cope with war, massive population movements, famine, or natural disasters; to send fact-finding teams to assess emergency needs; to deploy medical teams and logistics experts with specially designed, prepacked equipment; to provide health facilities, feeding centers and sanitation, vaccinations, and epidemiological surveillance in refugee camps; to deliver customized kits for shelter, communications, water and waste processing, sanitation, food, and power supplies; to store emergency logistics in areas at high risk; to rehabilitate hospitals and dispensaries, to establish rural health units, immunization programs, and sanitation facilities, and to train local medical, paramedical, and technical personnel; to provide quasi-permanent aid in countries where conflict, food shortages, and population movements are recurring phenomena, or where the immediate emergencies have ended but rehabilitation needs are still massive; to use logistical centers in Amsterdam, Bordeaux, and Brussels to purchase, test, and store equipment such as vehicles, communication equipment, water and sanitation equipment, surgical instruments, shelters, and tools; and to dispatch equipment kits from centers in Kenya, Thailand, and Costa Rica for more than 60 different kinds of emergencies.

Interagency Relationships. MSF cooperates with local health authorities and various international agencies, such as the UNDP, UNICEF, WHO, and UNHCR in refugee camps.

Organization. MSF is a network of 6 operational centers (Amsterdam, Barcelona, Brussels, Geneva, Luxembourg, and Paris), 12 delegate offices (Australia, Austria, Canada, Denmark, Germany, Greece, Hong Kong, Italy, Japan, Sweden, the United Kingdom, and the United States), and the Brussels-based international office. During emergencies or major crises, the operational centers combine forces, recruiting and dispatching volunteers as well as coordinating logistical support and finances with those in charge of operations. Each operational center is supported by logistics, medical, human resources, financial, communications, and fund-raising departments. The 12 delegate offices are responsible for recruitment, public advocacy, and fund-raising.

Point of Contact. Doctors Without Borders USA, Inc., 6 East 39th Street, 8th floor, New York, NY 10016

Tel: (212) 679-6800; Fax: (212) 679-7016

E-mail: *dwb@newyork.msf.org*

MERCY CORPS INTERNATIONAL

Overview. Mercy Corps is a nonprofit, voluntary agency that exists to assist the world's suffering, impoverished, and oppressed through emergency relief, self-help projects, and development education. Mercy Corps strives to promote self-reliance, productivity, and human dignity. Guided by

Christian values, Mercy Corps International seeks to motivate and educate the public about the plight of the poor and to work for peace and social justice. Since 1979, Mercy Corps International has provided over $300 million in assistance to more than 50 countries. Mercy Corps is known nationally and internationally for its quick-response, high-impact programs. Over 92 percent of the agency's resources are allocated directly to programs that help the poor. In 1998, Mercy Corps assisted families in Bosnia-Herzegovina, Kosovo, Macedonia, Lebanon, the West Bank and Gaza, North Korea, the Philippines, Honduras, Nicaragua, Afghanistan, Pakistan, Azerbaijan, Kazakhstan, Kyrgyzstan, Tajikistan, and Uzbekistan.

Capabilities. Mercy Corps provides emergency relief that assists people afflicted by conflict or disaster; sustainable community development that focuses on the needs of children and their care-givers, including microenterprise, agriculture and the environment, special education and literacy, and infrastructure and housing reconstruction; civil society initiatives that promote citizen participation, accountability, nonviolent conflict resolution, and the rule of law.

Point of Contact. Mercy Corps International, 3030 SW First Avenue, Portland, OR 97201

Tel: (503) 796-6800; Fax: (503) 796-6844

E-mail: *info@mercycorps.org*

Web site: *http://www.mercycorps.org*

MERCY SHIPS

Overview. Mercy Ships uses oceangoing vessels to bring spiritual and physical healing to the poor and needy in port cities around the world. The ministry encourages societal change by following Christ's example, mobilizing volunteers to serve others through medical and dental care, relief, community development, training, and evangelism.

Capabilities. Mercy Ships focuses on health, poverty and hunger, and religion.

Point of Contact. Mercy Ships, Highway 110 FM 16, Garden Valley, TX 75771

Tel: (903) 882-0887; Fax: (903) 882-0336

E-mail: *vanderwa@mercyships.org*

Web site: *http://www.mercyships.org*

NORTHWEST MEDICAL TEAMS INTERNATIONAL

Overview. Northwest Medical Teams International is a volunteer-driven agency expressing Christ's love to all people, locally and internationally, through disaster response, humanitarian assistance, and community development programs.

Capabilities. Northwest Medical Teams concentrates on children and youth, disaster relief, and health.

Point of Contact. Northwest Medical Teams International, 6955 SW Sandburg Street, Portland, OR 97223

Tel: (503) 624-1000; Fax: (503) 624-1001

E-mail: *nwmti@transport.com*

Web site: *http://www.nwmti.org*

OXFAM INTERNATIONAL (OI)

Overview. OI is a partnership of NGOs from 10 countries. It was established to allow the maximum impact to be made with available resources. Oxfam aims to relieve poverty, distress, and suffering throughout the world and to educate the public about the nature, causes, and effects of poverty. Through close collaboration among members, OI can have a far greater effect on these fundamental issues than could be achieved working separately. Although it will take time to organize this joint venture, significant results have already been achieved.

Capabilities. OI works to provide food, water, and shelter to people during natural disasters; to assist migrants with reception, short-term assistance, and housing; to assist people in their efforts to gain economic self-sufficiency; to administer charitable programs and link them to overseas aid efforts; to operate relief and development projects in agriculture, health, and education; and to market goods produced by small community groups in developing countries.

Interagency Relationships. Oxfam enjoys official relations with WHO and holds consultative status with the United Nations' Economic and Social Council. It has links with the Commonwealth Secretariat, European Development Fund, Global Information and Early Warning System on Food and Agriculture, International Bank for Reconstruction and Development, International Fund for Agricultural Development, UNHCR, WFP, the UN Relief and Works Agency for Palestine Refugees in the Near East, International Federation of Red Cross and Red Crescent Societies, and European Union. It cooperates with many NGOs and PVOs, including the Agency for Cooperation and Research in Development, African Medical and Research Foundation, Africa Network for Integrated Development, Aga Khan Foundation, Arab Women's Solidarity Association, Asian Disaster Preparedness Centre, Caribbean Organization of Indigenous Peoples, Catholic Fund for Overseas Development, Indian Council of South America, Latin American Association for Human Rights, PANOS Institute, Register of Engineers of Economic and Social Research, and Water, Engineering and Development Centre. *Organization.* The Oxfam International Secretariat is a small staff that coordinates communication and cooperation among the 11 members from its base in Oxford, UK. Each of the member organizations maintains its own staff. The Washington Advocacy Office, set up in 1995 with a staff of three, lobbies the World Bank, the International Monetary Fund, and the United Nations on issues agreed by the 11 members.

Points of Contact. Oxfam International Secretariat, 2nd floor, Prama House, 267 Banbury Road, Oxford, OX2 7HT UK

Tel: (44 1865) 31 39 39; Fax: (44 1865) 31 39 35

E-mail: *administration@oxfaminternational.org*

Web site: *http://www.oxfaminternational.org*

Oxfam International Advocacy, 1511 K Street, Suite 640, Washington, DC 20005

Tel: (202) 783-3331; Fax: (202) 783-5547

E-mail: *oxfamintdc@igc.apc.org*

Web site: *http://www.oxfaminternational.org*

REFUGEES INTERNATIONAL (RI)

Overview. Refugees International was founded in 1979 in Japan in response to the forced repatriation of thousands of Indo-Chinese refugees. It provides early warning in crises of mass exodus. RI also serves as an advocate for refugees. Since 1990, RI has moved from its original focus on Indo-Chinese refugees to refugee crises worldwide.

RI's mission is to bring refugees' plight to international attention. Unlike other NGOs and PVOs, RI concentrates exclusively on advocacy for refugee protection. RI is not a relief agency. It responds only to life-threatening emergencies that, in its view, are not being handled adequately by other organizations.

Capabilities. RI is available to launch a refugee emergency action mission to assess a crisis on-site and galvanize governments and international organizations to step in with lifesaving measures; to apprise policy makers about looming refugee emergencies; to make reliable recommendations for action; to pave the way for relief agencies and human rights organizations to intervene with lifesaving measures; and to promote better coordination and collaboration among operating voluntary agencies.

Interagency Relationships. Whenever refugees are in danger, RI attempts to spur governments, the United Nations, and voluntary agencies into action.

Organization. RI is headquartered in Washington, D.C. It is incorporated in the United States and maintains an office in Europe.

Point of Contact. Refugees International, 2639 Connecticut Avenue N.W., Suite 202, Washington, DC 20008

Tel: (202) 828-0110; Fax: (202) 828-0819

E-mail: *ri@refintl.org*

Web site: *http://www.refintl.org*

SAVE THE CHILDREN

Overview. Save the Children is a relief and development organization dedicated to improving the lives and futures of needy children and their families. From preventive healthcare to early childhood education, relief and rehabilitation to economic development, Save the Children's programs promote self-sufficiency and self-determination so that positive changes become permanent improvements.

Authority and Responsibilities. The UN Convention on the Rights of the Child and the 1923 Declaration of the Rights of the Child are the basis of Save the Children's work to ensure that children are the first to receive relief in times of distress and are protected against every form of exploitation. Emphasis is placed on early childhood development, primary and non-formal education, and care for children in especially difficult circumstances, but not necessarily for only the poorest.

Capabilities. Save the Children is equipped to provide emergency relief, including food, during major disasters and refugee migrations; to promote long-term development efforts with disabled children, disadvantaged children, and women, including literacy and skills training; to establish food security, distribution, transport management, and logistics; to provide healthcare management, refugee healthcare and healthcare management, health planning, epidemiology, "cold chain" management of vaccines, and nutritional surveillance; to develop social policy, juvenile justice, and legal reform; and to carry out community development by community-based rehabilitation, education, management of water resources, hydrogeological surveys, village-level maintenance of water facilities, water pump location and installation, and bridge and road building and repair.

Interagency Relationships. Save the Children cooperates with humanitarian agencies, government and intergovernmental organizations, other worldwide NGOs and PVOs, and communities and families.

Organization. Save the Children Federation, the U.S. member of the Save the Children Alliance, is located in Westport, Connecticut. Throughout the United States and in the 40 countries where Save the Children sponsors children and provides programs, field offices serve as the primary contact for program operations.

Save the Children Fund (UK), the oldest and currently the largest member of the alliance, is headquartered in London. A country program is coordinated by a field director. A network of regional offices provides technical support and advice to field offices.

The International Save the Children Alliance acts as a clearinghouse of information for the 25 members of the alliance.

Points of Contact. Save the Children Federation (U.S.), 54 Wilton Road, Westport, CT 06880

Tel: (203) 221-4000; Fax: (203) 227-5667

E-mail: *http://www.savethechildren.org/email.html*

Web site: *http://www.savethechildren.org/*

Save the Children Fund (UK), 17 Grove Lane, Camberwell SE5 8RD London UK

Tel: (44 171) 703-5400; Fax: (44 171) 703-2278

Web site: *http://www.scfuk.org.uk*

International Save the Children Alliance Web site:
http://www.savethechildren.org/alliance.html

SOS-KINDERDORF INTERNATIONAL

Overview. Founded in 1949, SOS Children's Villages is a private, non-political, and nondenominational welfare organization. SOS Children's Villages offers abandoned, orphaned, and destitute children—regardless of race, nationality, or creed—new and permanent homes, and prepares them for independence. SOS-Kinderdorf International is the umbrella organization with which all national SOS Children's Village Associations are affiliated. SOS Children's Villages and SOS Youth Facilities provide the children entrusted to their care with homes until they achieve self-reliance and are able to make their own way in life. SOS Children's Villages was active in 129 countries and territories as of May 1998. More than 40,000 children were being cared for permanently in 377 SOS Children's Villages and 380 SOS Youth Facilities worldwide. A total of more than 200,000 young people benefit from all 1,452 SOS Children's Village facilities.

In 1995, SOS-Kinderdorf International was classified as an NGO with consultative status with the Economic and Social Council of the United Nations.

Capabilities. SOS concentrates on children's issues.

Point of Contact. SOS-Kinderdorf International, Hermann-Gmeiner-Str. 51, P.O. Box 443A-6021, Innsbruck, Austria

Tel: (43 512) 33 10-0; Fax: (43 512) 33 10-27
E-mail: *com@sos-kd.org*
Web site: *http://www.sos-kd.org/index.htm*

WORLD CONCERN

Overview. World Concern is an international Christian relief and development organization committed to providing long-term solutions to poverty and hunger. Founded in 1955 as Medicine for Missions, the organization collected donations of medicines to be sent to those in greatest need throughout the world. Since then, the work has expanded to include not only contributions of medicines but also contributions of seeds and clothing and operation of feeding centers, medical clinics, and development projects. More than 4 million people are served annually in nearly 80 countries.

World Concern's mission is to work as a funding and resource agency in the areas of relief, rehabilitation, and development; to enable aid recipients in developing countries to achieve self-sufficiency and economic independence; and to form partnerships between Christian churches in North America and churches in less-developed countries. World Concern works in three regions: Asia (including the former Soviet Union), Africa, and Latin America and the Caribbean (Haiti).

Capabilities. World Concern works to provide water development, personnel training, leprosy care, primary healthcare, population planning, immunization, public health, rehabilitation therapy, administrative skills, mother and child healthcare, community health workers, AIDS counseling, and training; to increase income generation through food production and/or agribusiness, forestry and/or soil conservation, vocational training, human resource development, microenterprises, and animal husbandry; and to establish programs for child welfare, handicapped training, social work, radio outreach and/or education, and literacy and/or education.

Interagency Relationships. World Concern works with governments and all types of relief organizations and is funded by many organizations throughout the world.

Organization. World Concern's international headquarters is in Seattle, Washington. The headquarters also serves as the international arm of CRISTA Ministries. (Christianity in Action is a corporation of 10 ministries, one of which is World Concern.) World Concern's area offices are located in Bangkok, Thailand (World Concern Asia); Port-au-Prince, Haiti (World Concern Haiti); Santa Cruz, Bolivia (World Concern Latin America); and Nairobi, Kenya (World Concern Africa).

Point of Contact. World Concern, 19303 Fremont Avenue, North, Seattle, WA 98133

Tel: (206) 546-7201; Fax: (206) 546-7269

E-mail: *wconcern@crista.org*

Web site: *http://www.worldconcern.org*

WORLD VISION RELIEF AND DEVELOPMENT (WVRD)

Overview. World Vision was founded in 1950 in response to the needs of Korean War orphans. The organization provides emergency relief, community development, leadership training, Christian outreach, and public education in partnership with churches, community associations, and national development groups. World Vision fights poverty, hunger, and homelessness by volunteer programs such as the Student Mentoring Initiative and the Love for Children program.

Capabilities. World Vision provides emergency relief, medical assistance, community development, leadership training, Christian outreach, and public education with an annual budget of nearly $500 million. The organization provides its services to 97 countries through a network of field offices.

Interagency Relationships. World Vision collaborates closely with the U.S. government, with regular briefings at the Department of State, Department of Defense, and USAID/OFDA. It is also represented at meetings chaired by the UN Department of Humanitarian Affairs. Private funds for World Vision are raised through special television programming, mailings, public awareness programs, church and civic campaigns, and publications. World Vision's recent fund-raising has exceeded $250 million annually in the United States.

Organization. World Vision Relief and Development is headquartered in Tacoma, Washington.

Point of Contact. World Vision Relief, P.O. Box 78481, Tacoma, WA 98481-8481

Tel: (253) 815-1000

Web site: *http://www.worldvision.org*

Chapter 41

International and Intergovernmental Organizations

INTERNATIONAL RED CROSS AND RED CRESCENT MOVEMENT

Presently in some 160 countries, the International Red Cross and Red Crescent Movement (also known by its former title, the International Red Cross) is composed of the International Committee of the Red Cross (ICRC), the recognized national societies, and the International Federation of Red Cross and Red Crescent Societies (IFRC)

The components of the International Red Cross and Red Crescent Movement normally meet every four years, together with representatives of the states party to the Geneva Convention. This conference is the movement's highest deliberative assembly. It considers general problems, adopts resolutions, and assigns mandates.

The emblem of a red cross on a white background was created with a specific purpose: to ensure the protection of those wounded in war and those who care for them. The emblem's red cross, mentioned in the 1864 Geneva Convention, was adopted as a tribute to Switzerland; it was not intended to have any religious significance. However, a number of countries in the Islamic world have adopted the red crescent, which is recognized as having equal status with the red cross. The red crescent is mentioned in the 1949 Geneva Conventions and their additional protocols. Any abuse of these signs is a breach of international law and threatens the humanitarian protection granted by them. Any use of these emblems for commercial or publicity purposes is forbidden. These emblems are used to identify and protect medical and relief workers, military and civilian medical facilities, mobile units, and hospital ships. They are also used to identify the programs and activities of National Red Cross and Red Crescent Societies and those of the Magen David Adom (Red Shield of David) humanitarian society in Israel.

INTERNATIONAL COMMITTEE OF THE RED CROSS (ICRC)

Overview. Formed in 1863, the ICRC is a private, independent humanitarian institution, not a multinational organization, composed exclusively of Swiss nationals.

The ICRC acts as a neutral intermediary between belligerents on behalf of the victims of war. It brings assistance to victims by providing medical care; setting up hospitals and rehabilitation centers; and providing material aid as needed, such as food, shelter, and clothing. The ICRC also runs a Central Tracing Agency, whose main tasks are to trace persons whose families have no news of them or who have disappeared, arrange for the exchange of family messages when normal channels of communication have broken down, and organize family reunifications and repatriations. The ICRC may also offer its services in situations not covered by international humanitarian law, such as internal disturbances. It is responsible for promoting international humanitarian law and for overseeing its development. The ICRC plays an essential role in promoting respect for the humanitarian principles that guide the work of the International Red Cross and Red Crescent Movement, ensuring that they are observed and helping in their implementation and dissemination within the movement. It also declares the recognition of new national societies, which thus become members of the movement.

Authority and Responsibilities. The ICRC's mission is to provide care to persons not directly participating in hostilities, such as the sick, wounded, prisoners, or those in distress, without discrimination.

The 1949 Geneva Conventions and their 1977 Protocols confer on the ICRC what many nations believe is the right to take action (e.g., to visit prisoners of war) and to make proposals to states (e.g., to offer its services). Additionally, the International Red Cross and Red Crescent Movement's statutes recognize that the ICRC has a right of humanitarian initiative in situations not covered by the Geneva Conventions or their protocols. All these "rights" constitute the permanent mandate conferred on the ICRC by much of the international community. This specific mandate distinguishes it from other humanitarian organizations. However, although the ICRC and advocates of humanitarian law may argue that the 1977 Protocols to the Geneva Conventions of 1949 have gained universal application through the formative custom of international law, the United States does not agree. The United States has not ratified the 1977 Protocols and may not always agree with nor recognize as authoritative ICRC actions based on the protocols. Other nations that have acceded to these protocols are bound by them. This leads to a major problem for legal counsel in the international arena: not all participants are similarly bound to international law on very basic matters. There are numerous conventions of wide but not universal application. Adherence or nonadherence can make a mismatch of potential partners in humanitarian ventures.

Capabilities. The ICRC is available to care for the wounded on the battlefield, protect captives, assist civilians who have been displaced or have fallen into the hands of the enemy, and reunite families separated by events; to organize material and medical assistance programs to ensure the survival of certain categories of people (e.g., civilians, displaced persons, refugees in combat zones) affected by armed conflict; to protect prisoners of war, the wounded, and civilian internees and visit them wherever they are (e.g., camps, prisons, hospitals, labor camps); to provide material and moral support to the detainees visited, to civilians in enemy hands or in occupied territories, to displaced persons, or to refugees in combat zones and situations not covered by the Geneva Conventions (e.g., internal disturbances and tensions); to visit persons who have been detained for security reasons and could be victims of arbitrary treatment to assess their material and psychological conditions of detention, not the reasons for the detention; to distribute additional aid to prisoners and their families who, deprived of their means of support, often run into serious economic difficulties; to keep reports (drawn up by the ICRC following visits to places of detention) confidential with the detaining authorities or, in the case of visits to prisoners of war, to the prisoners' state of origin; to care for the wounded and supply medicine and medical equipment; to conduct disease prevention activities, nutrition programs, vaccination campaigns, water purification, and public hygiene; to recruit, select, and prepare the members of medical and surgical teams sent to the field to care for the wounded or participate in emergency relief programs; to maintain a shortwave radio network that is one of the world's largest nongovernmental telecommunications systems; to obtain and record all information that might enable dead, wounded, or missing persons to be identified and to pass information to next of kin; to facilitate correspondence between members of families separated by events when other means of communication have been interrupted; to trace people who are missing or who have not been heard from by their next of kin; and to issue various types of documents, such as certificates of captivity or death and travel papers.

Interagency Relationships. The ICRC and the IFRC keep each other informed of their respective activities and consult with each other regularly on the coordination and distribution of their work and on all matters of interest to the International Red Cross and Red Crescent Movement. The ICRC has enjoyed permanent observer status to the UN since 1991.

Funding. The ICRC has no resources or funds of its own. Funding comes from voluntary contributions from the states party to the Geneva Conventions and the European Union, the National Red Cross and Red Crescent Societies, private donors, and various gifts and bequests. Half of the ICRC's regular budget is financed by the Swiss government.

Organization. The ICRC is the founding institution of the International Red Cross and Red Crescent Movement, which, in addition to the ICRC, has two other components: the IFRC (see below) and the National Red Cross and Red Crescent Societies.

National Red Cross and Red Crescent Societies were originally created for service in time of war to help army medical personnel care for the wounded and the sick. Today, the national societies work within their countries as auxiliaries to the public authorities and have numerous responsibilities both in war and in peace as well as during natural disasters. The national society in the United States is the American Red Cross (see chapter 40).

The ICRC is headquartered in Geneva, Switzerland. The headquarters' Directorate of Operations includes the Relief and Medical Divisions and the Central Tracing Agency. All ICRC delegates have a university education and speak several languages, including English.

Point of Contact. International Committee of the Red Cross, Public Information Division, 19 avenue de la Paix, 1202 Geneva Switzerland

Tel: (41 22) 734-6001; Fax: (41 22) 733-2057; Telex: 414 226 CCR CH

E-mail: *com_dip.gva@icrc.org*

Press relations: *press.gva@icrc.org*

Web site: *http://www.icrc.org/*

INTERNATIONAL FEDERATION OF RED CROSS AND RED CRESCENT SOCIETIES (IFRC)

Overview. Founded in 1919 as the League of Red Cross Societies, the International Federation of Red Cross and Red Crescent Societies coordinates Red Cross and Red Crescent operations for relief of disaster victims, develops the humanitarian and health activities of national societies, and helps refugees outside war zones. In the early 1980s, the league changed its name to the League of Red Cross and Red Crescent Societies to better indicate its composition. In 1992, to more clearly reflect its global nature, the league became the International Federation of Red Cross and Red Crescent Societies, referred to as the Federation. The seven principles of the International Red Cross and Red Crescent Movement—humanity, impartiality, neutrality, independence, voluntary service, unity, and universality—guide all Federation actions.

The functions of the Federation are to organize, coordinate, and direct international relief actions; promote and support humanitarian activities; represent national societies on an international level; bring help to victims of armed conflicts, refugees, and displaced persons outside of conflict zones; encourage the creation and development of national societies; and reduce the vulnerability of people through development programs.

Capabilities. The IFRC is equipped to appeal to a select number of national societies for disaster relief, stating the amount and duration of assistance needed, the number of people requiring help, and the methods of providing that help; to coordinate the money and materials donated from the societies; to help national societies devise development and disaster preparedness programs; to provide national societies with support in areas such as blood donation, the prevention of disease and epidemics, first aid, social welfare, the prevention and treatment of AIDS, and information and communication systems; to bring the plight of refugees to public attention; to help refugees or displaced people by providing food, shelter, protection, and long-term assistance in education, medical care, and, in some cases, return to homes; and to send delegates who are specialists in logistics, nursing, telecommunications, information, and finance to disaster spots.

Interagency Relationships. The Federation Secretariat is at the heart of a global network that helps national societies develop and coordinate their work at the international level. Through its regional delegations and its many country delegations, the Secretariat is in regular contact with the national societies and keeps abreast of current field conditions. It enjoys consultative status (Category I) with the Economic and Social Council of the United Nations. In 1994, the UN General Assembly invited the Federation to become a permanent observer and participate in the work of the Assembly. Through its many delegations, the Federation maintains permanent contact, both in Geneva and in the field, with UN agencies, governments, the European Union (especially the Humanitarian Office), and other NGOs. The Federation has a delegation in New York City to maintain relations with UN agencies and diplomatic missions. In the field, Federation delegates maintain close contact with other humanitarian agencies, particularly with the ICRC, that are engaged in operations complementary to those of the Federation. The Federation, funded by annual contributions from all member national societies, represents the societies at the international level.

Organization. The Federation comprises more than 160 National Red Cross and Red Crescent Societies. It is headquartered in Geneva, Switzerland. The Federation, the individual national societies, and the ICRC together constitute the International Red Cross and Red Crescent Movement.

Points of Contact. International Federation of Red Cross and Red Crescent Societies, P.O. Box 372, CH-1211 Geneva 19 Switzerland

Tel: (41 22) 730-4222; Fax: (41 22) 733-0395; Telex: 412 133 FRC CH

Press relations: (41 22) 730-4214, (41 22) 730-4346

E-mail: *secretariat@ifrc.org*

Web site: *http://www.ifrc.org*

Disaster Relief and Operations Coordination, Tel: (41 22) 730-4277; Fax: (41 22) 733-0395

E-mail: *wahlstro@ifrc.org*

UNITED NATIONS CHILDREN'S FUND (UNICEF)

Overview. Founded in 1946 as a temporary body to provide emergency assistance to children in Europe and China following World War II, the United Nations Children's Fund is a semiautonomous agency of the United Nations that works for the well-being of children. Financial support for UNICEF is derived entirely from voluntary contributions made by governments, foundations, corporations, and individuals around the world—not dues paid by UN member governments. UNICEF is the only UN agency that relies heavily on private donations. Nearly 30 percent of UNICEF's income is provided by individuals, NGOs, and PVOs.

UNICEF advocates and works for the protection of children's rights, to help the young meet their basic needs and expand their opportunities to reach their full potential. The UNICEF Executive Board reaffirmed this mandate in January 1996, when it adopted the following statement on the mission of UNICEF: "[UNICEF] is guided by the Convention on the Rights of the Child and strives to establish children's rights as enduring ethical principles and international standards of behaviour towards children."

Authority and Responsibilities. UNICEF is charged with giving assistance, particularly to developing countries, in the development of permanent child health and welfare services. The UN International Children's Emergency Fund was changed to the UN Children's Fund, retaining the UNICEF acronym. UNICEF reports to the UN Economic and Social Council.

Capabilities. UNICEF is prepared to provide immunizations, to record and monitor cases of polio, measles, neonatal tetanus, and other infectious diseases, and to alert health officials to potential epidemics; to support programs to control acute respiratory infections (the largest cause of child death in the world); to train health workers to recognize and treat respiratory diseases and control diarrheal diseases; to support educational activities aimed at preventing the spread of HIV, especially among young people in and out of school; to combat malnutrition by controlling vitamin and mineral deficiencies, by promoting breast feeding and improved child-feeding practices, by ensuring community participation in developing activities that affect their daily lives, and by improving national nutrition information systems; to support family planning through efforts to improve the status of women, through support for breast feeding, basic education, and literacy, and through advocacy and social mobilization; to provide women throughout the developing world with pre- and postnatal care, safe delivery services, and protection against HIV and other sexually transmitted diseases; to encourage governments to increase the budget share for basic education, emphasizing low-cost ways of bringing education to poor, isolated communities, especially to female children; to provide artificial limbs and training to children who have been disabled in armed conflicts; to bring attention to the growing problem of child prostitution and street children; to reunite unaccompanied child victims of conflict with their families; to raise public awareness of child labor and to end it; to offer trauma counseling to children who have witnessed—or been forced to participate in—violent acts; to respond to natural disasters, such as floods and earthquakes, and other emergencies of ethnic and communal violence with emergency support; to emphasize primary environmental care and environmental education in countries whose ecosystems are at risk; and to support water supply and environmental sanitation projects.

Interagency Relationships. UNICEF works with numerous agencies, including the WHO, World Bank, Organization of American States, International Labor Organization, International Reference Center for Water and Sanitation at The Hague, German Agency for Technical Cooperation, USAID, European Union, Water and Sanitation for Health, International Water and Sanitation Center, McGill University, Harvard School of Public Health, All India Institute of Hygiene and Public Health, University Federal of Pelotas (Brazil), Honduran Water Authority, Family Care International, Freedom from Hunger, Public Interest International, International Baby Food Action Network, La Leche League International, International Code Documentation Center, International Lactation Consultant Organization, World Alliance for Breastfeeding Action, and Christian Children's Fund. UNICEF and its major relief partners, including UNHCR and the WFP, uphold the humanitarian principles of neutrality and impartiality when the United Nations is also politically and militarily involved in a civil conflict or war. Upholding these principles is becoming increasingly difficult for

UNICEF, and UNICEF staff members have been killed while serving children in emergency situations. This highlights the need for security forces in highly dangerous situations to protect those individuals dedicated to the delivery of humanitarian assistance.

Organization. UNICEF headquarters is located in New York City. It also has offices in Geneva, Switzerland; Tokyo, Japan; Sydney, Australia; Kathmandu, Nepal; Amman, Jordan; Bangkok, Thailand; Santa Fe de Bogota, Colombia; Abidjan, Cote d'Ivoire; and Nairobi, Kenya. UNICEF has national committees in 35 countries, including the United States. The U.S. Committee supports UNICEF-assisted programs, such as development education, emergency relief, social welfare, and public health, in certain countries throughout the developing world. The committee is headquartered at 333 East 38th Street, New York, NY, 10016.

Points of Contact. UNICEF House, 3 United Nations Plaza, 44th Street (between 1st and 2nd Avenues), New York, NY 10017

Tel: (212) 326-7000 (switchboard); Fax: (212) 888-7465 (primary), (212) 888-7454 (secondary)

E-mail: *gopher://gopher.unicef.org:70/11/.s2email*

Press relations: *media@unicef.org*

Web site: *http://www.unicef.org/*

Contact information: *http://www.unicef.org/uwwide/*

Emergency Programs: Tel: (212) 326-7163; Fax: (212) 326-7037

E-mail: *nkastberg@unicef.org*

UNITED NATIONS DEVELOPMENT PROGRAMME (UNDP)

Overview. Through a unique network of 134 country offices, the UNDP helps people in 174 countries and territories to help themselves, focusing on poverty elimination, environmental regeneration, job creation, and the advancement of women. In support of these goals, UNDP is frequently asked to assist in promoting sound governance and market development and to support rebuilding societies in the aftermath of war and humanitarian emergencies.

UNDP's overarching mission is to help countries build national capacity to achieve sustainable, human development, giving top priority to eliminating poverty and building equity.

Interagency Relationships. In administering its programs, UNDP draws on the expertise of developing-country nationals and NGOs, the specialized agencies of the UN system, and research institutes in every field. Eighty-five percent of UNDP staff is based in the countries where people need help.

Organization. At the country level, UNDP is responsible for the coordination of all UN development activity, and the head of the UNDP office in 134 program countries is designated as resident coordinator of the United Nations system's operational activities. Headquartered in New York, UNDP is governed by a thirty-six-member executive board, representing both developing and developed countries.

Points of Contact. United Nations Development Programme, One United Nations Plaza, New York, NY 10017

Tel: (212) 906-5315

Web site: *http://www.undp.org/*

Contact information:

   http://www.undp.org/toppages/discover/disframe.htm

Emergency Response Division: Tel: (212) 906-5193; Fax: (212) 906-5379; E-mail: *omar.bahket@undp.org*

Division of External Relations: Tel: (212) 906-6039; Fax: (212) 906-5776; E-mail: *nukhil.chandavarkar@undp.org*

Press relations: Tel: (212) 906-5382; Fax: (212) 906-5364

UNITED NATIONS FOOD AND AGRICULTURE ORGANIZATION (FAO)

Overview. The Food and Agriculture Organization of the United Nations is the largest of the UN specialized agencies. The FAO's 171 member nations have pledged to raise the level of nutrition and the standards of living of their peoples, improve the production and distribution of all foods and agricultural products, and improve the condition of rural people.

Authority and Responsibilities. The organization is a development agency, an information center, an adviser to governments, and a neutral forum. It is not an aid agency or agricultural bank but a unique source of expertise and information. The FAO's four main tasks are to carry out a major program of technical advice and assistance for the agricultural community on behalf of governments and development-funding agencies; collect, analyze, and disseminate information; advise governments on policy and planning; and provide opportunities for governments to meet and discuss food and agricultural problems.

Capabilities. The FAO is prepared to give direct, practical help in the developing world through technical assistance projects in all areas of food and agriculture; to mobilize international funding for agriculture; to help developing countries find the external capital they need to build up their agriculture; to help borrowers and lending institutions formulate and prepare investment projects; to help farmers resume production following floods, fires, outbreaks of livestock diseases, and other emergencies; to assess needs in close collaboration with local authorities and other UN agencies, with detailed assessments of damage and losses; to prepare assistance projects for external funding; to mobilize and coordinate for donor support of relief operations; to provide emergency relief in the form of agricultural inputs and equipment, veterinary and feed supplies, breeding stock, vehicles, storage facilities, and technical support; to provide information to farmers, scientists, technologists, traders, and government planners on every aspect of agriculture—including production, supply, demand, prices, and technology—so that they can make rational decisions on planning, investment, marketing, research, or training; to serve as a clearinghouse for data, which are published and made available in every medium; to advise governments on agricultural policy and planning, the administrative and legal structures needed for development, and ways of ensuring that national development strategies are directed toward rural development and the alleviation of poverty and malnutrition; and to help member nations share resources, skills, and capabilities.

Interagency Relationships. The FAO helps national governments cooperate through regional and subregional groupings, such as the Economic Community of West African States, South African Development Coordination Conference, Center for Integrated Rural Development in Asia and the Pacific, and Organization of Andean Pact Countries. The FAO cooperates with practically all the major multilateral funding institutions, including the World Bank, International Fund for Agriculture Development, African Development Bank and Fund, Asian Development Bank, Inter-American Development Bank, UN Capital Development Fund, most of the major Arab banks, and subregional institutions. The World Bank is the single most important source of financing for investment projects prepared by the FAO.

Organization. FAO headquarters is in Rome, Italy. It is staffed by more than 1,200 professional members. A similar number are employed on field projects and at country and regional offices in the Third World. The FAO has five regional offices and two liaison offices. The former are located in Accra, Ghana; Bangkok, Thailand; Rome, Italy; Santiago, Chile; and Cairo, Egypt. The Liaison Office for North America is located in Washington, D.C., while the Liaison Office with the United Nations is at UN Headquarters in New York City.

Point of Contact. Food and Agriculture Organization, Viale delle Terme di Caracalla, 00100 Rome, Italy

Tel: (39 6) 5705-1; Fax: (39 6) 5705-3152; Telex: 625852/625853/610181 FAO I

Telegrams: FOODAGRI ROME
Press relations: (39 06) 5705-3105
E-Mail: *Postmaster@fao.org*
Web site: *http://www.fao.org/*
Contact Information: *http://www.fao.org/inside/faohqe.htm*
Special Operations Service, Technical Cooperation Department: Tel:
(39 06) 5705-4936; Fax: (39 06) 5705-4941
Press Office: Tel: (39 06) 5705-3259 or 5705-3105; Fax: (39 06) 5705-
3699

UNITED NATIONS HIGH COMMISSION FOR HUMAN RIGHTS (UNHCHR)

Overview. In 1947, when the Commission on Human Rights met for the first time, its sole function was to draft the Universal Declaration of Human Rights. For the first 20 years (1947–66), the commission concentrated its efforts on standard-setting. Using the Universal Declaration as the basis, the commission set about drafting an impressive body of international human rights law, culminating in the adoption by the General Assembly in 1966 of the two human rights covenants: the International Covenant on Civil and Political Rights and the International Covenant on Economic, Social, and Cultural Rights. Together, the Universal Declaration and the two covenants are commonly referred to as the International Bill of Human Rights.

In 1967, the commission was specifically authorized (by the Economic and Social Council, and with the encouragement of the General Assembly) to start to deal with violations of human rights. Since then, the commission has set up an elaborate machinery and procedures—country-oriented or thematic (operating through special rapporteurs and working groups)—to monitor states' compliance with international human rights law and to investigate alleged violations of human rights by dispatching fact-finding missions anywhere in the world, to rich and poor, developing and developed countries alike. During the 1970s and 1980s, implementation of this fact-finding machinery and these procedures became the focus of the commission's attention.

In the 1990s, the commission increasingly turned its attention to states' need for advisory services and technical assistance to overcome obstacles to securing the enjoyment of human rights by all. At the same time, more emphasis was put on the promotion of economic, social, and cultural rights, including the right to development and the right to an adequate standard of living. Increased attention is also being given to the protection of the rights of vulnerable groups in society, including minorities and indigenous people, and to the protection of the rights of children and women, including the eradication of violence against women and the attainment of equal rights for women.

Capabilities. The UNHCHR promotes universal enjoyment of all human rights by giving practical effect to the will and resolve of the world community as expressed by the United Nations; plays the leading role on human rights issues and emphasizes the importance of human rights at the international and national levels; promotes international cooperation for human rights; stimulates and coordinates action for human rights throughout the UN system; promotes universal ratification and implementation of international standards; assists in the development of new norms; supports human rights organs and treaty-monitoring bodies; responds to serious violations of human rights; undertakes preventive human rights action; promotes the establishment of national human rights infrastructures; undertakes human rights field activities and operations; and provides education, information advisory services, and technical assistance in the field of human rights.

Organization. Fifty-three UN member nations belong to the Commission on Human Rights.

Points of Contact. United Nations High Commission for Human Rights, Palais des Nations, 8-14 avenue de la Paix, CH 1211 Geneva 10, Switzerland

Tel: (41 22) 917-3456; Fax: (41 22) 917-0213

Web site: *http://www.unhchr.ch/hchr_un.htm*

Activities and Programs Branch: Tel: (41 22) 917-3357; Fax: (41 22) 917-0092

Media, press, or public relations: Tel: (41 22) 917-3309; Fax: (41 22) 917-0286

UNITED NATIONS HIGH COMMISSIONER FOR REFUGEES (UNHCR)

Overview. The Office of the United Nations High Commissioner for Refugees was established by the UN General Assembly in 1951 to protect refugees and to promote lasting solutions to refugee problems. UNHCR has two closely related functions: to protect refugees and to promote durable solutions to their problems. UNHCR assists all refugees who have fled their countries because of well-founded fears of persecution for reasons of their race, religion, nationality, political opinion, or membership in a particular social group, and who cannot or do not want to return.

Authority and Responsibilities. UNHCR's mission is to protect refugees against physical harm, to protect their basic human rights, and to make sure that they are not forcibly returned to countries where they could face imprisonment, torture, or death. The latter mission—UNHCR's most important function, known as "international protection"—means that the organization strives to ensure that no refugee is returned involuntarily to a country where he or she has reason to fear persecution. Initially, UNHCR's mandate was limited to people outside their country of origin. Over time, however, as part of its duty to ensure that voluntary repatriation schemes are sustainable, it has become involved in assisting and protecting returnees in their home countries. UNHCR assists internally displaced people—usually referred to as "persons of concern"—who have not crossed an international border but are in a refugee-like situation inside their country of origin.

Capabilities. UNHCR is empowered to ensure that applications for asylum are examined fairly and that asylum-seekers are protected while their requests are being examined against forcible return to a country where their freedom or lives would be endangered; to ensure that refugees are treated in accordance with recognized international standards and receive an appropriate legal status, including, whenever possible, the same economic and social rights as nationals of the country in which they have been given asylum; to help refugees cease being refugees either through voluntary repatriation to their countries of origin or, if this is not feasible, through the eventual acquisition of the nationality of their country of residence; to help reintegrate refugees returning to their home countries in close consultation with the governments concerned, and to monitor amnesties, guarantees, or assurances on the basis of which they have returned home; to promote the physical security of refugees, asylum seekers, and returnees, particularly their safety from military attacks and other acts of violence; to promote the reunification of refugee families; and to maintain emergency response teams that are dispatched to cope with refugees and displaced people and make arrangements to position and stockpile relief supplies.

Interagency Relationships. From the outset, UNHCR's work was intended to be undertaken jointly with other members of the international community. As its activities have increased and diversified, UNHCR's relations with other organs and agencies of the UN system, intergovernmental organizations, NGOs, and PVOs have become increasingly important. UNHCR draws on the expertise of other UN organizations in matters such as food production (FAO), health measures (WHO), education (UN Educational, Scientific, and Cultural Organization), child welfare, and vocational training (International Labour Organization). When refugees have not been able to return home, the World Bank, International Fund for Agricultural

Development, and UNHCR have joined forces to plan, finance, and implement projects that aim to promote self-reliance.

Organization. UNHCR is headquartered in Geneva, Switzerland. The UNHCR Branch Office for the United States is located in Washington, D.C. UNHCR employs over 4,400 people, including short-term staff. Of the total personnel, some 3,500 serve in the field and the rest at headquarters. UNHCR, funded almost entirely by voluntary contributions from donor governments, has offices in over 110 countries. The High Commissioner for Refugees is elected every five years by the UN General Assembly on the nomination of the Secretary-General. The High Commissioner follows policy directives from the General Assembly and the UN Economic and Social Council. The Executive Committee of the High Commissioner's Programme, a body composed of almost 50 governments, oversees UNHCR's budgets and advises on refugee protection.

Points of Contact. United Nations High Commissioner for Refugees, Case Postale 2500, 1211 Geneva 2 Switzerland

Tel: (41 22) 739-8111; Fax: (41 22) 739-7314/15/16

E-mail: *hqpi00@unhcr.ch*

Cable: HICOMREF Geneva

Press relations: (41-22) 739-8502

Web site: *http://www.unicc.org/unhcr/*

Emergency Preparedness and Response Section: Tel: (41 22) 739-8181; Mobile Tel: (079) 202-2315; Fax: (41 22) 739-7301

Emergency Operations Centre or duty officer: (41 22) 739-8969/8967/8966

Inter-Organizational Affairs and Secretariat Services: Tel: (44 21) 739-8605; Fax: (44 21) 739-7349; Emergency tel: (41 22) 731-0244

U.S. Office, 1775 K Street, N.W., Suite 300, Washington, DC 20006

UNITED NATIONS OFFICE FOR THE COORDINATION OF HUMANITARIAN AFFAIRS (OCHA)

Overview. In 1991, the UN General Assembly recognized the need to strengthen interagency coordination for rapid response and make more effective the efforts of the international community—particularly those of the UN system—to provide humanitarian assistance to victims of natural disasters and complex emergencies. To perform this task, the UN Secretary-General established the UN Department of Humanitarian Affairs in 1992, incorporating the former Office of the UN Disaster Relief Coordinator, the various UN emergency units dealing with emergency programs, and the Secretariat for the International Decade for Natural Disaster Reduction

(IDNDR). Prior to the establishment of OCHA in 1997, the predecessor Department of Humanitarian Affairs (DHA) responded to 416 natural disasters from 1992 through 1997.

Authority and Responsibilities. OCHA's mission is to coordinate and facilitate international relief assistance following sudden disasters and similar emergencies. At the international level, the DHA provides a framework for the interagency coordination of relief assistance by UN agencies, bilateral donors, NGOs, and PVOs. At the country level, the UNDP's resident coordinator and the UN disaster management team (DMT) are the first line of response to disasters and emergencies. The resident coordinator normally coordinates humanitarian assistance at the country level. OCHA assumes immediate UN systemwide relief coordination responsibility when a disaster strikes, including the role of on-site coordination. OCHA utilizes the Interagency Standing Committee (IASC) to formulate and coordinate policy, the Central Emergency Revolving Fund (CERF) as a quick source of emergency funding, and the Consolidated Appeals Process (CAP) to assess the needs in a critical situation and prepare a comprehensive interagency response strategy.

Interagency Standing Committee. The IASC is composed of the executive heads of relevant UN organizations: UNDP, UNHCR, UNICEF, WFP, WHO, and FAO. The International Organization for Migration, International Committee of the Red Cross, International Federation of Red Cross and Red Crescent Societies, and three of the largest humanitarian consortia—the International Council of Voluntary Agencies, American Council for Voluntary International Action, and Steering Committee for Humanitarian Response—are also members. Representatives of relevant NGOs, PVOs, and UN departments are invited to participate in IASC discussions on an ad hoc basis.

Central Emergency Revolving Fund. The CERF is a cash-flow mechanism for use by UN operational organizations, especially during the critical initial stages of emergencies. The CERF is financed by voluntary contributions and managed by OCHA. UN agencies draw on the CERF and repay the advances they receive as donors respond to their own fund-raising efforts.

Consolidated Appeals Process. The CAP helps the international community identify the most critical needs of affected people and determines the most appropriate ways to provide assistance.

Capabilities. OCHA is equipped to arrange the mission assessment and coordination support to governments; to maintain a warehouse in Pisa, Italy, that holds a comprehensive emergency stockpile and serves as an assembly center for international relief shipments for OCHA and other UN agencies; to collect and share information and provide independent and reliable telecommunications links on short notice; to develop the means for interaction among the political, peacekeeping, and humanitarian components of UN operations in complex emergencies through procedures for cooperation, information, joint planning, and logistics; to address issues such as access to victims, security of personnel and relief supplies, humanitarian imperatives in conflict situations, special needs arising from application of UN sanctions, demobilization of former combatants, removal of land mines, resource mobilization, assistance to internally displaced persons, field coordination of international humanitarian responses, and the transition from relief to development; to help governments and international agencies prepare for and provide quick response to sudden disasters, as well as to increase the overall capacity for emergency management; to operate the International Search and Rescue Advisory Group, the UN Disaster Assessment and Coordination Stand-by Teams, and the IDNDR; to provide country-specific training on disaster management; to formulate, coordinate, and implement de-mining schemes in a number of countries; to maintain centralized information management systems for humanitarian emergencies (the International Emergency Readiness and Response Information System and the Humanitarian Early Warning System); and to maintain the Central Register of Disaster Management Capacities, including the Register of Emergency Stockpiles.

Interagency Relationships. OCHA has close interagency relationships with a variety of forums, but especially through the IASC and the CAP. OCHA maintains close contact with the Department of Political Affairs and the UN Department for Peacekeeping Operations with regard to security, political and humanitarian dimensions of complex emergencies to promote joint policy planning, and coordination. OCHA also works closely with operational organizations of the UN system (such as UNICEF and WFP) and other humanitarian agencies, providing emergency operational support to governments, coordinating international relief activities during emergencies, and promoting and assisting activities relating to disaster mitigation. In the event of a complex emergency, the UN emergency relief coordinator and/or the Undersecretary-General for Humanitarian Affairs consults with IASC members before either confirming the resident coordinator as humanitarian coordinator or designating another official to perform that function. A small UN disaster assistance coordination stand-by team is rapidly deployed, often with an OCHA relief coordination mission, following sudden natural disasters.

OCHA has increasingly come to appreciate the role of NGOs. Since NGOs are often indispensable implementers of emergency programs and often have more detailed knowledge of and are closer to affected populations,

OCHA has learned that NGOs should be part of the early warning effort, initial requirements assessment and programming, CAPs, DMTs, disaster management training programs, and other coordinating bodies for prevention, preparedness, and local capacity building.

OCHA realizes that the use of military and civil defense assets (MCDA) contributes significantly to disaster relief. OCHA acknowledges that military and civil defense teams are well suited to assist emergency relief operations because they are perhaps the best organized to provide support to a full range of public services—including civil engineering, communications, transportation, emergency medicine, healthcare services, and search and rescue—that are all intrinsic to the military. As outlined in Project 213/3, OCHA appreciates using MCDA in disaster relief because of the tremendous logistic potential they can bring to an operation—a potential that has not been effectively utilized so far.

Organization. OCHA is headquartered at the UN office in Geneva, Switzerland. OCHA can also be contacted at UN Headquarters in New York City. The OCHA staff in Geneva and New York is involved in policy planning and early warning functions, emergency operational support and relief coordination, and disaster mitigation. The UN Under Secretary-General of Humanitarian Affairs serves concurrently as the UN emergency relief coordinator. Whereas the main responsibility of the under secretary-general is to head OCHA, the main responsibility of the emergency relief coordinator is to develop rapid-response procedures and teams for use in international humanitarian emergencies.

OCHA currently maintains field coordination arrangements in 16 countries and one region: Afghanistan, Angola, Armenia, Azerbaijan, Bosnia and Herzegovina, Burundi, Democratic Peoples Republic of Korea, Democratic Republic of the Congo, Georgia, Great Lakes, Republic of the Congo, Russian Federation, Rwanda, Sierra Leone, Somalia, Sudan, and Tajikistan.

Points of Contact. Office for the Coordination of Humanitarian Affairs, United Nations, S-3600, New York, NY 10017

Tel: (212) 963-1234; Fax: (212) 963-1312

Press relations: Tel: (212) 963-4832

Advocacy and External Relations Unit: Tel: (212) 963-4832 and 963-1608

Geneva Office, Office for the Coordination of Humanitarian Affairs, United Nations, Palais des Nations, 1211 Geneva 10 Switzerland

Tel: (41 22) 917-1234; Fax: (41 22) 917-0023

In case of emergency: (41 22) 917-2010

Press relations: (41 22) 917-2336, (41 22) 917-2300; Fax: (41 22) 917-0030

E-mail: *info@dha.unicc.org*

Web sites: OCHA On-Line: *http://www.reliefweb.int/dha_ol/index.html;*
ReliefWeb: *http://wwwnotes.reliefweb.int/*

Disaster Response Branch (Natural Disasters): Tel: (41 22) 917-1724;
Fax: (41 22) 917-0401

Complex Emergency Response/Consolidated Appeal Process (CER/
CAP) Branch: Tel: (41 22) 788-7600; Fax: (41 22) 788-6389

UNITED NATIONS WORLD FOOD PROGRAMME (WFP)

Overview. Founded in 1963, the World Food Programme is the food aid
organization of the United Nations. The WFP's assistance is targeted at the
poorest sections of the population in low-income, food-deficit countries,
particularly vulnerable groups such as women and children. Although the
WFP has increasingly been called on to provide disaster relief assistance, it
believes that development projects have been and should remain the core of
its work to help poor people become more self-reliant.

Authority and Responsibilities. The program's mandate is to help poor
people by combating world hunger and poverty. The WFP works on two
fronts: as the principal international channel providing fast, efficient relief
assistance to victims of natural and man-made disasters, and as a major sup-
plier of food aid to poor people in developing countries aimed at building
self-reliant families and communities. In both emergency operations and
development projects, WFP is responsible for assessing food aid needs,
mobilizing contributions from donors, transporting commodities, and managing overall distribution on a countrywide basis. But final distribution to
beneficiaries is undertaken either by government agencies or by local and
international NGOs and PVOs.

Capabilities. The WFP is available to promote rural development and
provide help in the area of agricultural and food production, environmental
protection, resettlement of communities, health and nutrition, education and
human resources development, forestry, infrastructure and transportation,
and fisheries; to support development projects involving and benefiting poor
women; to administer the International Emergency Food Reserve and work
in the operation of its own bilateral emergency food aid programs; to coordinate emergency supplies from all sources through its transportation and
logistics operations; to carry out vulnerability mapping, emergency training,
food needs assessment missions, and the design of appropriate development
projects and quick-action rehabilitation projects in the program's emergency
response capacity; to mitigate disasters by identification and design of
appropriate projects, vulnerability mapping, and emergency training; to

transport relief food by land, sea, and air; to arrange the purchase and transport of food aid provided bilaterally by individual countries; to improve the environment through such measures as afforestation and soil conservation; and to alleviate the effects of structural adjustment programs on the poor, particularly those that involve reductions in public spending and in subsidies for basic foods.

Interagency Relationships. The WFP cooperates with other UN agencies, NGOs, PVOs, and regional and international organizations. It also works with the international financial institutions (especially the World Bank) and bilateral agencies. The WFP collaborates with several hundred NGOs and PVOs in emergencies to get food to the needy. NGOs and PVOs are often contracted to transport and distribute food. Special measures have been emphasized to form stronger partnerships with NGOs and PVOs. These include more formal arrangements in countries where collaboration with NGOs and PVOs has taken place on an ad hoc basis. Among other things, these arrangements cover monitoring, reporting, and financial accountability in the implementation of actual food distribution, while also maintaining some flexibility to allow freedom of action of the partners. For example, the WFP has signed country-specific agreements with the Mozambican Red Cross, Cooperative for Assistance and Relief Everywhere, World Vision, Oxfam, and Save the Children Federation.

Particularly close interagency coordination has been established with the UNDHA and the UNHCR in responding to emergency situations. The WFP actively participates in UNDHA-led meetings, particularly the IASC and the IASC Working Group. The WFP also strongly supports UNDHA through the temporary assignment of senior emergency management staff to UNDHA's New York and Geneva offices, participation in UNDHA's CAP and interagency assessment missions, and the use of UNDHA's CERF.

The WFP and UNHCR have working arrangements that make the former responsible for the mobilization of all basic food commodities and the funds to pay for transport costs for all UNHCR-managed refugee relief operations. The program's involvement in conflict zones results in greater interaction with UN peacekeeping forces around the world. Such interaction is instrumental in ensuring the de-mining of access routes, a key requirement for the delivery of large amounts of relief supplies. Peacekeeping forces also assist in the delivery of relief aid in humanitarian convoys across military lines.

Organization. The WFP is headquartered in Rome, Italy. At WFP headquarters, the Operations Department has six regional bureaus coordinated by three divisions for development, emergencies, and transport and logistics. Operational responsibility for emergency operations is integrated into the regional bureaus, which receive technical support from the Emergency Division. The Transport and Logistics Division has line responsibility for transport, logistics, and insurance operations. Eighty-five country offices fall under the six regional bureaus. Composed of 42 member governments, the Committee on Food Aid Policies and Programmes (CFA) is WFP's governing body and also a forum for intergovernmental consultations on all food aid matters. The CFA is responsible for the supervision and direction of the WFP, including policy, administration, operations, funds, and finances. The WFP is funded through voluntary contributions from donor countries and intergovernmental bodies, such as the European Union. Contributions are made in commodities, cash, and services.

Points of Contact. World Food Programme, Via Cesare Giulio Viola, 68, Parco dei Medici, Rome 00148 Italy

Tel: (39 06) 6513-1; Fax: (39 06) 6590-632 / 637; Telex: 626675 WFP I; Cable: WORLDFOOD I

Press relations: (39 06) 6513-2602 or (39 06) 6513-2971

Web site: *http://www.wfp.org*

Contact information: *http://www.wfp.org/Telecom/index.html*

Technical Support Service, Operations Department: Tel: (39 06) 6513-2014; Fax: (39 06) 6513-2837

External Relations: Tel: (39 06) 6513-2602; Fax: (39 06) 6513-2840

UNITED NATIONS WORLD HEALTH ORGANIZATION (WHO)

Overview. The World Health Organization is an intergovernmental organization within the UN system. WHO's objective is "the attainment by all peoples of the highest possible level of health." WHO was given its mandate as the United Nations' specialized agency for international health work in 1946, with a constitution that took effect on 7 April 1948. That date is now commemorated each year as World Health Day.

Authority and Responsibilities. WHO's main constitutional functions are to act as the directing and coordinating authority on international health work; to ensure valid and productive technical cooperation for health among member states; and to promote research. WHO's responsibilities are to assist governments, upon request, in strengthening health services; to establish and maintain such administrative and technical services as may be required, including epidemiological and statistical services; to provide information, counsel, and assistance in the field of health; to stimulate the eradication of epidemic, endemic, and other diseases; to promote improved nutrition, housing, sanitation, working conditions, and other aspects of environmental hygiene; to promote cooperation among scientific and professional groups that contribute to the enhancement of health; to propose international conventions and agreements on health matters; to promote and conduct research in the field of health; to develop international standards for food, biological, and pharmaceutical products; and to assist in developing an informed public opinion among all peoples on matters of health.

Capabilities. WHO's capabilities include the following: to provide education on health problems and the methods of preventing and controlling them; to promote food supply, proper nutrition, adequate supply of safe water, basic sanitation, and maternal and child healthcare, including family planning; to conduct immunization against the major infectious diseases; to prevent and control locally endemic diseases; to provide appropriate treatment and essential drugs for common diseases and injuries; to coordinate UN authority on international health work with emergency assistance using national and international resources and to provide necessary emergency aid, especially health services and facilities; to report on outbreaks of communicable diseases; to coordinate the international health aspects of disaster preparedness; to guide UN member states in strengthening national capabilities in emergency preparedness; to help provide early warning of disasters to the UN system; to act as a clearinghouse for all kinds of health information; to constantly check air and water pollution and measure contaminants in food and levels of radioactivity in the human environment; to disseminate valid information on health matters throughout the world, including food, biological and pharmaceutical standards, standardized diagnostic procedures, environmental health criteria, and the international nomenclature and classification of diseases; and to promote the research required to develop appropriate health technologies and to identify social and behavioral approaches that could lead to healthier lifestyles in both developed and developing countries.

Interagency Relationships. As a cooperative organization, WHO is the collective expression of the health aspirations and actions of the UN membership. Besides providing technical cooperation for individual UN member states, WHO facilitates technical cooperation between countries, both developed and developing. For example, WHO's Global Programme on AIDS works with more than 150 countries to provide financial and technical support. WHO's Action Programme on Essential Drugs collaborates with all countries to ensure the regular supply of drugs at the lowest possible cost and the rational use of a select number of safe and effective drugs and vaccines of acceptable quality. Since WHO has a constitutional requirement to "establish and maintain effective collaboration with the United Nations," it coordinates its international activities with the UN system in the field of health and socioeconomic development, working closely with other UN organizations, including UNICEF, UN Environment Programme (UNEP), International Atomic Energy Agency, International Labour Organization (ILO), International Programme on Chemical Safety, FAO, the Joint FAO/WHO Meeting on Pesticide Residues, and the Joint WHO/FAO Codex Alimentarius Commission, which ensures the safety of food moving in trade and provides guidelines for national food control.

WHO maintains close working relationships with NGOs and PVOs. Some 160 NGOs and PVOs have official relations with WHO. In addition, more than 1,000 leading health-related institutions around the world are officially designated as WHO Collaborating Centres.

Organization. WHO is headquartered in Geneva, Switzerland. It performs its functions through three principal bodies: the World Health Assembly, the Executive Board, and the Secretariat. The WHO Liaison Office to the United Nations is located in New York City.

WHO operates in six regions, each consisting of a Regional Committee and a Regional Office. At the head of each Regional Office is a regional director. The Regional Offices are responsible for formulating regional policies and for monitoring regional activities. In many countries, there is a resident WHO representative who is responsible for WHO's activities in the country and who supports the government in the planning and management of national health programs.

The six Regional Offices are the Regional Office for Africa, Brazzaville, Congo; Regional Office for the Americas/Pan American Health Organization, Washington, D.C.; Regional Office for South-East Asia, New Delhi, India; Regional Office for Europe, Copenhagen, Denmark; Regional Office for the Eastern Mediterranean, Alexandria, Egypt; and Regional Office for the Western Pacific, Manila, Philippines.

Points of Contact. World Health Organization, Avenue Appia 20, 211 Geneva 27 Switzerland
Tel: (41 22) 791-2111; Fax: (41 22) 791-0746; Telex: 415 416; Telegraph: UNISANTE GENEVA
E-mail: *info@who.ch*
Web site: *http://www.who.int*
Contact Information: *http://www.who.int/home/hq.html*

Division of Emergency and Humanitarian Action: Tel: (41 22) 791-2752 or (41 22) 791-2727; Fax: (41 22) 791-4844

Emergency duty officer number: (41 79) 200-58 78 (mobile)

Inter-Agency Cooperation (in emergencies): Tel: (41 22) 791-2756 / (41 22) 791-2754; Mobile: (41 79) 218-9802; Fax: (41 22) 791-4844

Press relations: Tel: (41 22) 791-3223; Fax (41 22) 791-4858

WHO Liaison Office to the United Nations, 2 UN Plaza, DC-2 Building, New York, NY 10017

Chapter 42

U.S. Government Agencies

CENTRAL INTELLIGENCE AGENCY (CIA)

Overview. The Central Intelligence Agency collects, evaluates, and disseminates vital information on foreign political, military, economic, scientific, and other developments. Overseas, the CIA is responsible for coordinating the nation's intelligence activities and for developing intelligence that affects the national security.

Authority and Responsibilities. The Central Intelligence Agency was established by the National Security Act of 1947. Executive Order 12333, issued by President Reagan on 4 December 1981, gives the Director of Central Intelligence (DCI) authority to develop and implement the National Foreign Intelligence Program (NFIP) and to coordinate the tasking of all intelligence community collection elements. The DCI is both the head of the intelligence community and the director of the CIA. The DCI acts as the principal intelligence adviser to the President and the National Security Council (NSC) and heads a group of intelligence components comprising the CIA; the National Security Agency (NSA); the Defense Intelligence Agency (DIA); the Bureau of Intelligence and Research of the Department of State; Army, Navy, Marine Corps, and Air Force intelligence offices; the counterintelligence component of the FBI; the Department of the Treasury; and the Department of Energy.

The DCI has four major intelligence community responsibilities: to serve as the senior intelligence officer of the U.S. government, to establish requirements and priorities for community efforts, to develop and justify the NFIP budget, and to ensure the protection of intelligence sources and methods.

A number of specialized committees deal with intelligence matters of common concern. Chief among these groups are the National Foreign Intelligence Board and the National Foreign Intelligence Council, which the DCI chairs.

Capabilities of U.S. Government Agencies

	USAID	DOD	DOJ	FEMA	CIA
Food and Water	X	X			
Sanitation	X	X			
Clothing & Shelter		X			
Emergency Medicine		X			
Healthcare Services		X			
Communications	X	X	X		X
Transportation	X	X			
Refugee Services					
Search & Rescue		X			X
Firefighting		X			
Civil Engineering		X			
Hazardous Materials		X			
Financial Assistance	X				X
Information & Planning	X	X	X	X	X
Energy		X			
Nutrition Services					
Agricultural Development					
Environmental Recovery					
Public Information		X			X
Interagency Coordination	X	X	X	X	X

The CIA has no police, subpoena, or law enforcement powers or internal (domestic) security functions. The CIA, under the direction of the President or the NSC, is responsible for the following: Advising the NSC regarding national security-related intelligence activities and the coordination of those activities; correlating and evaluating intelligence related to the national security and providing for its appropriate dissemination; collecting, producing, and disseminating counterintelligence and foreign intelligence, as well as intelligence on foreign aspects of narcotics production and trafficking; conducting counterintelligence activities outside and within the United States in coordination with the FBI; coordinating counterintelligence activities and the collection of information not otherwise obtainable when conducted outside the United States by other departments and agencies; and conducting special activities approved by the President.

Capabilities. The CIA's reconnaissance and intelligence assessment capabilities are essential ingredients to interagency strategic and operational planning. It provides real-time response in the quest for essential information to form the basis for interagency action.

Interagency Relationships. The CIA is involved with other agencies of the U.S. government on a regular basis, including the NSC Senior Interagency Group, the National Intelligence Council (NIC), and the national intelligence support team (NIST). The NIST is staffed by members of the CIA, DIA, and NSA, who provide specialized capabilities useful to the joint force commanders, including the following: technical intelligence collection systems supporting both national and defense intelligence requirements, coordination of intelligence-sharing arrangements with foreign governments, human intelligence activities, and counterintelligence operations outside the United States.

Point of Contact. Central Intelligence Agency (CIA), Washington, DC 20505

Tel: (703) 482-5868; Fax: (703) 482-2243

Web site: *http://www.odci.gov/cia/ciahome.html*

DEPARTMENT OF JUSTICE (DOJ)

Overview. Established in 1870, the Department of Justice provides legal advice to the President, represents the Executive Branch in court, investigates federal crimes, enforces federal laws, operates federal prisons, and provides law enforcement assistance to states and local communities.

Authority and Responsibilities. The Attorney General heads the Department of Justice; supervises U.S. attorneys, U.S. marshals, clerks, and other officers of the federal courts; represents the United States in legal matters; and makes recommendations to the President concerning appointments to federal judicial positions and to positions within the DOJ, including U.S. attorneys and U.S. marshals.

Capabilities and Organization. DOJ personnel includes nearly 8,000 attorneys located primarily in the Antitrust, Civil, Civil Rights, Environment and Natural Resources, and Tax Divisions. The bulk of the remaining litigation is performed by the nearly 100 U.S. attorneys and their staffs dispersed throughout the country. Within the Criminal Division, the Internal Security Section supervises the investigation and prosecution of cases affecting national security, foreign relations, and the export of strategic commodities and technology. Its cases involve espionage, sabotage, neutrality, atomic energy, and violations of the Classified Information Procedures Act.

Among the law enforcement offices of the DOJ is the Drug Enforcement Administration (DEA), the primary narcotics enforcement agency for the U.S. government. Its Domestic and International Criminal Law Sections are major interagency players in criminal investigation policies, procedures, and legislation. The DEA operates with the Customs Service, the Internal Revenue Service, the Coast Guard, and the 11-agency National Narcotics Intelligence Consumers Committee. It also manages the El Paso Intelligence Center, using personnel from 13 federal agencies.

The Federal Bureau of Investigation (FBI) investigates violations of certain federal statutes, collects evidence in cases in which the United States is or may be an interested party, and performs other duties imposed by law or presidential directive. The FBI also maintains liaison posts abroad in a number of foreign countries in its effort to quell organized crime, drugs, foreign counterintelligence, white-collar crime, terrorism, and violent crime. The FBI has extensive intelligence and operational assets available both domestically and overseas.

The International Criminal Police Organization–United States National Central Bureau (INTERPOL-USNCB)–facilitates international law enforcement cooperation as the United States' representative to INTERPOL, an intergovernmental organization of 169 member countries. The functions of the INTERPOL-USNCB include coordinating information for international investigations and providing efficient communications between U.S. domestic law enforcement agencies at the federal, state, and local levels and the National Central Bureaus of other member countries.

The United States Marshals Service (USMS) supervises our nation's oldest federal law enforcement office, the U.S., which serves in 94 judicial districts in the 50 states, the District of Columbia, Guam, Puerto Rico, and the U.S. Virgin Islands. Marshals provide prisoner transportation, service and execution of court orders, federal court and judicial security, witness protection, maintenance and disposal of forfeited assets, federal fugitive apprehension, foreign extradition, security and law enforcement assistance during movement of cruise and intercontinental ballistic missiles, and emergency response by the USMS Special Operations Group. The marshals assume a special role when natural disasters or civil disturbances threaten the peace of the United States.

The International Criminal Investigative Training Assistance Program (ICITAP) was established within the DOJ in 1986 in an effort to enhance investigative capabilities in democracies throughout Latin America. ICITAP is funded through the annual economic support fund appropriations to USAID. The Department of State provides policy guidance and oversight, while responsibility for design, development, and implementation of projects rests with the DOJ. ICITAP directs its assistance primarily at police agencies, but an important focus is the relationship among the police, judges, and prosecutors. Through training courses, conferences, and seminars, greater coordination among the three criminal justice sectors is sought.

The Immigration and Naturalization Service (INS) plays a significant role in interagency response to migrant operations, including those involving Cuban, Haitian, and Chinese nationals. The Coast Guard routinely deploys with INS agents and interpreters during scheduled migrant interdiction operations.

Point of Contact. U.S. Department of Justice (DOJ), 950 Pennsylvania Avenue, N.W., Washington, DC 20530-0001

Tel: (202) 514-2000; Fax (202) 514-4371

Web site: *http://www.usdoj.gov/*

DEPARTMENT OF THE TREASURY

Overview. The Department of the Treasury performs four basic functions: formulates and recommends economic, financial, tax, and fiscal policies; serves as financial agent for the U.S. government; enforces the law; and manufactures coins and currency. It manages and superintends the nation's finances.

Authority, Responsibilities, and Capabilities. The Treasury Department was created 2 September 1789. Its Secretary is a major policy adviser to the President and oversees the execution of the broad departmental responsibilities described above. The Assistant Secretary (Enforcement) is responsible for the Office of Financial Enforcement and the Office of Foreign Assets Control and supervises four operating bureaus:

The Bureau of Alcohol, Tobacco, and Firearms (ATF) enforces laws relating to interstate trafficking in contraband cigarettes, commercial arson, trafficking in illicit distilled spirits, firearms, destructive devices, and explosives. Since many crimes of violence are drug related, ATF directs a significant portion of its resources to fighting the war on drugs.

The U.S. Customs Service (USCS) is specifically charged with the following: to assess and collect customs duties, excise taxes, fees, and penalties due on imported merchandise; to interdict and seize contraband, including narcotics and illegal drugs; to process persons, carriers, cargo, and mail into and out of the United States; to detect and apprehend persons engaged in fraudulent practices designed to circumvent customs and related copyright, patent, and trademark provisions and quotas; to oversee marking requirements for imported merchandise; to enforce export control laws and report requirements of the Bank Secrecy Act; to intercept illegal high-technology and weapons exports; and to conduct border enforcement and a wide range of public safety and quarantine matters.

The mission of the U.S. Secret Service (USSS) is to protect the President, the Vice President, members of their immediate families, visiting heads of foreign states or governments, and other distinguished foreign visitors to the United States. Lesser known responsibilities pertain to laws of the United States relating to currency, coins, obligations, and securities of the United States or foreign governments; forgery; violations of the Federal Deposit Insurance Act, the Federal Land Bank Act, and the Government Losses in Shipment Act; and laws pertaining to electronic funds transfer frauds credit and debit card fraud, false identification documents or devices, computer access fraud, and U.S. Department of Agriculture food coupons.

The Federal Law Enforcement Training Center provides law enforcement training for personnel of more than 70 federal law enforcement agencies and for selected state and local law enforcement personnel. The center conducts advanced programs in areas of common need, such as white-collar crime, the use of microcomputers as an investigative tool, advanced law enforcement photography, international banking and/or money laundering, marine law enforcement, and several instructor training courses.

The Office of the Commissioner of Internal Revenue was established 1 July 1862. The Internal Revenue Service (IRS) is responsible for administering and enforcing the internal revenue laws and related statutes, except those relating to alcohol, tobacco, firearms, and explosives.

The undersecretary for international affairs deals with several national security issues, including financial transactions associated with terrorism, illegal drugs, and rogue states.

Interagency Relationships. The Treasury Department collaborates and assists the Office of Management and Budget, the Council of Economic Advisors, and other U.S. government agencies regarding economic forecasts and law enforcement matters. Interagency functions include the following: to act as liaison between the Secretary and other U.S. government agencies with respect to their financial operations and conduct governmentwide accounting and cash management activities; to provide financial services, information, and advice to taxpayers, the Treasury Department, federal program agencies, and government policy makers; to interact regularly with the FAA, the airports, and the air carriers; to assist in the administration and enforcement of some 400 provisions of law on behalf of more than 40 U.S. government agencies; to cooperate with other federal agencies and foreign governments in suppressing the traffic of illegal narcotics and pornography; and to provide direction and support to the Drug Law Enforcement System and serve as an integral component of the counterdrug Joint Interagency Task Forces (JIATF) East and West.

Organization. The ATF has its headquarters in Washington, D.C. Beneath the headquarters level are five regional offices that are concerned with compliance operations and 22 district law enforcement offices in principal cities within the continental United States.

The headquarters of the USCS is in Washington, D.C. The 50 states, plus the U.S. Virgin Islands and Puerto Rico, are divided into seven Customs Regions. Within these regions are 44 subordinate district or area offices under which there are approximately 240 ports of entry. The Customs Service maintains foreign field offices in Bangkok, Bonn, Dublin, Hermosillo, Hong Kong, London, Mexico City, Milan, Monterrey, Ottawa, Panama City, Paris, Rome, Seoul, Singapore, Tokyo, Vienna, and The Hague and represents U.S. Mission to the European Community in Brussels.

The USSS has two echelons of activities: headquarters in Washington, D.C., and district offices. There are 115 district offices in the United States (including Hawaii and Alaska) and Puerto Rico, and six overseas district offices are located in Bangkok, Bonn, London, Manila, Paris, and Rome. The USSS interacts extensively with federal, state, and local agencies while accomplishing its protective service responsibilities.

Point of Contact. Department of the Treasury, Office of Public Correspondence, 1500 Pennsylvania Avenue, N.W., Washington, DC 20220
Tel: (202) 622-2000; Fax: (202) 622-6415
Web site: *http://www.treas.gov*

FEDERAL EMERGENCY MANAGEMENT AGENCY (FEMA)

Overview. The Federal Emergency Management Agency is the focal point for emergency planning, preparedness, mitigation, response, and recovery. It works closely with state and local governments by funding emergency programs and providing technical guidance and training and oversees the development and execution of policies and programs for overall emergency management, national emergency readiness, disaster planning, emergency training and education, fire prevention and control, floodplain management, and insurance operations.

Authority and Responsibilities. FEMA was established in 1979. It develops and coordinates national policy and programs and facilitates the delivery of effective emergency management during all phases of national security and catastrophic emergencies through the comprehensive Federal Response Plan (FRP), coordinated with 28 U.S. government departments and agencies. The FRP applies to all U.S. government departments and agencies that are tasked to provide response assistance in disaster or emergency situations. It describes federal actions to be taken in providing immediate response assistance to one or more affected states.

Capabilities. FEMA's capabilities and core competencies include the following: to administer programs in support of state and local governments that are designed to improve emergency planning preparedness, mitigation, response, and recovery capabilities; to administer the National Flood Insurance Program and the Federal Crime Insurance Program; and to provide leadership, coordination, and support for the agency's urban search and rescue, fire prevention and control, hazardous materials, and emergency medical services activities.

The FRP describes the basic mechanisms and structures by which the U.S. government mobilizes resources and conducts activities to augment state and local response efforts. To facilitate the provision of federal assistance, the plan uses a functional approach to group the types of federal assistance that a state is most likely to need under 12 emergency support functions (ESFs). Each ESF is headed by a primary agency that has been selected based on its authorities, resources, and capabilities in the functional area. Other agencies are designated as support agencies for one or more ESFs, based on their resources and capabilities to support the functional area. The 12 ESFs serve as the primary mechanism through which federal response assistance is provided to a state. The federal assistance effort is controlled by the federal coordinating officer (FCO), who is appointed by the director of FEMA on behalf of the President. Upon activation of an ESF, a primary agency is authorized, in coordination with the FCO and the state, to initiate and continue actions to carry out the ESF missions described in the ESF annexes to the FRP, including tasking designated support agencies to carry out assigned ESF missions.

Interagency Relationships. The FRP was developed through the efforts of 28 departments and agencies at both the national and regional levels. FEMA continues to work with these organizations to develop, maintain, and enhance the federal response capability.

Organization. FEMA's organizational structure mirrors the functions that take place in the life cycle of emergency management: mitigation, preparedness, and response and recovery. FEMA also contains the U.S. Fire Administration, which supports the nation's fire service, and the Federal Insurance Administration, which provides flood insurance to property owners nationwide. In addition, a director of strategic communication reports to the FEMA director.

Point of Contact. Federal Emergency Management Agency (FEMA), 500 C Street, S.W., Washington, DC 20472

Tel: (202) 646-3923; Fax: (202) 646-3930

Web site: *http://www.fema.gov/*

PEACE CORPS

Overview. The Peace Corps' purpose is to promote world peace and friendship, to help other countries in meeting their needs for trained labor, and to help promote understanding between the American people and other peoples served by the Peace Corps. The Peace Corps Act emphasizes the Peace Corps' commitment to programming to meet the basic needs of those living in the countries in which it operates.

Authority and Responsibilities. The Peace Corps is an independent federal agency. President John F. Kennedy created the Peace Corps by executive order in 1961.

Capabilities. The Peace Corps focuses on agriculture—food production, storage, distribution, marketing, sustainable agriculture, aquaculture, and pest management; education—English, mathematics, science, business studies, and special, vocational, and nonformal educational activities for adults and at-risk youth; the environment—community work, the importance of resource conservation and sustainable management techniques; reforestation, and forestry and watershed management; health—primary healthcare services, maternal and child health activities, nutrition, community health education, guinea worm eradication, water and sanitation projects, and HIV/AIDS education and prevention; small business—local economic development through self-sustaining income- and employment-producing practices, business management, commercial banking and related skills, and assisting efforts to establish free market economies; and urban development—housing, solid waste management, urban planning, and urban youth development projects.

Interagency Relationships. Peace Corps volunteers, by nature of their commitment and responsibilities, traditionally work as members of a team. Through its collaborative agreements with U.S. government agencies, ongoing cooperation and coordination with NGOs and PVOs, and self-help grants to indigenous groups, the Peace Corps strengthens and increases its impact. To maximize foreign assistance funds, the Peace Corps works closely with USAID, U.S. Department of Agriculture (USDA), USDA/Forest Service, U.S. Department of the Interior (DOI), DOI/ Park Service, Environmental Protection Agency (EPA), and U.S. Department of Health and Human Services. In many countries, the Peace Corps coordinates its efforts with NGOs and PVOs that also receive support from the U.S. Government.

Organization. The Peace Corps is headquartered in Washington, D.C. Fifteen offices in major U.S. cities help thousands of Peace Corps applicants compete for placement as volunteers. The Peace Corps' international operations are divided into four regions: Africa; Asia and the Pacific; Europe, Central Asia, and the Mediterranean; and Inter-America. Approximately 7,000 Peace Corps volunteers and trainees serve in over 90 countries in Asia, the Pacific, Africa, the Middle East, Central and South America, the Caribbean, Central and Eastern Europe, and the former Soviet Union. Since 1961, over 140,000 Peace Corps volunteers have served in over 100 countries worldwide.

Point of Contact. Peace Corps, 1990 K Street, N.W., Washington, DC 20526

Tel: (202) 606-3010; Fax: (202) 606-3110

Web site: *http://www.peacecorps.gov/home.html*

U.S. AGENCY FOR INTERNATIONAL DEVELOPMENT/OFFICE OF U.S. FOREIGN DISASTER ASSISTANCE (USAID/OFDA)

Overview. USAID plays both a major role in U.S. foreign policy and a principal role in interagency coordination. It is an autonomous agency under the policy direction of the Secretary of State through the International Development Cooperation Agency, which is headed by the administrator of USAID. USAID administers and directs the U.S. foreign economic assistance program and acts as the lead federal agency for U.S. foreign disaster assistance. USAID works largely in support of the Department of State and manages a worldwide network of country programs for economic and policy reforms that generate sound economic growth, encourage political freedom and good governance, and invest in human resource development. Response to natural and man-made disasters is one of the agency's primary missions.

Authority and Responsibilities. USAID administers a wide variety of programs in the developing world, Central and Eastern Europe, and the newly independent states of the former Soviet Union. It administers two kinds of foreign assistance: development assistance and economic support funds. It provides funding for extraordinary economic assistance in developing countries and manages several "Food for Peace" assistance programs.

USAID focuses much of its efforts on six areas of special concern: agriculture, the environment, child survival, AIDS, population planning, and basic education. It directs all developmental assistance programs under the Foreign Assistance Act of 1961, Public Law 480 ("Food for Peace") and similar legislation.

USAID is also the principal agency charged with coordinating the U.S. government response to declared disasters and emergencies worldwide. Through OFDA, the agency administers the President's authority to provide emergency relief and long-term humanitarian assistance in response to disasters as declared by the ambassador (also known as the chief of mission) within the affected country or higher Department of State authority. USAID/OFDA may also expedite interventions at the operational and tactical levels through NGOs, PVOs, regional and international organizations, and other sources of relief capacity.

The administrator of USAID, as the special coordinator for international disaster assistance, has delegated the authority to coordinate the response to international disasters to OFDA, which is organized under the agency's Bureau for Humanitarian Response. The director of OFDA has primary responsibility for initiating this response. USAID/OFDA responsibilities include organizing and coordinating the total U.S. government disaster relief response; responding to embassy and/or mission requests for disaster assistance; initiating necessary procurement of supplies, services, and transportation; and coordinating assistance efforts with operational-level NGOs and PVOs.

Capabilities. USAID/OFDA's capabilities include the following: to respond to longer-term, complex emergencies such as civil strife, population displacement, and other man-made disasters; to provide useful, and at times critical, information in these areas through its collection of data on U.S. disaster assistance, world disaster histories, U.S. and other donor country actions in case reports, country preparedness reports, and commodity use; to obligate up to $25,000 in cash, in cooperation with the U.S. Embassy or mission, for supplies or services to assist disaster victims (the agency's international disaster assistance budget includes a $75 million appropriation each year for contingency operations); to make cash grants to local government relief organizations or international voluntary agencies handling emergency relief; to purchase needed relief supplies; to access important data through its Disaster Assistance Logistics Information System; to transport relief supplies to the affected country; to reimburse other U.S. government agencies for disaster relief services; to acquire disaster relief supplies from OFDA stockpiles; to provide additional funds to support activities in the following essential sectors: shelter, water and sanitation, health, food, logistics, and technical assistance; and to maintain stockpiles of standard relief commodities in Maryland (United States), Panama, Italy, Guam, and Thailand.

Interagency Relationships. USAID/OFDA has established relationships with several U.S. government agencies and dozens of NGOs, PVOs, and international organizations. In carrying out its responsibilities, USAID/OFDA draws on these agencies and organizations, as required, to coordinate the response to foreign disasters. Similarly, these agencies and organizations look to USAID/OFDA for advice and assistance, as appropriate, in handling their assigned responsibilities. USAID/OFDA currently has agreements with the following:

- The Department of Agriculture's U.S. Forest Service and the Interior Department's Bureau of Land Management, for emergency managers, logisticians, communicators, and firefighting experts.
- The U.S. Public Health Service and the Centers for Disease Control and Prevention, for health assessment and to provide medical personnel, equipment, and supplies.
- The U.S. Geological Survey, for notification and assessment of earthquakes and volcanic eruptions.
- The NOAA, for typhoon, hurricane, and cyclone reporting and assessment.
- FEMA, for training in disaster management, emergency preparedness, and relief for host-country disaster specialists.
- The DOD, for matters concerning defense equipment and personnel provided to the affected country and for arranging DOD transportation.

DOD Directive 5100.46, Foreign Disaster Relief, establishes the relationship between the DOD and USAID/OFDA. The Deputy Assistant Secretary of Defense (Humanitarian and Refugee Affairs) is the DOD's primary point of contact. The Joint Staff point of contact for the DOD Foreign Disaster Relief/Humanitarian Assistance Program is the chief, Logistics Readiness

Center, J-4. When USAID/OFDA requests specific services from the DOD (typically airlift), USAID/OFDA pays for those services or commodities. The geographic combatant commander can directly coordinate with OFDA to obtain military and civilian assistance efforts. Additionally, the DOD independently has statutory authority to respond to overseas man-made or natural disasters when necessary to prevent loss of life. Under the statute's implementing executive order, the Secretary of Defense provides such assistance at the direction of the President or in consultation with the Secretary of State.

Organization. USAID consists of a central headquarters staff in the Washington, D.C., area and a large number of overseas missions, offices, and regional organizations.

Staff Offices and Functional Bureaus. Four staff offices and five functional bureaus are responsible for USAID's overall policy formulation, program management, planning, inter- and intraagency coordination, resource allocation, training programs, and liaison with Congress. International disaster assistance activities are coordinated by OFDA.

Geographic Bureaus. Four bureaus (Africa, Asia and the Near East, Europe and the Newly Independent States, and Latin America and the Caribbean) are the principal USAID line offices, with responsibility for the planning, formulation, and management of U.S. economic development and/or supporting assistance programs in their areas. There are three types of country organizations; USAID Missions, Offices of USAID Representative, and USAID sections of the embassy.

Office of U.S. Foreign Disaster Assistance. OFDA consists of the Office of the Director and three functional divisions: Prevention, Mitigation, and Preparedness Division; Disaster Response Division; and Operations Support Division. It also operates a Crisis Management Center to coordinate disaster assistance operations when necessary, 24 hours a day.

OFDA Regional Advisers. OFDA has regional advisers stationed in Addis Ababa, Ethiopia; San Jose, Costa Rica; Manila, Republic of the Philippines; and Suva, Fiji. They are emergency response experts and consultants with long experience with USAID. All have security clearances and are known to government officials and UN, ICRC, NGO, and PVO representatives, as well as senior officials in U.S. embassies and USAID missions and offices.

Disaster Assistance Response Teams (DARTs). These teams are the OFDA's method of providing a rapid response to international disasters. A DART provides specialists trained in a variety of disaster relief skills to assist U.S. embassies and USAID missions with the management of the U.S. government response to international disasters. The structure of a DART is dependent on the size, complexity, type, and location of the disaster and on the needs of the embassy and/or USAID mission and the affected country.

Points of Contact. U.S. Agency for International Development (USAID), Ronald Reagan Building, Washington, DC 20523-0016

Tel: (202) 647-4000; Fax: (202) 647-0148

Web site: *http://www.info.usaid.gov/*

Office of U.S. Foreign Disaster Assistance (OFDA): Tel: (202) 647-5916; Fax: (202) 647-5269

U.S. INFORMATION AGENCY (USIA)

Overview. The USIA is an independent foreign affairs agency within the Executive Branch responsible for the U.S. government's overseas information, cultural, and educational exchange programs. Public diplomacy—the USIA mission—complements and reinforces traditional diplomacy by communicating U.S. interests directly to foreign publics, including strategically placed individuals and institutions. Since 1953, the USIA has been charged with the conduct of public diplomacy within the policy parameters set by the Secretary of State. The director of USIA reports directly to the President. USIA is known overseas as the U.S. Information Service (USIS). The USIA foreign service officers and staff operate at virtually all U.S. embassies and consulates abroad and also operate cultural and information resource centers in many countries. USIS posts are responsible for managing press strategy—including press releases and press contacts—for all U.S. government elements operating abroad under the authority of the U.S. ambassador. USIA is also responsible for the Voice of America, broadcasting worldwide in more than 40 languages; Radio Free Europe and Radio Liberty; the WORLDNET satellite television system; radio and television broadcasting to Cuba; the Fulbright Scholarship, International Visitor and other educational and cultural exchange programs; the U.S. Speakers Program; and the Wireless File, a daily compendium of policy statements and opinions.

Authority and Responsibilities. The mission of USIA is to understand, inform, and influence foreign publics in the promotion of the national interest and to broaden the dialogue between Americans and U.S. institutions and their counterparts abroad. USIA is prohibited by its enacting legislation (except when granted a specific exception) from conducting information programs or disseminating its information products within the United States.

Capabilities. USIA is equipped to contribute to press and public information planning during preparation for employment of U.S. forces in crisis response or contingency operations, and to significantly contribute to implementation of press and public information strategy during the operational phase; to assist civil affairs personnel in the development of popular support and the detection and countering of conditions and activities that distort or hinder U.S. operations; and to similarly assist psychological operations personnel.

Interagency Relationships. Operating as the USIS overseas, USIA has primary responsibility for the dissemination of information and related materials about the United States to foreign countries. Press activities of all U.S. government elements operating at U.S. diplomatic missions abroad are cleared and coordinated by USIS posts at those missions. USIA tracks foreign media coverage of issues of U.S. national interest and advises on foreign public opinion. USIS posts can assist in publicizing U.S. military and civilian achievements in a given foreign country. Plans involving civil affairs should include coordination with USIA-USIS planners. When requested by the Secretary of Defense, USIA will provide a senior representative to any established interagency planning or oversight committee.

Organization. The agency's overseas offices and personnel operate as an integral part of the U.S. diplomatic mission in each country. Each country operation (or USIS post) is headed by a public affairs officer (PAO), who reports to the ambassador in the field and to the appropriate area director within USIA. The PAO serves as a member of the country team. USIS posts usually include additional American foreign service officers in the positions of information officer and cultural affairs officer and are assisted by a staff of foreign national employees. Working with their staffs, PAOs supervise the operational aspects of U.S. public diplomacy activities overseas and maintain important contacts in the media and in the political, educational, cultural, and business communities. The PAO serves as the embassy's principal spokesperson and provides the ambassador and other mission elements with advice and expertise on matters of public diplomacy. All press releases, press contacts, and related public affairs activities by all U.S. government elements operating abroad under the authority of the U.S. ambassador—including Defense Attaché Offices and DOD military assistance and advisory offices—are directly managed or coordinated by USIS.

International Broadcasting Bureau. The Voice of America, Radio Free Europe and Radio Liberty, WORLDNET Television and Film Service, and the Office of Cuba Broadcasting form the International Broadcasting Bureau (IBB). The IBB, along with the grantees Radio Free Europe and Radio Liberty, forms the broadcasting arm of USIA. Each is a distinct programming service that shares an integrated engineering, technical, and administrative infrastructure.

Bureau of Educational and Cultural Affairs. This bureau manages academic exchanges of American and foreign graduate students, teachers, scholars, and specialists and short-term programs for foreign leaders and professionals in the United States. It also administers a variety of programs to support the study of the United States and of the English language overseas and to promote U.S. cultural presentations and exchanges.

Bureau of Information. The Bureau of Information creates and acquires those products and services that best communicate American values abroad. It generates a wide range of programs, publications, and services to provide information about the United States and its policies for use by USIS posts abroad. These include American experts who travel abroad as speakers, academic specialists, and professionals-in-residence; the Wireless File (which contains policy statements and other authoritative information); a variety of publications; and information resource services.

The Geographic Offices. The directors of USIA's six geographic area offices are responsible for the formulation, content, direction, resource management, and effectiveness of the overseas mission programs in the countries of their assigned areas. They are the prime Washington sources of expertise for their areas on the public diplomacy aspects of U.S. policy formulation and execution. They are in constant contact with the Department of State and other government agencies on regional matters.

The Office of Research and Media Reaction. This office conducts assessments of foreign attitudes on policy issues for U.S. government officials both in the United States and abroad, measures foreign audiences for the IBB, and prepares daily summaries of foreign media commentary on U.S. policies, major international events, and special foreign policy topics.

Point of Contact. U.S. Information Agency (USIA), Office of Public Liaison, 301 4th Street S.W., Room 602, Washington, DC 20547

Tel: (202) 619-6194; Fax: (202) 205-0484

Web site: *http://www.usia.gov/*

Chapter 43

Miscellaneous Organizations

ACTION WITHOUT BORDERS

Overview. Action Without Borders is a nonprofit organization that promotes the sharing of ideas, information, and resources to help build a world where all people can live free, dignified, and productive lives.

Capabilities. Action Without Borders maintains Idealist, the most comprehensive directory of nonprofit and volunteering resources on the World Wide Web, and publishes *Ideas in Action,* a biweekly E-mail newsletter with news and pointers to useful resources for volunteers and nonprofit professionals around the world. It also trains nonprofit and community organizations on how best to use the Internet in their work.

Point of Contact. Action Without Borders, Inc., 350 Fifth Avenue, Suite 6614, New York, NY 10118
Tel: (212) 843-3973; Fax: (212) 564-3377
E-mail: *info@idealist.org*
Web site: *http://www.idealist.org/*

DISASTERRELIEF.ORG

Overview. DisasterRelief.org is a web site with the mission of providing worldwide disaster relief information via the Internet. The site includes current reports on developing stories related to U.S. and international disasters and conflicts, reports of interest to any person or organization involved in or affected by disasters, and reports on disaster relief efforts and disaster prevention and mitigation. One of the critical functions of the web site is to provide timely, accurate information as disasters occur. The organization wants to encourage people to get involved in disaster relief activity by illustrating the scope of the disasters, their effects on everyday people's lives, and the "human side" of disasters through firsthand accounts and images from disaster areas. DisasterRelief.org is a collaborative effort among the

American Red Cross, IBM, and CNN Interactive. The site is managed and operated by the American Red Cross; IBM provides funding, technical support, and site hosting; and CNN Interactive is the primary news partner.

Capabilities. DisasterRelief.org focuses on media, disaster relief, community service, and volunteering.

Point of Contact. DisasterRelief.org, 111 Gatehouse Road, Floor 4, Falls Church, VA 22042

Tel: (703) 206-8869

E-mail: *disrelweb@usa.redcross.org*

Web site: *http://www.disasterrelief.org*

INTERACTION: AMERICAN COUNCIL FOR VOLUNTARY INTERNATIONAL ACTION

Overview. InterAction is a coalition of more than 150 U.S.-based PVOs engaged in international humanitarian efforts, including sustainable development, disaster relief, refugee assistance, advocacy, and education in 165 countries around the world. InterAction's goal is to enhance the effectiveness and professional capacities of its members engaged in international humanitarian efforts, and to foster partnership, collaboration, and leadership among them as they strive to achieve a world of self-reliance, justice, and peace.

Capabilities. InterAction's capabilities include the following: to provide up-to-date information on members' programs and finances through *InterAction Member Profiles 1993,* 4th ed., (Washington, DC: InterAction, 1993); to publish a biweekly publication containing news and commentary on changing global events that affect humanitarian work; to provide up-to-date information on international disaster response efforts through its reports on complex emergencies; and to bring PVOs together for briefings or planning sessions on short notice.

Interagency Relationships. InterAction conducts PVO-to-PVO coordination and is a member of the International Council of Voluntary Agencies (ICVA), which includes PVOs from all over the world.

InterAction conducts PVO-to-UN coordination, with monthly meetings for its members with the UN Department of Humanitarian Affairs and regular meetings of the UN Interagency Standing Committee (IASC), bringing together the heads of UN relief organizations as well as the International Committee of the Red Cross and several international PVO coalitions.

InterAction also conducts PVO-to-U.S. government coordination. The organization communicates with USAID/OFDA, and the Departments of State and Defense to build an understanding of PVO capabilities and operations. InterAction has worked extensively with a number of military units to build a better and broader understanding within the U.S. military of PVO capabilities and operations. InterAction has organized the participation of NGOs and PVOs in numerous training activities, including peace enforcement training exercises at the Joint Readiness Training Center at Fort Polk. InterAction has briefed many civil affairs units on the activities of NGOs and PVOs, as well as a number of the U.S. military schools, including the U.S. Army Peacekeeping Institute and the Command and General Staff College at Fort Leavenworth. InterAction staff have traveled with the Secretary of Defense and with the Chief of Staff of the Army on two trips to Rwanda to review the progress of relief operations. In addition, InterAction staff traveled to Fort Drum to participate in planning for the CMOC and HACC in Haiti and assisted in the production of a U.S. military video on CMOCs to be distributed to NGOs and PVOs.

Organization. InterAction is headquartered in Washington, D.C. It has approximately 30 staff members and is not operational overseas. InterAction's Program Officer for Disaster Response provides staff support for the PVOs active on InterAction's Disaster Response Committee. This committee deals most directly with peace operations and often acts as a functional liaison with organizations such as the U.S. military and United Nations peacekeeping operations.

Point of Contact. InterAction, 1717 Massachusetts Avenue, N.W., Suite 801, Washington, DC 20036
   Tel: (202) 667-8227; Fax: (202) 667-8236
   E-mail: *ia@interaction.org*
   Web site: *http://www.interaction.org/*

RELIEFNET
Overview. ReliefNet is a nonprofit organization dedicated to helping humanitarian organizations raise global awareness and encourage support for relief efforts via the Internet.

Capabilities. ReliefNet focuses on economic development, disaster relief, computers, and technology.

Point of Contact. ReliefNet, 409 3rd Street #1, Brooklyn, NY 11215-2850
   Tel: (718) 832-3114
   E-mail: *cland@netbox.com*
   Web site: *http://www.reliefnet.org*

Appendix A

Acronyms

AARs	after action reviews
A&P	administrative and personnel
ABCA	American, British, Canadian, and Australian
ACE	Allied Command Europe
ACLANT	Allied Command Atlantic
ACSA	acquisition cross-service agreement
ADL	armistice demarcation line
ADMIN	administrative
ADRA	Adventist Development and Relief Agency
AE	aeromedical evacuation
AFCENT	Allied Forces Central Europe
AFMIC	Armed Forces Medical Intelligence Center
AFRTS	Armed Forces Radio and Television Service
AFSATCOM	Air Force Satellite Communications System
AICF/USA	Action Internationale Contre la Faim (International Action against Hunger)
AIDS	acquired immunodeficiency syndrome
AJWS	American Jewish World Service
AMC	Air Mobility Command
AME	air mobile element
AMF(L)	ACE Mobile Force (Land) (NATO)
AOR	area of responsibility
APC	armored personnel carrier
ARC	American Red Cross
ARRC	Allied Command Europe Rapid Reaction Corps (NATO)
ARTI	American Rescue Team International
ASD(ISA)	Assistant Secretary of Defense (International Security Affairs)

ASD(S&R)	Assistant Secretary of Defense (Strategy and Requirements)
ASD(SO/LIC)	Assistant Secretary of Defense (Special Operations/Low-Intensity Conflict)
AT	antiterrorism
ATF	Bureau of Alcohol, Tobacco, and Firearms (TREAS)
B-H	Bosnia-Herzegovina
BIO	Bureau of International Organizations
BN	battalion
C of S	chief of staff
C2	command and control
C3	command, control, and communications
C4	command, control, communications, and computers
CA	civil affairs
CAAS	Civil Affairs Area Study
CAO	chief administrative officer
CAP	Consolidated Appeals Process (UN)
CARE	Cooperative for Assistance and Relief Everywhere
CCC	Cross-Cultural Communications Course
CCIR	commander's critical information requirements
CCP	civilian collection point
CD	counterdrug
CDRG	Catastrophic Disaster Response Group (FEMA)
CERF	Central Emergency Revolving Fund (UN)
CFA	Committee on Food Aid Policies and Programmes (UN)
CFS	coalition forces support team
CI	counterintelligence
CIA	Central Intelligence Agency (USG)
CiCSI	Chairman of the Joint Chiefs of Staff Instruction
CiCSM	Chairman of the Joint Chiefs of Staff Manual
CIMIC	Civil-Military Cooperation concept
CINC	commander of a combatant command; commander in chief
CISO	counterintelligence support officer
CIV	civilian
CJCS	Chairman of the Joint Chiefs of Staff
CJTF	commander, joint task force

CLPSB	CINC Logistical Procurement Support Board
CMO	civil-military operations; chief military observer
CMOC	civil-military operations center
CNN	Cable News Network
COA	course of action
COCOM	combatant command (command authority)
CONEX	container express
cont.	continued
CONUS	continental United States
CONUSA	continental United States Army
COS	Chief of Staff
CRS	Catholic Relief Services
CS	chief of staff
CT	counterterrorism
DAO	Defense attaché office
DART	Disaster Assistance Response Team (USAID/OFDA)
DATT	defense atttaché
DC	dislocated civilian
DCI	Director of Central Intelligence
DCJTF	deputy commander, joint task force
DCMO	deputy chief military observer
DCO	defense coordinating officer
DDA	Deputy Director for Administration (CIA)
DDCI	Deputy Director of Central Intelligence (CIA)
DDI	Deputy Director for Intelligence (CIA)
DDO	Deputy Director for Operations (CIA)
DDS&T	Deputy Director for Science & Technology (CIA)
DEA	Drug Enforcement Administration
DFC	deputy force commander
DFO	disaster field office (FEMA)
DHHS	Department of Health and Human Services
DIA	Defense Intelligence Agency
DIRMOBFOR	director of mobility force
DLA	Defense Logistics Agency
DMPITS	Deployment Mass Population Identification and Tracking System
DMT	disaster management team (UN)
DOC	Department of Commerce
DOD	Department of Defense

DOE	Department of Energy
DOI	Department of the Interior
DOJ	Department of Justice
DOMS	Director of Military Support
DOS	Department of State
DOT	Department of Transportation
DPC	Defense Planning Committee (NATO)
DPKO	Department of Peacekeeping Operations
DRMO	Defense Reutilization Marketing Office
DSAA	Defense Security Assistance Agency
DSCS	Defense Satellite Communications System
DZ	drop zone
EAP	Emergency Action Plan
ECC	Evacuation Control Center
ECOSOC	Economic and Social Council (UN)
EEZ	exclusive economic zones
EOD	explosive ordnance disposal
EPA	Environmental Protection Agency (USG)
EPW	enemy prisoner of war
ERT	emergency response team (FEMA)
ESF	emergency support function (FEMA)
ESG	executive steering group
EST	emergency support team (FEMA)
EU	European Union
EXDIR	Executive Director (CIA)
EXDIR/ICA	Executive Director for Intelligence Community Affairs (USG)
FAA	Federal Aviation Administration
FALD	Field Administration and Logistics Division
FAO	Food and Agriculture Organization (UN)
FAS	Foreign Agricultural Service (USDA)
FBI	Federal Bureau of Investigation
FC	force commander
FCE	forward command element
FCO	federal coordinating officer (USG)
FEMA	Federal Emergency Management Agency
FHA	Bureau for Food and Humanitarian Assistance; Federal Highway Administration

FHI	Food for the Hungry International
FID	foreign internal defense
FLSG	Force Logistics Support Group
FLTSATCOM	fleet satellite communications
FM	field manual
FOD	Field Operations Division
FPA	foreign policy adviser
FRA	Federal Railroad Administration (DOT)
FRMAC	Federal Radiological Monitoring and Assessment Center (DOE)
FRP	Federal Response Plan (USG)
G-5	civil affairs, military government
GCCS	Global Command and Control System
GPS	Global Positioning System
HA	humanitarian assistance
HACC	humanitarian assistance coordination center
HAO	humanitarian assistance operations
HAST	humanitarian assistance survey team
HCA	humanitarian and civic assistance
HEDP	high-explosive/dual-purpose
HIV	human immunodeficiency virus
HLZ	helicopter landing zone
HN	host nation
HNS	host-nation support
HOC	humanitarian operations center; human intelligence operations cell
HQ	headquarters
HRA	humanitarian relief agencies
HSS	health service support
HUMINT	human intelligence
IAEA	International Atomic Energy Agency (UN)
IAPSO	Interagency Procurement Services Office
IASC	Interagency Standing Committee (UN)
IAW	in accordance with
IBB	International Broadcasting Bureau
ICD	International Cooperation and Development Program (USDA)

ICITAP	International Crime Investigative Training Assistance Program (DOJ)
ICRC	International Committee of the Red Cross
ICVA	International Council of Voluntary Agencies
ID	identification
IDAD	internal defense and development
IDF	Israeli Defense Forces
IDNDR	International Decade for Natural Disaster Reduction (UN)
IFOR	implementation force (Bosnia)
IFRC	International Federation of Red Cross and Red Crescent Societies
IFV	infantry fighting vehicle
IG	inspector general
ILO	International Labor Organization (UN)
IMC	International Medical Corps
IMF	International Monetary Fund (UN)
INA	Immigration and Naturalization Act
INF	infantry
INL	International Narcotics and Law Enforcement Affairs (USG)
INS	Immigration and Naturalization Service (USG)
INTERPOL-USNCB	
	International Criminal Police Organization–United States National Central Bureau (DOJ)
IO	international organization, information operation
IOM	International Organization for Migration
IRC	International Rescue Committee
IRS	Internal Revenue Service
ISB	intermediate staging base
ITV	in-transit visibility
IWG	Interagency Working Group (NSC)
J-1	Manpower and Personnel Directorate of a joint staff
J-2	Intelligence Directorate of a joint staff
J-2X	Joint Force J-2 Counterintelligence/Human Intelligence Staff Element
J-3	Operations Directorate of a joint staff

J-4	Logistics Directorate of a joint staff
J-5	Plans Directorate of the Joint Staff or a CINC's joint staff; Civil Military Operations section of a joint task force staff
J-6	Command, Control, Communications, and Computer Systems Directorate of a joint staff
JBPO	Joint Blood Program Office
JCMEB	Joint Civil-Military Engineering Board
JCMOTF	Joint Civil-Military Operations Task Force
JCS	Joint Chiefs of Staff
JDISS	Joint Deployable Intelligence Support System
JEL	Joint Electronic Library
JFC	joint force commander
JFSOCC	joint force special operations component commander
JFUB	Joint Facilities Utilization Board
JIATF	joint interagency task force (DOD)
JIB	Joint Information Bureau
JIC	joint intelligence center
JISE	joint intelligence support element
JMC	Joint Movement Center, joint military commission
JMFU	Joint METOC Forecast Unit
JOA	joint operations area
JOC	joint operations center
JOPES	Joint Operation Planning and Execution System
JPG	joint planning group
JPMRC	Joint Patient Movement Requirement Center
JPO	Joint Petroleum Office
JPOTF	joint psychological operations task force
JPRC	joint personnel reception center
JSCP	Joint Strategic Capabilities Plan
JSOA	joint special operations area
JSOTF	joint special operations task force
JTF	joint task force
JTTP	joint tactics, techniques, and procedures
JVB	joint visitors bureau
JWICS	Joint Worldwide Integrated Communications System
KSARNG	Kansas Army National Guard

LA	legal advisor
LAW	light antitank weapon
LEA	law enforcement agency
LFA	lead federal agency
LIC	low-intensity conflict
LNO	liaison officer
LOC	logistics operations center
LOCs	lines of communications
LOG	logistics
LOGCAP	Logistics Civil Augmentation Program
LOGSTAT	logistics status report
LRC	logistics readiness center
LWR	Lutheran World Relief
LZ	landing zone
MACDIS	military assistance for civil disturbances
MC&G	mapping, charting, and geodesy
MCDA	military and civil defense assets (UN)
MCM	Marine Corps Manual; manual for courts-martial
MDA	multinational deployment agency; Magen David Adom
MEDCAP	medical civic assistance program
MEDEVAC	medical evacuation
METOC	meteorological and oceanographic
METT-TC	mission, enemy, time, terrain–troops available, civil considerations
MFO	multinational force and observers
MI	military intelligence
MIF	maritime interdiction force
MILOBs	military observers
MILSATCOM	military satellite communications
MILVAN	military van (container)
MIST	military information support team
MNF	multinational force
MOA	memorandum of agreement
MOOTW	military operations other than war
MOU	memorandum of understanding
MP	military police
MRI	magnetic resonance imaging
MSC	major subordinate command
MSCA	military support to civil authorities

MSCLEA	military support to civilian law enforcement agencies
MSF	Medecins Sans Frontieres (Doctors without Borders)
MTG	meeting
NAC	North Atlantic Council (NATO)
NATO	North Atlantic Treaty Organization
NBC	nuclear, biological, and chemical
NCA	national command authorities
NCO	noncommissioned officer
NCOIC	noncommissioned officer in charge
NEO	noncombatant evacuation operation
NEOPACKS	NEO passengers
NESDIS	National Environmental Satellite, Data and Information Service (DOC)
NFIP	National Foreign Intelligence Program (CIA); National Flood Insurance Program (FEMA)
NGO	nongovernmental organization
NIC	National Intelligence Council
NIST	national intelligence support team
no.	number
NOAA	National Oceanic and Atmospheric Administration
NSA	National Security Agency
NSC	National Security Council
NSC/DC	National Security Council/Deputies Committee
NSC/IWG	National Security Council/Interagency Working Group
NSC/PC	National Security Council/Principals Committee
NWS	National Weather Service (DOC)
OAS	Organization of American States
OASD(PA)	Office of the Assistant Secretary of Defense (Public Affairs)
OATSD(PA)	Office of the Assistant to the Secretary of Defense (Public Affairs)
OASD(SO/LIC)	Office of the Assistant Secretary of Defense (Special Operations/Low-Intensity Conflict)
OAU	Organization of African Unity
OCDETF	Organized Crime Drug Enforcement Task Force
OCHA	Office for the Coordination of Humanitarian Affairs (UN)

OCONUS	outside the continental United States
OES	Office of Emergency Services
OFDA	Office of United States Foreign Disaster Assistance
OFOESA	Office of Field Operational and External Support Activities
OI	Oxfam International
OIC	officer in charge
OJE	Operation Joint Endeavor
ONDCP	Office of National Drug Control Policy
OP	observation post
OPBAT	Operation Bahamas, the Turks, and Caicos Islands (DEA)
OPCON	operational control
OPLAN	operation plan
OPORD	operation order
OPS	operations
OPSEC	operations security
OSCE	Organization on Security and Cooperation in Europe
OSD	Office of the Secretary of Defense
OSPA	Office for Special Political Affairs
PA	public affairs
PAO	public affairs office, public affairs officer
PCRTS	primary casualty receiving and treatment ship
PDD	presidential decision directive
PE	peace enforcement
PEO	peace enforcement operation
PERMREP	permanent representative (NATO)
PIO	press information officer
PK	peacekeeping
PKO	peacekeeping operation
PM	provost marshal
PO	peace operation
POC	point of contact
POL	petroleum, oils, and lubricants
POLAD	political adviser
POW	prisoner of war
PRC	populace and resource control
RPD	presidential review directive
PSYOPS	psychological operations

PUB	publication
PVO	private voluntary organization
PZ	pick-up zone
QRF	quick reaction force
RAP	Radiological Assistance Program (DOE)
RCA	riot control agents
RCO	Regional Coordinating Officer (DOE)
REAC/TS	Radiation Emergency Assistance Center/Training Site (DOE)
REMBASS	remotely-monitored battlefield sensor system
RET	retired
RI	Refugees International
RM	risk management
ROE	rules of engagement
ROWPU	reverse osmosis water purification unit
RSO	reconnaissance staff officer
S-2	intelligence staff officer
S-3	operations staff officer
S-4	logistics staff officer
S-5	civil affairs staff officer
SA	security assistance; senior adviser
SACEUR	Supreme Allied Command, Europe (NATO)
SACLANT	Supreme Allied Command, Atlantic (NATO)
SALUTE	size, activity, location, unit, time, and equipment
SAM	surface-to-air missile
SAO	Security Assistance Office
SAR	search and rescue
SASO	stability and support operations
SATCOM	satellite communications
SCF(UK)	Save the Children Fund (United Kingdom)
SCF/US	Save the Children Fund/United States
SCIF	Special Compartmented Information Facility
SCO	state coordinating officer
SCRAG	Senior Civilian Representative of the Attorney General
SDA	Seventh-Day Adventist (ADRA)
SECSTATE	Secretary of State

SHAPE	Supreme Headquarters Allied Powers Europe (NATO)
SITREP	situation report
SJA	staff judge advocate
SO	special operations
SOF	special operations forces
SOFA	status-of-forces agreement
SOMA	status-of-missions agreement
SOP	standard operating procedure
SPT	support
SROE	standing rules of engagement
SRSG	special representative to the Secretary-General
SSM	surface-to-surface missile
STANAVFORLANT	
	Standing Naval Forces Atlantic (NATO)
TAACOM	Theater Army Area Command
TACON	tactical control
TCC	transportation component command
TCN	third-country national
TFCICA	Task Force Counterintelligence Coordinating Authority
TOR	terms of reference
TOW	tactical antitank missile
TPMRC	Theater Patient Movement Requirements Center
TRADOC	United States Army Training and Doctrine Command
TREAS	Department of the Treasury
UAV	unmanned aerial vehicle
UCMJ	Uniform Code of Military Justice
UK	United Kingdom
UK(I)	United Kingdom and Ireland
UKAR	United Kingdom Army
UN	United Nations
UNCTAD	United Nations Conference on Trade and Development
UNDHA	United Nations Department of Humanitarian Affairs
UNDP	United Nations Development Programme
UNDPKO	United Nations Department of Peacekeeping Organizations

UNEF	United Nations Emergency Force
UNEP	United Nations Environmental Programme
UNHCHR	United Nations High Commission for Human Rights
UNHCR	United Nations High Commissioner for Refugees
UNICEF	United Nations Children's Fund
UNIFIL	United Nations Interim Force in Lebanon
UNITAF	Unified Task Force (Somalia)
UNITAR	United Nations Institute for Training and Research
UNLOC	United Nations Logistics Course
UNMIH	United Nations Mission in Haiti
UNMILPOC	United Nations Military Police Course
UNMOC	United Nations Military Observers Course
UNMOVCC	United Nations Movement Control Course
UNPROFOR	United Nations Protection Force
UNRWA	United Nations Relief and Works Agency for Palestine Refugees in the Near East
UNSC	United Nations Security Council
UNSOC	United Nations Staff Officers Course
UNTAC	United Nations Transitional Authority in Cambodia
UNTSO	United Nations Truce and Supervision Organization
U.S.	United States
USA	United States Army
USACOM	United States Atlantic Command
USAF	United States Air Force
USAID	United States Agency for International Development
USC	United States Code
USCG	United States Coast Guard
USCINCACOM	
	Commander in Chief, U.S. Atlantic Command
USCINCPAC	Commander in Chief, U.S. Pacific Command
USCINCSOUTH	
	Commander in Chief, U.S. Southern Command
USCINCTRANS	
	Commander in Chief, U.S. Transportation Command
USCS	United States Customs Service (TREAS)
USDA	United States Department of Agriculture (USG)
USDAO	United States Defense Attaché Office
USDR	United States Defense Representative
USG	United States government
USIA	United States Information Agency

USIC	United States Interdiction Coordinator (USG)
USIS	United States Information Service (USG)
USMC	United States Marine Corps
USMS	United States Marshals Service (DOJ)
USN	United States Navy
USNR	United States Navy Reserve
USPACOM	United States Pacific Command
USSOUTHCOM	
	United States Southern Command
USSS	United States Secret Service (TREAS)
USTRANSCOM	
	United States Transportation Command
USUN	U.S. Mission to the United Nations
UXO	unexploded ordnance
VBSS	visit, board, search, and seizure
VIP	very important person
V/STOL	vertical/short take off and landing aircraft
VTC	video teleconferencing
WEU	Western European Union
WFP	World Food Programme (UN)
WHO	World Health Organization (UN)
WLG	Washington Liaison Group (DSO)
WMD	weapons of mass destruction
WVRD	World Vision Relief and Development

Appendix B

Glossary

The following definitions are based on Joint Pub. 1-02, *Dictionary of Military Terms.*

antiterrorism (AT). Defensive measures used to reduce the vulnerability of individuals and property to terrorist acts, including limited response and containment by local military forces.

armistice. In international law, a suspension or temporary cessation of hostilities by agreement between belligerent powers.

centers of gravity. Those characteristics, capabilities, or localities from which a military force derives its freedom of action, physical strength, or will to fight.

chain of command. The succession of commanding officers from a superior to a subordinate through which command is exercised. Also called command channel.

civil affairs. The activities of a commander that establish, maintain, influence, or exploit relations between military forces and civil authorities, both governmental and nongovernmental, and the civilian populace in a friendly, neutral, or hostile area of operations in order to facilitate military operations and consolidate operational objectives. Civil affairs may include performance by military forces of activities and functions normally the responsibility of local government. These activities may occur prior to, during, or subsequent to other military actions. They may also occur, if directed, in the absence of other military operations.

civil-military operations. Group of planned activities in support of military operations that enhance the relationship between the military forces and civilian authorities and population, and that promote the development of favorable emotions, attitudes, or behavior in neutral, friendly, or hostile groups.

civil-military operations center (CMOC). An ad hoc organization, normally established by the geographic combatant commander or subordinate joint force commander, to assist in the coordination of activities of engaged military forces, other U.S. government agencies, nongovernmental organizations, private voluntary organizations, and regional and international organizations. There is no established structure, and its size and composition are situation dependent.

coalition force. A force composed of military elements of nations that have formed a temporary alliance for some specific purpose.

combat service support. The essential capabilities, functions, activities, and tasks necessary to sustain all elements of operating forces in theater at all levels of war. Within the national and theater logistic systems, it includes but is not limited to that support rendered by service forces in ensuring the aspects of supply, maintenance, transportation, health services, and other services required by aviation and ground combat troops to permit those units to accomplish their missions in combat. Combat service support encompasses those activities at all levels of war that produce sustainment to all operating forces on the battlefield.

combat support. Fire support and operational assistance provided to combat elements.

combatant command (command authority) (COCOM). Nontransferable command authority established by title 10 ("Armed Forces"), USC, section 164, exercised only by commanders of unified or specified combatant commands unless otherwise directed by the President or the Secretary of Defense. Combatant command (command authority) cannot be delegated and is the authority of a combatant commander to perform those functions of command over assigned forces involving organizing and employing commands and forces, assigning tasks, designating objectives, and giving authoritative direction over all aspects of military operations, joint training, and logistics necessary to accomplish the missions assigned to the command. Combatant command (command authority) should be exercised through the commanders of subordinate organizations. Normally this authority is exercised through subordinate joint force commanders and service and/or functional component commanders. Combatant command (command authority) provides full authority to organize and employ commands and forces as the combatant commander considers necessary to accomplish assigned missions. Operational control is inherent in combatant command (command authority).

combatant commander. A commander in chief of one of the unified or specified combatant commands established by the President.

combating terrorism. Actions, including antiterrorism (defensive measures taken to reduce vulnerability to terrorist acts) and counterterrorism (offensive measures taken to prevent, deter, and respond to terrorism), taken to oppose terrorism throughout the entire threat spectrum.

combined. Between two or more forces or agencies of two or more allies. (When all allies or services are not involved, the participating nations and services are identified, e.g., Combined Navies.)

command, control, communications, and computer (C4) systems. Integrated systems of doctrine, procedures, organizational structures, personnel, equipment, facilities, and communications designed to support a commander's exercise of command and control across the range of military operations.

common user airlift service. The airlift service provided on a common basis for all Department of Defense agencies and, as authorized, for other agencies of the U.S. government.

Continental United States Army (CONUSA). A regionally oriented command with geographic boundaries under the command of United States Army Forces Command. The Continental United States Army is a numbered Army and is the Forces Command agent for mobilization, deployment, and domestic emergency planning and execution.

counterdrug (CD). Those active measures taken to detect, monitor, and counter the production, trafficking, and use of illegal drugs.

counterintelligence (CI). Information gathered and activities conducted to protect against espionage, other intelligence activities, sabotage or assassinations conducted by or on behalf of foreign governments or elements thereof, foreign organizations, or foreign persons, or international terrorist activities.

counterterrorism (CT). Offensive measures taken to prevent, deter, and respond to terrorism.

country team. The senior in-country United States coordinating and supervising body, headed by the chief of the United States diplomatic mission, and composed of the senior member of each represented United States department or agency, as desired by the chief of the U.S. diplomatic mission.

course of action. A plan that would accomplish, or is related to, the accomplishment of a mission.

crisis. An incident or situation involving a threat to the United States, its territories, citizens, military forces, and possessions or vital interests that develops rapidly and creates a condition of such diplomatic, economic, political, or military importance that commitment of U.S. military forces and resources is contemplated to achieve national objectives.

developmental assistance. U.S. Agency for International Development function chartered under Chapter 1 of the Foreign Assistance Act of 1961, primarily designed to promote economic growth and the equitable distribution of its benefits.

Disaster Assistance Response Team (DART). USAID/OFDA provides this rapidly deployable team in response to international disasters. The team provides specialists, trained in a variety of disaster relief skills, to assist U.S. embassies and USAID missions with the management of the U.S. government response to disasters.

displaced person. A civilian who is involuntarily outside the national boundaries of his or her country. See also *refugee*.

doctrine. Fundamental principles by which the military forces or elements thereof guide their actions in support of national objectives. It is authoritative but requires judgment in application.

end state. What the national command authorities want the situation to be when operations conclude—both military operations and those in which the military is supporting other instruments of national power.

executive agent. A term used in DOD and service regulations to indicate a delegation of authority by a superior to a subordinate to act on behalf of the superior. An agreement between equals does not create an executive agent. For example, a service cannot become a DOD executive agent for a particular matter simply by the agreement of the other services; such authority must be delegated by the Secretary of Defense. Designation as executive agent, in and of itself, confers no authority. The exact nature and scope of the authority delegated must be stated in the document designating the executive agent. An executive agent may be limited to providing only administration and support or coordinating common functions, or it may be delegated authority, direction, and control over specified resources for specified purposes.

federal coordinating officer (FCO). Appointed by the director of the Federal Emergency Management Agency, on behalf of the President, to coordinate federal assistance to a state affected by a disaster or emergency. The source and level of the federal coordinating officer usually depend on the nature of the federal response.

force protection. Security program designed to protect soldiers, civilian employees, family members, facilities, and equipment, in all locations and situations, accomplished through planned and integrated application of combating terrorism, physical security, operations security, and personal protective services and supported by intelligence, counterintelligence, and other security programs.

foreign assistance. Assistance ranging from the sale of military equipment to donations of food and medical supplies to aid survivors of natural and man-made disasters; U.S. assistance takes three forms—development assistance, humanitarian assistance, and security assistance.

foreign disaster. An act of nature (such as a flood, drought, fire, hurricane, earthquake, volcanic eruption, or epidemic) or an act of man (such as a riot, violence, civil strife, explosion, fire, or epidemic) that is or threatens to be of sufficient severity and magnitude to warrant U.S. foreign disaster relief to a foreign country, foreign persons, or an international organization.

foreign disaster relief. Prompt aid that can be used to alleviate the suffering of foreign disaster victims. Normally it includes humanitarian services and transportation; the provision of food, clothing, medicine, beds, and bedding; temporary shelter and housing; the furnishing of medical materiel and medical and technical personnel; and repairs to essential services.

foreign internal defense (FID). Participation by civilian and military agencies of a government in any of the action programs taken by another government to free and protect its society from subversion, lawlessness, and insurgency.

host nation. A nation that receives the forces and/or supplies of allied nations and/or NATO organizations to be located on, to operate in, or to transit through its territory.

host-nation support. Civil and/or military assistance rendered by a nation to foreign forces within its territory during peacetime, crises, emergencies, or war, based on agreements mutually concluded between nations.

humanitarian and civic assistance. Assistance to the local populace provided by predominantly U.S. forces in conjunction with military operations and exercises. This assistance is specifically authorized by Title 10, USC Section 401, and funded under separate authorities. Assistance provided under these provisions is limited to (1) medical, dental, and veterinary care provided in rural areas of a country; (2) construction of rudimentary surface transportation systems; (3) well drilling and construction of basic sanitation facilities; and (4) rudimentary construction and repair of public facilities. Assistance must fulfill unit training requirements that incidentally create humanitarian benefit to the local populace.

humanitarian assistance. Programs conducted to relieve or reduce the results of natural or man-made disasters or other endemic conditions such as human pain, disease, hunger, or privation that might present a serious threat to life or that can result in great damage to or loss of property. Humanitarian assistance provided by U.S. forces is limited in scope and duration. The assistance provided is designed to supplement or complement the efforts of the host-nation civil authorities or agencies that may have primary responsibility for providing humanitarian assistance.

information. Facts, data, or instructions in any medium or form.

intelligence. 1. The product resulting from the collection, processing, integration, analysis, evaluation, and interpretation of available information concerning foreign countries or areas. 2. Information and knowledge about an adversary obtained through observation, investigation, analysis, or understanding.

interagency coordination. Within the context of Department of Defense involvement, the coordination that occurs between elements of the Department of Defense and engaged U.S. government agencies, nongovernmental organizations, private voluntary organizations, and regional and international organizations for the purpose of accomplishing an objective.

internal defense and development (IDAD). The full range of measures taken by a nation to promote its growth and protect itself from subversion, lawlessness, and insurgency. It focuses on building viable institutions (political, economic, social, and military) that respond to the needs of society.

international organization. Organizations with global influence, such as the United Nations and the International Committee of the Red Cross.

joint force commander (JFC). A general term applied to a combatant commander, subunified commander, or joint task force commander authorized to exercise combatant command (command authority) or operational control over a joint force.

joint staff. 1. The staff of a commander of a unified or specified command, subordinate unified command, joint task force, or subordinate functional component (when a functional component command will employ forces from more than one military department), which includes members from the several services constituting the force. These members should be assigned in such a manner as to ensure that the commander understands the tactics, techniques, capabilities, needs, and limitations of the component parts of the force. Positions on the staff should be divided so that service representation and influence generally reflect the service composition of the force. 2. Joint Staff. The staff under the Chairman of the Joint Chiefs of Staff as provided for in the National Security Act of 1947, as amended by the Goldwater-Nichols Department of Defense Reorganization Act of 1986. The Joint Staff assists the Chairman and, subject to the authority, direction, and control of the Chairman, the other members of the Joint Chiefs of Staff and the Vice Chairman in carrying out their responsibilities.

joint tactics, techniques, and procedures (JTTP). The actions and methods that implement joint doctrine and describe how forces will be employed in joint operations. They are promulgated by the Chairman of the Joint Chiefs of Staff, in coordination with the combatant commands, services, and Joint Staff.

joint task force (JTF). A joint force that is constituted and so designated by the Secretary of Defense, a combatant commander, a subunified commander, or an existing joint task force commander.

lead agency. Designated among U.S. government agencies to coordinate the interagency oversight of the day-to-day conduct of an ongoing operation. The lead agency chairs the interagency working group established to coordinate policy related to a particular operation. The lead agency determines the agenda, ensures cohesion among the agencies, and is responsible for implementing decisions.

letter of assist. A contractual document issued by the UN to a government authorizing it to provide goods or services to a peacekeeping operation; the UN either agrees to purchase the goods or services or authorizes the government to supply them subject to reimbursement by the UN.

liaison. That contact or intercommunication maintained between elements of military forces or other agencies to ensure mutual understanding and unity of purpose and action.

logistic assessment. An evaluation of (1) the logistics support required for particular military operations in a theater of operations, country, or area, or (2) the actual and/or potential logistics support available for the conduct of military operations within the theater, country, or area or located elsewhere.

logistics. The science of planning and carrying out the movement and maintenance of forces. In its most comprehensive sense, those aspects of military operations that deal with (1) design and development, acquisition, storage, movement, distribution, maintenance, evacuation, and disposition of materiel; (2) movement, evacuation, and hospitalization of personnel; (3) acquisition or construction, maintenance, operation, and disposition of facilities; and (4) acquisition or furnishing of services.

military civic action. The use of preponderantly indigenous military forces on projects useful to the local population at all levels in such fields as education, training, public works, agriculture, transportation, communications, health, sanitation, and others contributing to economic and social development, which would also serve to improve the standing of the military forces with the population. (U.S. forces may at times advise or engage in military civic actions in overseas areas.)

military department. One of the departments within the Department of Defense created by the National Security Act of 1947, as amended.

military operations other than war (MOOTW). Operations that encompass the use of military capabilities across the range of military operations short of war. These military actions can be applied to complement any combination of the other instruments of national power and occur before, during, and after war.

military options. A range of military force responses that can be projected to accomplish assigned tasks. Options include one or a combination of the following: civic action, humanitarian assistance, civil affairs, and other military activities to develop positive relationships with other countries; confidence building and other measures to reduce military tensions; military presence; activities to convey threats to adversaries and truth projections; military deceptions and psychological operations; quarantines, blockades, and harassment operations; raids; intervention operations; armed conflict involving air, land, maritime, and strategic warfare operations; support for law enforcement authorities to counter international criminal activities (terrorism, narcotics trafficking, slavery, and piracy); support for law enforcement authorities to suppress domestic rebellion; and support for insurgencies, counterinsurgency, and civil war in foreign countries.

multinational operations. A collective term to describe military actions conducted by forces of two or more nations, typically organized within the structure of a coalition or alliance.

nation assistance. Civil and/or military assistance rendered to a nation by foreign forces within that nation's territory during peacetime, crises, emergencies, or war, based on agreements mutually concluded between the nations. Nation assistance programs may include, but are not limited to, security assistance, foreign internal defense, other USC Title 10 (DOD) programs, and activities performed on a reimbursable basis by federal agencies or international organizations.

national command authorities (NCA). The President and the Secretary of Defense or their duly deputized alternates or successors.

noncombatant evacuation operations (NEOs). Operations conducted to relocate threatened noncombatants from locations in a foreign country. These operations normally involve U.S. citizens whose lives are in danger and may also include selected foreign nationals.

nongovernmental organizations (NGOs). Transnational organizations of private citizens that maintain a consultative status with the Economic and Social Council of the United Nations. Nongovernmental organizations may be professional associations, foundations, multinational businesses, or simply groups with a common interest in humanitarian assistance activities (development and relief). This term is normally used by non-U.S. organizations.

operational control. Transferable command authority that may be exercised by commanders at any echelon at or below the level of combatant command. Operational control is inherent in combatant command (command authority). Operational control may be delegated and is the authority to perform those functions of command over subordinate forces involving organizing and employing commands and forces, assigning tasks, designating objectives, and giving authoritative direction necessary to accomplish the mission. Operational control includes authoritative direction over all aspects of military operations and joint training necessary to accomplish missions assigned to the command. Operational control should be exercised through the commanders of subordinate organizations. Normally this authority is exercised through subordinate joint force commanders and service and/or functional component commanders. Operational control normally provides full authority to organize commands and forces and to employ those forces as the commander in operational control considers necessary to accomplish assigned missions. Operational control does not, in and of itself, include authoritative direction for logistics or matters of administration, discipline, internal organization, or unit training.

peace operations. Encompasses peacekeeping operations and peace enforcement operations conducted in support of diplomatic efforts to establish and maintain peace.

peacekeeping. Military operations undertaken with the consent of all major parties to a dispute, designed to monitor and facilitate implementation of an agreement (cease-fire, truce, or other such agreement) and support diplomatic efforts to reach a long-term political settlement.

preventive diplomacy. Diplomatic actions taken in advance of a predictable crisis to prevent or limit violence.

private voluntary organizations (PVOs). Private, nonprofit humanitarian assistance organizations involved in development and relief activities. Private voluntary organizations are normally U.S.-based. This term is often used synonymously with "nongovernmental organizations."

psychological operations (PSYOPS). Planned operations to convey selected information and indicators to foreign audiences to influence their emotions, motives, and objective reasoning and, ultimately, the behavior of foreign governments, organizations, groups, and individuals. The purpose of psychological operations is to induce or reinforce foreign attitudes and behavior favorable to the originator's objectives.

refugee. A civilian who, by reason of real or imagined danger, has left home to seek safety elsewhere.

rules of engagement (ROE). Directives issued by competent military authority that delineate the circumstances and limitations under which U.S. forces will initiate and/ or continue combat engagement with other forces encountered.

sabotage. An act or acts with intent to injure, interfere with, or obstruct the national defense of a country by willfully injuring or destroying, or attempting to injure or destroy, any national defense or war material, premises, or utilities, including human and natural resources.

security assistance. Group of programs authorized by the Foreign Assistance Act of 1961, as amended, and the Arms Export Control Act of 1976, as amended, or other related statutes by which the United States provides defense articles, military training, and other defense-related services by grant, loan, credit, or cash sales in furtherance of national policies and objectives.

special operations (SO). Operations conducted by specially organized, trained, and equipped military and paramilitary forces to achieve military, political, economic, or psychological objectives by unconventional military means in hostile, denied, or politically sensitive areas. These operations are conducted during peacetime competition, conflict, and war, independently or in coordination with operations of conventional, nonspecial operations forces. Political-military considerations frequently shape special operations, requiring clandestine, covert, or low-visibility techniques and oversight at the national level. Special operations differ from conventional operations in degree of physical and political risk, operational techniques, mode of employment, independence from friendly support, and dependence on detailed operational intelligence and indigenous assets.

status-of-forces agreement (SOFA). An agreement that defines the legal position of a visiting military force deployed in the territory of a friendly state. Agreements delineating the status of visiting military forces may be bilateral or multilateral. Provisions pertaining to the status of visiting forces may be set forth in a separate agreement, or they may be part of a more comprehensive agreement. These provisions describe how the authorities of a visiting force may control members of that force and the amenability of the force or its members to the local law or to the authority of local officials. To the extent that agreements delineate matters affecting the relations between a military force and civilian authorities and population, they may be considered civil affairs agreements.

strategy. The art and science of developing and using political, economic, psychological, and military forces as necessary during peace and war, to afford the maximum support to policies, in order to increase the probabilities and favorable consequences of victory and to lessen the chances of defeat.

supported commander. The commander having primary responsibility for all aspects of a task assigned by the Joint Strategic Capabilities Plan or other joint operation planning authority. In the context of joint operation planning, this term refers to the commander who prepares operation plans, campaign plans, or operation orders in response to requirements of the Chairman of the Joint Chiefs of Staff.

supporting commander. A commander who provides augmentation forces or other support to a supported commander or who develops a supporting plan. Includes the designated combatant commands and defense agencies as appropriate.

terrorism. The calculated use of violence or threat of violence to inculcate fear, intended to coerce or to intimidate governments or societies in the pursuit of goals that are generally political, religious, or ideological.

unified command. A command with a broad continuing mission under a single commander and composed of significant assigned components of two or more military departments, which is established and so designated by the President, through the Secretary of Defense with the advice and assistance of the Chairman of the Joint Chiefs of Staff. Also called unified combatant command.

United States country team. The senior, in-country, U.S. coordinating and supervising body, headed by the Chief of the U.S. diplomatic mission, usually an ambassador, and composed of the senior member of each represented U.S. department or agency.

Index

Notes

Notes

Notes

About the Authors

The authors first met during their service in the same rifle platoon of the 82d Airborne Division at Fort Bragg, North Carolina.

Lieutenant Colonel Keith E. Bonn, USA (Ret.), served in infantry, airborne infantry, and light infantry units in the States and overseas. His firsthand experience with MOOTW was in peacekeeping operations in the Korean DMZ (where he commanded an infantry company at Camp Greaves) and counterdrug, nation assistance, and humanitarian operations in Central America, where he served as Director of Operations (J-3) of Joint Task Force–Bravo. His final Army tour was as Special Assistant for Doctrine to the Commanding General, U.S. Army Training and Doctrine Command. A ranger and master parachutist, he holds a B.S. from the U.S. Military Academy, West Point, and an M.A. and Ph.D. (both in history) from the University of Chicago.

Master Sergeant Anthony E. Baker, USAR (Ret.), served in airborne infantry, special forces, and civil affairs units. His experience with MOOTW includes personal participation in the humanitarian relief efforts in the wake of Hurricane Andrew, and dislocated civilian operations in Operation Desert Shield/Desert Storm, Operation Provide Comfort (Kurdistan), and Operation Safe Haven (Panama). A veteran of over 20 years of active duty (RA and AGR), he is a special forces and civil affairs qualified master parachutist and holds an A.S. from the Community College of Rhode Island.

STACKPOLE
BOOKS

Military Professional Reference Library

Armed Forces Guide to Personal Financial Planning
Air Force Officer's Guide
Airman's Guide
Army Officer's Guide
Army Dictionary and Desk Reference
Career Progression Guide
Combat Service Support Guide
Combat Leader's Field Guide
Enlisted Soldier's Guide
Guide to Effective Military Writing
Guide to Military Operations Other Than War
Job Search: Marketing Your Military Experience
Military Money Guide
NCO Guide
Reservist's Money Guide
Serviceman's Legal Guide
Soldier's Guide to a College Degree
Today's Military Wife
Veteran's Guide to Benefits
Virtual Combat: A Guide to Distributed Interactive Simulation

Professional Reading Library

Fighting for the Future: Will America Triumph?
by Ralph Peters

Roots of Strategy Books 1, 2, 3, and 4

Street Without Joy
by Bernard Fall

A Tale of Three Wars
by Edward B. Atkeson